GANGBUSTER

GANGBUSTER

ONE MAN'S BATTLE AGAINST CRIME, CORRUPTION, AND THE KLAN

ALAN PRENDERGAST

CITADEL PRESS
Kensington Publishing Corp.
www.kensingtonbooks.com

CITADEL PRESS BOOKS are published by

Kensington Publishing Corp.
119 West 40th Street
New York, NY 10018

All Kensington titles, imprints, and distributed lines are available at special quantity discounts for bulk purchases for sales promotions, premiums, fund-raising, educational, or institutional use. Special book excerpts or customized printings can also be created to fit specific needs. For details, write or phone the office of the Kensington sales manager: Kensington Publishing Corp., 119 West 40th Street, New York, NY 10018, attn: Sales Department; phone 1-800-221-2647.

CITADEL PRESS and the Citadel logo are Reg. U.S. Pat. & TM Off.

ISBN: 978-0-8065-4212-6

First Citadel hardcover printing: April 2023

10 9 8 7 6 5 4 3 2 1

Printed in the United States of America

Library of Congress Control Number: 2022948698

ISBN: 978-0-8065-4214-0 (e-book)

For Lisa

Contents

Prologue

It was something the Colonel hammered into his investigators: Find out all you can about your target. Start by identifying his associates. You can learn a lot about a crook, he told them, if you discover who his friends are. By his friends you shall know him.

The same could not be said about an honest man. More often than not, an honest man will have few friends. A truly incorruptible one might have none. If the Colonel himself was ever to be investigated, you'd be better off studying his enemies. There were so many of them.

Consider a single confounding episode, long after the Colonel's gangbusting days were over. Shortly before midnight on July 19, 1943, Philip Sidney Van Cise—also known as the Colonel, in recognition of his military service in World War I—takes the streetcar home after a long evening at his law office in downtown Denver. Fifty-eight years old, portly and balding, he bears little resemblance to the trim, dapper war hero who ran for district attorney twenty-three years earlier, proclaiming himself "A Fighting Man for a Fighting Job." As he walks the last two blocks to his house in the Cheesman Park neighborhood, a stately, turn-of-the-century three-story, he notices two men keeping pace with him on the opposite side of the street.

Van Cise reaches the steps of his house. The men break into a run and catch up to him on the porch. One grabs him by the tie and snarls, like a Hollywood hood, "We want you to come with us." The other man keeps his hand in his coat pocket, pointing something at the lawyer's belly.

Van Cise is dog-tired and having none of it. Croaking out half-strangled cries for help, he wrestles with the goon yanking on his tie. The other man joins in the struggle, pulling his hand out of his pocket.

No gun.

Van Cise hollers and thrashes. The commotion sends dogs barking and neighbors to their windows. The men flee.

When the police arrive, Van Cise tells them he didn't recognize the men. He doesn't know why anybody would want to kidnap him—but this isn't the first time it's happened, either. Possibly, he suggests, it was an attempt at payback by someone he put away when he was Denver's top prosecutor, back in the Roaring Twenties.

Two decades is a long time to hold a grudge. Yet District Attorney Van Cise did his job so well, with favor toward none, that the list of potential suspects is staggering. In addition to prosecuting murderers, rapists, and thugs of all stripes, the Colonel set out to smash two sprawling criminal conspiracies during his single eventful term in office. The first battle made him one of the most admired and feared gangbusters in the country. The second cost him his job and almost cost him his life.

Van Cise became Denver's district attorney at a critical moment in the city's history. It was a time when prostitution, gambling, and bootlegging thrived under police protection, when Denver's teeming underworld was ruled by Lou "The Fixer" Blonger—a shrewd ex-lawman who had something on everybody. Among the nation's top con artists, Denver was known as the Big Store, the place where a well-connected grifter could fleece rich marks out of hundreds of thousands of dollars without any interference from the law, as long as the Fixer got his cut.

Blonger attempted to buy off Van Cise even before he took office, a move he soon regretted. In defiance of the police and a mobbed-up city administration, Van Cise declared war on Blonger and his "Million Dollar Bunco Ring." He embarked on months of secret, often perilous investigation, involving techniques that were decades ahead of their time: electronic surveillance, undercover operatives, around-the-clock stakeouts and communications intercepts, even counterintelligence measures—all to track and expose a confidence game so elaborate that some victims never realized that they'd been swindled. The effort brought down the gang, upended the state's power structure and made national headlines.

At the time of the bunco ring trial, Van Cise was the most celebrated figure in Colorado, and powerful men pleaded with him to run for mayor or governor. When he left office two years later, he was, by his own account, "the most unpopular man in the state." This reversal of fortune says less about Van Cise than it does about the great political and social upheaval that swept across the country in the years after World War I. After prosecuting Blonger, the emboldened DA went on to investigate the workings of a resurgent Ku Klux Klan in Colorado. Employing the tactics he'd developed for busting the confidence game, he sent undercover agents to infiltrate KKK meetings and launched a grand jury probe of the group's well-cloaked leadership and political connections. He was grappling with a rapidly spreading disease, far more insidious than traditional crime syndicates. His audacious campaign to rid

Colorado of the Klan exposed corruption at the highest levels of state government, but it had been largely forgotten by the time the two men tried to seize him from his porch.

It's hard to believe that any member of the bunco ring or the KKK would still be gunning for the Colonel in 1943, so long after the main event. Con men don't usually get involved in rough stuff like assault and abduction, and it seems unlikely that the few Klansmen who remained in Denver would attempt such a move. But Van Cise managed to attract trouble—and lasting rancor—simply by being his stiff-necked self. Just a few weeks before the bungled kidnapping, the *Rocky Mountain News* ran a short, begrudging profile of the former DA, comparing him to Julius Caesar. "Abrupt, incisive, a bit inclined to deal with people as if he were a drill sergeant," the anonymous scribe observed. "A zealot and a crusader . . . Refused to be a candidate for mayor in 1923 when he could have been elected without question . . . The sort that repels familiarities . . . His back, even at times of triumph, is seldom slapped."

Some people go along to get along and end up with slapped backs and testimonial dinners. Others follow their own moral compass, at great personal risk, and are ridiculed as "the sort that repels familiarities." They might even be attacked on the street for no apparent reason. The mystery of the attempted kidnapping was never solved. It hangs there, unexplained, an echo of dangerous times, a grim reminder that a man who dares to do what Van Cise did will be looking over his shoulder for years to come.

The kind of criminal conspiracies he fought are still with us, in more sophisticated guises, and so are the deceptions that go with them. But we can learn a great deal about how to fight them from his example—the methods he employed, the determination he showed, the ways he snatched victory from defeat without getting snatched himself. He had a singular talent for sniffing out a con and exposing it, whether it was a stock exchange that existed only in the minds of its victims or a fat little man hiding behind a curtain, demanding that all bow and pay tribute to the Imperial Wizard. And, as his would-be abductors found out that summer evening long ago, if you showed up at his house uninvited, intending to take him by force, then that had better be a real gun in your pocket.

The Colonel was just the man to call your bluff.

PART ONE

GRIFTERS

Lies were the foundation of my schemes. A lie is an allurement, a fabrication, that can be embellished into a fantasy. It can be clothed in the raiments of a mystic conception.

—JOSEPH R. WEIL, as told to W. T. Brannon,
Con Man: A Master Swindler's Own Story

1

—

The Fighting Man

Like many American soldiers coming home from the Great War, Philip Van Cise found himself at loose ends. The war and his part in it had not gone the way he expected, and the return to civilian life was not as gratifying as he'd imagined it would be. It was fine to have people fussing over your uniform, your ribbons and medals—including, in Van Cise's case, a Distinguished Service Medal, honoring his "exceptional ability" as an intelligence officer—but settling into the peace was more difficult than he anticipated.

By the time he stepped off the train in Denver's Union Station in July of 1919, shortly after his discharge, the victory parades had all been marched, the speeches delivered, the thanks of a grateful nation bestowed. He was thirty-four years old and had been gone for more than two years, including sixteen months in France. The experience had been, for the most part, a disappointment. Having previously commanded a company in the Colorado National Guard, he'd sailed through officer training, received a commission as a captain of infantry, and patiently waited for a posting to a front-line battalion. But his superiors considered him to be more valuable as an administrator; he was promoted to major and assigned to supply services and office work. In letters to a cousin in Iowa, he complained of being stuck in a series of paper-pushing, do-nothing jobs, with too much time on his hands—time he spent learning French, reading Ibsen, exploring the countryside, and even, on one occasion, hunting boar.

"About all I can say is that I am practically my own boss, can go for a horseback ride, auto ride, or an airplane ride whenever I want to, and work on an average about one hour a day," he wrote. "It is a shame the great number of officers who are over here with absolutely nothing to do."

He finally "went over the top," as the trench soldiers called it, in the Battle of Saint-Mihiel, the first American-led offensive of the war. He emerged unscathed and was put in charge of intelligence for the Eighty-First Division, gathering information on the enemy's strength, location, and intentions. Promoted to lieutenant colonel and detailed to the general staff of the American Expeditionary Forces, he remained on active duty overseas for months after the armistice.

In Denver, he had a wife and two small children, a son and a daughter. The youngest, Edwin, had been scarcely three months old when Van Cise enlisted. A widowed mother, an ailing sister, and a much-neglected law practice also demanded his attention—along with the city itself, a city that Van Cise had embraced, brooded over, bragged about, and quarreled with most of his adult life.

At first glance, postwar Denver made quite an impression. It was the largest, most prosperous metropolis between Kansas City and San Francisco, home to a quarter million residents—roughly one out of every four people in the entire state. A regional hub for industry and agriculture, it also offered abundant amenities for tourists, including thousands of acres of urban and mountain parks; a mild and sunny climate; a well-lit downtown teeming with elegant hotels, shops, restaurants, and movie palaces, served by an extensive electric trolley system; and spectacular views of the rugged foothills and towering Rockies to the west. Tuberculosis patients came to Denver for its dry, clean air; immigrants, primarily from eastern Europe and Russia, came seeking jobs in its factories, stockyards, and smelters (where the air was not so clean). Civic boosters touted Denver as the Top of the World, the Mile High City, and the Paris of the West.

The official version of how the Paris of the West got so grand, the one recited by tour guides, tended to focus on colorful prospectors who struck it rich and blessed their adopted home with magnificent acts of philanthropy. The real story of how Denver evolved from a frontier settlement to a bustling city with cosmopolitan pretensions was a much tawdrier tale. It began in the late 1850s, when gold hunters established a clump of primitive encampments along Cherry Creek and the South Platte River. The gold petered out quickly, and civic progress stalled during the turmoil of the Civil War. But more substantial gold and silver strikes in the nearby mountains brought a flood of miners and speculators to the region. In the 1870s, the railroads and statehood came calling, and in the following decade the city's population tripled. Denver transformed itself from gold-camp backwater to mining supply capital, providing equipment, outfitting, engineering, legal and financial expertise, amusements and diversions—a gauntlet of services and investment opportunities designed to separate newcomers from their cash.

Not all the offerings were strictly legal. Laws against gambling and prostitution had been on the books since territorial days, but they were rarely enforced. In a red-light district known as The Row, hundreds of women worked in brothels, ranging from fancy bawdy houses to ramshackle "cribs," scarcely larger than a jail cell. A short stroll away was a procession of saloons and gambling halls. At most of them, the house had not simply an edge but a guarantee, thanks to loaded dice, rigged wheels, and faro dealers who were skilled mechanics. One reporter concluded that, of the hundreds of games of chance operating in Denver in 1885, all but six were crooked.

Suckers who steered clear of the gambling dens had a good chance of losing their bankroll elsewhere. Three-card monte dealers worked the street corners, and even the more respectable hotels and saloons had their share of gold-brick salesmen and promoters of salted mines. The most brazen of the con men, Jefferson Randolph "Soapy" Smith, drew throngs to his corner stand by offering large bills—twenties, fifties, even the occasional hundred—as "prizes" wrapped around bars of cheap soap, which were then packaged in paper and presented for purchase alongside other prize-less bars. After watching an ecstatic winner or two come away waving cash, frantic customers might pay five dollars a bar—or even more, once Smith started auctioning off the dwindling pile. But the prize winners were all shills, Smith deftly palmed each bill as he wrapped the bars in paper, and there was never anything in the suckers' packages but soap. Smith made enough at the racket and other schemes to own a piece of the Tivoli Club, one of the town's premiere clip joints.

Bunco artists like Smith couldn't have operated so openly without official sanction and protection, a trail of greased palms that went from the cop on the beat to high-ranking city officials. In 1894, a new Colorado governor, Davis Waite, attempted to do something about Denver's graft-riddled Fire and Police Board, replacing the worst offenders with his own appointees. The fired board members refused to step down. Waite called out the state militia, which trained cannons and Gatling guns on City Hall. Deputized in response to the emergency, Soapy Smith brought men, guns, and explosives to the besieged building, determined to defend the city's right to embrace corruption as it saw fit. The tense standoff ended with Waite ordering his troops to withdraw.

Pressure from business interests eventually did what the militia could not. Robert Speer, a land developer turned Democratic party boss, ascended to the mayor's office on promises of cleaning up the city, literally and figuratively. Under the Speer administration, squalid Cherry Creek became a greenway along a grand boulevard, an abandoned cemetery became a regional park, the city center became a whirl of new public buildings rising above a neoclassical amphitheater and plaza—and Denver became a showcase of the City Beautiful movement. Speer also launched sporadic crusades against the most conspicuous gambling halls and the cribs along The Row. The makeover did wonders for his town's image, but how deep the changes went was open to question. Speer was a realist, not a reformer; the idea was to control vice, not eradicate it.

"What evils we have thus far been unable to rid ourselves of are at least not hidden evils," he boasted in one public address. "Of course, there is graft in Denver, but I believe all efforts are being made to keep it at a minimum."

Speer's own ties to the not-so-hidden evils of the town were intricate and far-flung. He had friends and donors among the real-estate interests that stood to benefit most from the civic improvements, friends in charge of the major utility franchises

that made millions off the city, friends among the town's most
notorious gamblers and gangsters. Reporters openly referred to
him as "Bunco Bob." Weary of machine politics, voters opted
for a reform candidate in 1912, a shift to a Progressive agenda
that saw Denver shutter its red-light district and Colorado enact
its own version of Prohibition. Yet the more cynical element in
town regarded these bouts of moral purification as temporary at
best. Denver had seen waves of reform, but they never lasted. The
gamblers and the madams and the opium peddlers hadn't been
purged, merely dispersed to more discreet locales. The ban on
booze, five years before the Volstead Act, gave local bootleggers
a head start on the rest of the country. As if to underscore the
fragility of reform, in 1916 the voters threw out the do-gooders
and brought Speer back as mayor. He died of pneumonia two
years later, halfway through his third term.

Van Cise arrived back in Denver just weeks after the election of Speer's successor, Dewey Bailey, a Republican. At first,
he was too preoccupied to pay much attention to local politics,
too busy rebuilding his law practice and fielding invitations
from civic groups eager to hear about his war experiences. In
early 1920, he was asked to introduce the commander of the
American Expeditionary Forces, General John J. Pershing, at
a reception at the City Auditorium. He worked painstakingly
on his brief role in the event, which was attended by twelve
thousand veterans. But as he watched the new city administration fumble around, promising a crackdown on crime that it
couldn't seem to deliver, he began to take an interest in Mayor
Bailey. Even more intriguing was the city's district attorney,
William Foley, who was said to be reluctant, if not entirely
derelict, in the pursuit of his duties. A Democrat, Foley was
described in the *Rocky Mountain News* as "too good a fellow to
make a successful prosecutor."

Van Cise gave the situation careful study. Then he wrote a letter to a long list of friends and acquaintances, making sure the newspapers received copies. "I hereby announce my candidacy for the Republican nomination for the office of district attorney," he wrote. "Good government and good citizenship result from the certain and swift enforcement of the law. I believe in action rather than promises."

=====

As he readily admitted in later years, Van Cise didn't know what he was getting into when he set his sights on becoming Denver's top law enforcement official. He was restless, cocky, ambitious, to be sure. At the same time, he wasn't quite as naive as he sounded. He knew something about the forces and people shaping local and state politics from years of sharing an office with his father, Edwin, another restless man of high ideals and multiple occupations. Father and son also shared a painfully earnest civic-mindedness, born of inflexible personal convictions about right and wrong and proprietary pride in their adopted town. A crime or scandal that shamed their city was like an assault on their family name, or a dinner guest who spat on the floor; it was an outrage that had to be addressed.

Born in 1842 in Adams County, Pennsylvania, Edwin Van Cise moved to Iowa as a teen. He taught in a country school, joined a Union regiment of volunteers, worked as a reporter and editor at the *Burlington Hawk Eye*, traveled Europe as a correspondent for several other newspapers, and picked up a license as a Universalist minister before deciding that his true calling was the law. In 1877, he moved to the Dakota Territory and became a county attorney in Rapid City and a special prosecutor under the Hayes administration, charged with investigating fraud perpetrated by whites on the Pine Ridge reservation. He then opened his own practice in Deadwood. In 1881, he married twenty-year-old Adele McBrine, the daughter of Irish immigrants.

Two years later, the couple had a daughter, Ethel. Philip was born the following year, on October 25, 1884. Deadwood's most notorious residents, including Wild Bill Hickock and Calamity Jane, had already died or moved on, but the place still had its rough edges. In his youth Phil encountered Sioux families camped on the edge of town, displaced by the Black Hills gold rush. He and other white boys bartered with the Sioux boys, trading kitchen utensils for arrowheads and tomahawks. According to family lore, the elder Van Cise represented members of the tribe *pro bono* in their claims against the mining companies, but as the mines began to play out, so did Edwin's law practice. In 1900, the family moved to booming Denver. Edwin set up a firm downtown, joined the law school faculty at the University of Colorado, served on the city's new Public Utilities Commission, and became affiliated with the Progressive Party.

A gawky adolescent, Phil loved fishing, the outdoors, and trouncing all comers as the star of the debate team at Denver's East High School. He graduated in 1903, then went to Boulder to study at the university. During the summer he worked as a reporter for the *Rocky Mountain News* and as house manager for his fraternity. In 1909 he collected his law degree from CU and joined his father's firm, Van Cise and Grant.

Yet he wasn't ready to settle into a career behind a desk. Just months out of school, he became one of the organizers of an all-college-man company in the Colorado National Guard. The sixty reservists of Company K soon established a reputation as the most disciplined and well-drilled outfit in the state. Their captain, Van Cise, was outspoken in his contempt for some of the other companies, a slovenly collection of Spanish-American War vets and ex-mercenaries. What was needed in the Guard, he insisted, was true professionalism. It was a cry that would be taken up by others, but only after a bloody clash between soldiers and civilians in a desolate place called Ludlow, a tragedy that reverberated throughout Colorado and much of the nation.

On September 23, 1913, eleven thousand miners working in southern Colorado's coal fields went on strike, after years of enduring the deadliest working conditions in the country. The mine owners brought in strikebreakers and private security companies to keep the mines operating. Evicted from the company towns, the strikers set up tent colonies near the railroad lines and tried to prevent imported "scabs" from reaching the mines. Local police agencies, which were closely aligned with the mine owners, were incapable of stemming the violent confrontations that followed. Under mounting pressure from the coal companies to intervene, Governor Elias Ammons called out the Colorado National Guard under the command of General John Chase, a Denver eye doctor. More than a thousand troops arrived in the southern fields at the end of October, setting up garrisons in Trinidad and Walsenburg and establishing an outpost just a few hundred yards from the largest tent colony of them all, Ludlow—a makeshift village of twelve hundred men, women, and children.

At first the strikers welcomed the soldiers as peacekeepers. Upon arrival at Ludlow, Company K was greeted with a band and union songs. Van Cise, who'd grown a substantial chin-warmer, was known as "the captain with a beard," and his men played baseball and football with the colonists. But the relationship quickly frayed. General Chase ordered the tents searched and all weapons seized. The strikers responded by hiding guns in storage pits dug under the tents and smuggling in more. An order prohibiting the troops from escorting strikebreakers to the mines was rescinded; the strikers, mostly southern and eastern European immigrants, started calling the soldiers "scab herders." Even more alarming, former mine guards and local deputies, sworn enemies of the strikers, began showing up in National Guard uniforms.

The most despised of them all was Lieutenant Karl "Monte" Linderfelt, commander of Company B. An army veteran who'd seen combat in the Philippines and as a mercenary in Mexico, Linderfelt had been working as a deputy in Las Animas County—in other words, in service to the mine owners—when he'd been called back to active duty in the Guard, along with his two brothers. In the months that followed, Linderfelt threatened or assaulted several strikers, earning particular ill will from the Greeks in the Ludlow colony, whom he referred to as "dagos" and "rednecks" (communists). "He rages violently upon little or no provocation, and is wholly unfit to bear arms and command men, as he has no control over himself," declared a State Federation of Labor report to Governor Ammons, urging that Linderfelt be removed. Van Cise thought Linderfelt was the worst man the army could have put in command of a company at Ludlow because of his "insane hatred" of the strikers. It didn't escape his notice that while the men from Company K could visit the tent colony unarmed, Linderfelt's men always went in armed to the teeth, expecting an ambush.

The strike dragged on through one of the harshest winters Colorado had ever seen. In the spring, eager to end the costly military occupation of two counties and believing that the strikers were close to capitulation, Ammons began recalling the troops. Van Cise's Company K went home in March. By mid-April only a skeleton force remained at the military encampment at Ludlow, including Linderfelt's Company B. On April 20, the day after Greek Easter, the colony erupted in gunfire, explosions, and flames.

No one knows who fired the first shot or what provoked it. It might have been strikers seeking retaliation against Linderfelt, or a soldier reacting to a surge of armed men pouring out of the camp, who were reacting to reports that soldiers were trying to arrest Louis Tikas, a leader of Ludlow's Greek community. Within minutes the militia had set up a machine gun on a rise overlooking the colony, and bullets were flying in all directions. Toward evening, soldiers began to move through the colony, setting the tents on fire and burning the place to the ground. By morning, twenty people had died, including two women and eleven children who'd taken refuge from the gunfire in an earthen cellar beneath a tent and suffocated there as the fire raged over them. Also among the dead were a soldier shot in the neck and three prisoners of the militia, supposedly killed while trying to escape. One of the dead prisoners was Louis Tikas, who had been shot three times in the back and had his skull fractured by a heavy blow.

Over the next ten days, the strikers exacted a terrible vengeance for their dead. They dynamited mine entrances, shot suspected scabs, and engaged the militia in battle on the hogback above Walsenburg. It was one of the most violent insurrections since the Civil War, claiming the lives of at least six strikers and twenty-four mine employees, and it didn't stop until President Woodrow Wilson sent in federal troops.

Van Cise returned to southern Colorado on Friday, April 24, well ahead of the federals. He was a man on a mission. The months of strike duty had postponed his plans to wed Sara Reeves, a twenty-eight-year-old piano teacher and the daughter of a prominent Denver realtor; now the wedding was only a day

away, but he'd been ordered back to the strike zone to learn all
he could about what would become known as the Ludlow Massacre. He sought out enlisted men from Company B, who told
him that Linderfelt had ordered the execution of the prisoners
and smashed Tikas in the head with his rifle, breaking the stock.
Van Cise reported back to Governor Ammons on Saturday
morning and married Sara that evening. He had to cut short the
reception after learning that he'd been appointed to a military
commission charged with investigating the killings and was
required back in the field. Van Cise accepted the appointment
reluctantly, making it plain that he believed court-martial proceedings should be brought against Linderfelt and every militia
member who participated in the burning of the colony.

To his surprise, court-martial hearings were held. To no
one's surprise, the hearings ended in acquittal of every one of
the soldiers charged—except for Linderfelt, who was found
to have assaulted Tikas, but without any intent of "criminal-
ity." He received a mild reprimand. After barely a week of
inquiry, the three-man commission issued a report claiming
that the strikers had started the firefight. Some blame, the
report added, "lies with the coal operators, who established
in an American industrial community a numerous class of
ignorant, lawless, and savage south-European peasants." That
ringing condemnation didn't reflect the complexity of Van
Cise's view of the matter. Although his own writings about
Ludlow included a call for tougher immigration laws, he also
denounced the Guard's efforts to investigate itself as a "whitewash" and referred to Lieutenant Colonel Edward Boughton,
the head of the commission and the principal author of the
report, as a crook. When not in uniform, Boughton earned
his bread as an attorney for mining companies.

Van Cise resigned from the Guard in the fall of 1914,

shortly after the death of his father at the age of seventy-two from complications of diabetes. His father had taught him about the law and justice, but Ludlow had been his education in the absence of such things: No justice for Tikas, for Linderfelt, for the women and children asphyxiated in the pit, for the men killed in the ten-day rampage that followed. His own role as inquisitor and whistleblower had won him few allies. Curiously, though, the bitter episode would not be the last time he sought out such a thankless mission—and ended up caught in the middle between labor and capital, trying to keep the peace and outraged by the lawlessness of both sides. The sequel came six years later, in the heat of his campaign to become Denver's district attorney.

———

ON AUGUST 1, 1920, LOCAL 746 of the streetcar workers' union voted 887–10 to strike against the Denver Tramway Company. Cutting the six-cent fares by a penny had been among the campaign promises of Mayor Bailey; to accomplish this, the company lopped wages, laid off employees, and trimmed routes. Facing more looming job losses and struggling to keep up with the rising cost of living on less than fifty cents an hour, the remaining workers saw no other choice but to walk out.

The move left thousands without transportation. The company summoned professional strikebreaker John "Black Jack" Jerome, who brought in scores of armed men to operate the most vital routes. The situation deteriorated quickly. Strike supporters surrounded one of the few trolleys running downtown and derailed it. Strikebreakers sprayed fire extinguishers on the attackers. Autos filled with strikebreakers were pelted with rocks and bricks. Arrests multiplied. So did the violence.

On the fifth day of the strike, a crowd of thousands marched into downtown in support of the union. It started quietly enough, but by evening, the demonstration had devolved into a series of scrums involving strikers, strikebreakers, and police. Throngs engulfed two streetcars, overturned and demolished them. Another contingent stormed the downtown "car barns," where the trolleys were stored, only to be met with gunfire. Two streetcars were attacked outside the Catholic cathedral on Colfax Avenue, forcing strikebreakers to take refuge in the church. An assault on another car barn on the south side led to more shooting. Hundreds poured into the *Denver Post* headquarters that night, enraged at the newspaper for its support of the company, and tried to wreck the presses and set the building on fire. At one in the morning, after huddling with the governor, Mayor Bailey put out a call for volunteers to help his overwhelmed police force maintain order.

The next day hundreds of army veterans showed up in uniform at the city's American Legion posts, reporting for special duty. They were sworn in as deputies by a police magistrate and issued white brassards to wear on the right arm, signifying that they were part of a peacekeeping force. Van Cise was one of them. Monte Linderfelt was another.

Van Cise was put to work coordinating deployment of the volunteers, who were supposed to patrol residential areas and free up the police to concentrate on quelling any disturbances downtown. Linderfelt, hailed in the *Rocky Mountain News* as "hero of many a hard fight," roamed the streets with his own entourage. He claimed to have seventy-five crack riflemen and gunners under his command, eager to respond to any assault on law and order.

The legionnaires formed cordons, closed streets, and told roving packs of belligerent young men to go home. Van Cise caught a ride in a truck with a machine gun mounted in the back and got no arguments from anyone. But after sunset, trouble boiled on the east side of town, where hundreds of strikers and onlookers had gathered outside a car barn packed with scabs. A touring car full of strikebreakers roared onto the scene and was met with a hail of bricks. Gunmen inside the building fired into the crowd, killing five and wounding at least a dozen more, including several women and children.

That night the mayor made the call he'd refused to make the night before. Within hours, Denver was under martial law. Federal troops rode the streetcars and occupied key positions across the city. The strikebreakers were disarmed. The union called off the strike, but most of the strikers lost their jobs anyway. The riots, which in two nights had resulted in seven dead and more than fifty wounded, came to an abrupt end.

District Attorney Foley summoned a special grand jury to investigate the strike violence. Some of the rioters who'd trashed private property were indicted. But no one was ever charged for the slaughter outside the eastside car barn. Van Cise was stunned.

It was Ludlow all over again.

———

HE HAD NO REASON TO EXPECT that he might win the race for district attorney. He had little experience with criminal law and no political pull at all. All he had was his late father's sterling reputation, a few friends in the legal community, and whatever support he could drum up by touting his war record. His campaign brochures presented him as "A Fighting Man for a Fighting Job," someone who'd served his country honorably and would be a fearless prosecutor—in contrast, say, to William Foley. Van Cise blasted the incumbent for failing to prosecute Denver Tramway's murderous hired guns and for his anemic courtroom performance in general. One third of the criminal cases Foley had filed during his four years in office were dismissed. Foley had personally tried only two cases— and lost them both.

Foley wasn't his chief worry, though. The Republicans had their machine politics, just like the Democrats, and the insiders loathed Van Cise for running without their approval. The party leadership had its own ideas about who the next DA was going to be, and it wasn't a self-promoting nobody from Deadwood who didn't know how to keep his nose out of messes like Ludlow or the Tramway strike. But Van Cise's timing for his dark-horse run couldn't have been better. The boys at City Hall backed one candidate for DA, Henry May, and U.S. Senator Lawrence Phipps backed another, Omar Garwood. When the GOP primary rolled around, the party loyalists were split. Van Cise drew enough votes from people who didn't care for May or Garwood to emerge with the nomination.

Alarmed at the upset, some of the Republican faithful began working to get the incumbent Democrat reelected rather than back Van Cise. Others set out to put an independent on the ballot, denouncing Van Cise as a pseudo-reformer and a martinet. ("His mind travels along a lone track—the rigidity of military discipline, all elements of humaneness obliterated," one of his critics wrote in an open letter to the public. "Force, brutality, egotism run amuck constitute a complete mental analysis of the candidate.") In spite of all this, a stream of supplicants sought out the Fighting Man, figuring he might have a shot at winning. A few days after the primary, Leonard DeLue showed up at Van Cise's law office, all smiles and good wishes.

DeLue had been a deputy sheriff in Denver back in the bad old days of the 1890s, involved in strikebreaking and street clashes over which gang of duly deputized toughs was going to control the ballot-stuffing at the city's polling places. He now ran the biggest private investigation agency in town, an enterprise built on his extensive knowledge of the local power structure and his access to people from all strata of society. He offered Van Cise his congratulations and said he had a friend who wanted to meet him, someone who "can do more to elect you than any man in Denver."

DeLue didn't name his friend, and Van Cise resisted his attempts to set up a meeting. He didn't like DeLue and didn't see any reason to curry favor with his friends. But DeLue persisted. He persuaded another attorney to intercede on his behalf, urging Van Cise to "be sociable" if it would help him get votes. Van Cise agreed to meet the mysterious kingmaker in DeLue's office one morning. He arrived at the appointed time and found Lou Blonger waiting for him.

Blonger was heavy-set, with thick-lidded eyes and coarse features. His face was dominated by a bulbous, oversized nose, like a misshapen potato, that was both unnerving and comical. He was seventy-one and had been a fixture in the city for more than thirty years, with interests at various times in saloons, gambling halls, and related rackets. Van Cise had met him years ago, in the course of his work as a cub reporter, but knew hardly anything about him. There were all sorts of stories about Blonger and his shady connections on both sides of the street, from judges and party bosses to legendary gunmen and outlaws like Wyatt Earp, Bat Masterson, and Soapy Smith. Like his city, Blonger had ostensibly cleaned up his act in recent years. He kept an office on Seventeenth Street these days, in the heart of the city's financial district, and referred to himself as a mining investor. Yet the moment Van Cise stepped into DeLue's office and saw Blonger there, he knew something unsavory was in the works.

Blonger was soft-spoken and genial. He boasted that he was a Civil War veteran and had marched in Memorial Day parades alongside the candidate's late father, a "grand old man." It was important for the vets to stick together, he said, and he was keenly interested in supporting the only candidate in the race who'd seen combat in France. He asked blunt questions about the state of Van Cise's law practice and his campaign funds. Van Cise admitted that neither was thriving.

"Have you any rich friends who are putting up for you?" Blonger asked.

"I've paid my own way so far," Van Cise replied, adding that he didn't think the campaign would cost more than two thousand dollars, tops.

"Two thousand dollars! It'll cost twenty-five if it costs a cent," Blonger declared. "I guess I am a sentimental fool, but . . . because you are the only soldier on any ticket, I'll put up that twenty-five thousand. You can either have it now or call on me as you need it."

Keeping his expression as deadpan as he could, Van Cise struggled to craft a response. The job of district attorney paid less than a hundred dollars a week. Twenty-five grand was better than five years' salary. It was graft on a grand scale. But what was expected in return? He had to find out.

"I don't know how to thank you," he said. "I don't need your money now. But I may need it, and if it costs as you say it does, I will certainly call upon you."

That seemed to satisfy Blonger. He chatted amiably and to no apparent purpose for a few minutes. Then he began to talk about young men he knew, grandsons of old chums, who were rising stars in the stock business. Their dealings were "perfectly legitimate," but occasionally a client got rattled and made a complaint, dragging in the district attorney over nothing, and putting Blonger in the position of posting bond until the matter was cleared up. It would save him a lot of inconvenience, he suggested, if Van Cise would agree to set the bond in such situations at a thousand dollars.

Once again, the candidate had to pick his words carefully. Low bail for peddlers of dubious stocks, so they could skip town without having to forfeit more than a fraction of their take—that was the ask? It was a clumsy play, and there was no way Van Cise could deflect it without declaring himself.

"I don't know anything about bonds," he said. "But my hunch would be to fix the bond at double the amount the defendant is said to have stolen. Then there would be no question about his appearance at the trial."

His frankness seemed to chase all the hail-fellow-soldier camaraderie out of the room. The gleam of interest in Blonger's eyes faded. There was no more talk of donations or bonds, and Van Cise soon departed.

On election night he took Sara to the Republican party headquarters to await the returns. The early count, based on ballots from the central business district, favored Foley. Van Cise could hear the cheers from the Republican county chairman's office, where the chairman was hosting Blonger and a deputy sheriff named Tom Clarke. Then the returns from other parts of the city started to trickle in. Van Cise surged ahead and stayed there, ultimately carrying close to 60 percent of the vote. Around midnight, Blonger and Clarke made a noisy, profanity-strewn exit.

Over the next few weeks, as Van Cise wound down his law practice and prepared to take office, he had occasion to reflect on his conversation with Blonger and pick at its implications. One December day he phoned the man and asked him to come to his office. Blonger arrived in minutes, perhaps hopeful that the district attorney–elect had decided to take him up on his offer of financial assistance. For long moments the men sat in cautious silence, eyeing each other.

"Lou," Van Cise began, "what is your honest opinion of the conversation we had in September?"

Blonger hesitated, as if looking for the trick in the question. But there was no equivocation in his reply. "That was the damnedest fool stunt I ever pulled in my life," he said.

Van Cise nodded. As soon as he was in office, he explained, he would be going after the illegal gambling operations in town. Those with a financial interest in such businesses could expect to be shut down and prosecuted.

Blonger listened with evident bafflement. He didn't have anything to do with gambling joints anymore, he protested. Not for years.

"Well, Lou, I just wanted to give you notice to quit while the quitting is good," Van Cise said.

"You do what you want," Blonger snapped.

Soon he was out the door—and off to the races, he said, in Hot Springs, Arkansas. The reaction Van Cise had hoped to elicit from him had failed to materialize. Whatever the old scoundrel was seeking to protect with his spurned $25,000 donation, it wasn't a rigged roulette wheel or card game. It was something much bigger.

Van Cise realized he was going to have to find out a lot more about Lou Blonger.

2

—

The Big Store

The man to see about how things worked in Denver was Hamilton Armstrong, the long-suffering police chief. Ham, as his friends called him, had been in and out of political favor over the past quarter century and knew all the players. No one had a better grasp of how crime was organized in the city or of the private arrangements among cops, politicians, and criminals that kept the smell of rot from permeating downtown and driving away the tourists. Shortly after his triumph in the election, Van Cise walked into City Hall, asked for the chief, and was granted an audience.

Armstrong was sixty-four years old, a gray, sunken fellow with an imposing walrus mustache; it was as if the job had worn him down, like a relentless rain, leaving only the mustache. He had been a bookbinder and a state senator before taking the chief's job in 1894 as Governor Waite's personal choice to oversee a shake-up of the force and a crackdown on illegal gambling. He had been brought back into office during subsequent spasms of reform and was now on his fourth nonconsecutive appointment as chief. Known for spurning bribes and leading vice raids himself, he was good copy for reporters and a widely trusted public figure in a town where such men were in short supply. Months before the 1920 Tramway strike, he'd been selected as an impartial arbiter, tasked with trying to broker a deal between the company and its workers. When the strike turned ugly, he'd been on the front lines and caught a flying brick in the face. Despite the chief's habit of calling everyone "son," Van Cise liked him and considered him a straight shooter.

But Armstrong wasn't inclined to share what he knew with just anybody. He suggested that the new district attorney see the situation firsthand before they had a serious talk. He summoned a police captain and introduced him to Van Cise. "Take him out and show him the town," he said.

"What part?" the captain asked.

"Every damn bit," the chief replied.

For several nights Van Cise and the captain explored downtown's seamier corners. They knocked on anonymous doors, got eyeballed through peepholes, and waited long minutes before admission, by which time any gambling equipment or booze in the vicinity had disappeared. They dropped in on rooming establishments that contained a suspicious number of single females but no gentleman callers. In Hop Alley, the remnant of a once-thriving Chinese community, they visited fan-tan parlors that seemed to have emptied of patrons just moments before they arrived, clouds of tobacco smoke still lingering over the tables.

Bewildered, Van Cise came back to Armstrong for an explanation. Despite what the law said, despite decades of alleged reforms, Denver was still a wide-open town—that much was obvious. It was also clear that the police knew about the gambling, prostitution, and speakeasy operations, and that a system of lookouts and barred doors had developed to spare the cops, the clientele, and the operators any embarrassment. But why did Armstrong put up with it?

The chief responded patiently, like a father explaining an unpleasant fact of life to a child. The lookouts Van Cise had encountered were only the beginning. There were lookouts on the police force, too, and in the district attorney's office. "When officers can get money for not seeing things, it takes an unusual man not to get blind once in a while," he said.

He ticked off names. Ike Goldman, the city constable who supervised jury selection in the misdemeanor courts, took payoffs from many of the gambling houses and brothels. Tom Clarke, the chief deputy sheriff whom Van Cise had seen hunkered with Lou Blonger on election night, collected from others. The bootleggers spread cash around several precincts, and the best bonded stuff in town could be found stored in the basement of the city auditorium, Mayor Bailey's private stock for lavish parties.

"What would happen if you raided all these places?" Van Cise asked.

"Say, you *are* green," Armstrong mused. "My raids would all be tipped off, and I'd arrest a lot of people but have no evidence. And Denver would have a new chief of police."

The problem wasn't just a payoff here and there, the chief explained. The web of graft and corruption had been evolving for years and now spanned the city, from the courts to the jails to the mayor's office. And behind it all was the Fixer, Lou Blonger, the man who could spring crooks with one phone call and whose own operations were so well-protected that Armstrong was powerless to oppose him. Blonger and his right-hand man, Adolph Duff, ran some kind of stock racket, but Armstrong didn't know the details. He'd once arrested Duff, only to see him released within hours, after Tom Clarke "went upstairs." Mayor Bailey had then informed Armstrong that he was to stay away from Blonger and his associates and was not to raid gambling houses or brothels "except on notice and for publicity purposes." Other than that, he could chase all the crooks he wanted.

"What Blonger says goes," Armstrong said. He named two police detectives who were almost certainly on Blonger's payroll. "Look out for them. They are Blonger's men, and he has a lot of others in this burg."

Van Cise listened raptly. He and the chief made a pact that evening; sick of tiptoeing around the graft, Armstrong agreed to work with him to bring down the whole mess, and damn the consequences. Van Cise went home that evening eager to get started. But he lost his most important ally before the plan could be put into motion. On January 10, 1921, a day before the new DA was sworn in, Ham Armstrong died of heart failure at his home. He'd been battling cancer and a bad heart for some time, but the *Denver Times* attributed his death to the frustration and heartbreak of his job: "Handicapped in the conduct of his office by political influence, unable to proceed vigorously against law offenders who were protected by pull, discouraged at the general public apathy toward vice, his spirit, according to his intimates, was crushed."

Speculation about who would replace the chief abounded. One article mentioned six possible successors. Three of them— Deputy Sheriff Tom Clarke, Captain of Detectives Washington Rinker, and Detective George Sanders—were names Van Cise already knew. Armstrong had called them Blonger's men.

———

MURDERS AND OTHER MAJOR FELONY CASES commanded most of Van Cise's attention during his first months in office. In his spare time, he began building a file on Blonger and his activities. It was a lonely pursuit. Mindful of what Armstrong had said about lookouts everywhere, he was wary of enlisting anyone in his office in his investigation, from the career staff to the youthful team of deputy prosecutors he'd recruited himself, for fear of tipping off his target. But information came to him anyway, in fragments and scraps, gleaned from old records or innocently volunteered by veteran attorneys drawn into reminiscing about local history. Reporters tended to have the best stories about Blonger, but it was hard to say how many of those stories were true. Blonger had cut a wide swath across the frontier West, a time and place so richly slathered in legend and romance that it was difficult to extract a reliable fact or two.

Born in 1849 in Vermont, Blonger grew up in a large family that would produce several rogues and hard cases. The family soon moved to Wisconsin. When Lou was ten, his mother died while giving birth to her thirteenth child. At fifteen, Lou joined the Union Army as a fifer. After the Civil War he headed west with his older brother Sam, whom he idolized. The pair gambled, drank, and embarked on a string of business ventures, never lingering in one place for long: A billiard parlor in Iowa. A gambling hall in Salt Lake City. Two saloons in Nevada, another in California. Prospecting in New Mexico and Colorado. In 1879, Sam Blonger ran for mayor of Leadville, Colorado, and lost. Three years later he was the city marshal in Albuquerque, with Lou as his deputy. At some point Sam lost an eye in a gunfight and took to wearing blue-tinted glasses to hide the injury.

In the late 1880s, the Blonger brothers moved to Denver, dividing their time between working mining claims in the mountains and running a series of saloons in town. The pair had attempted modest swindles of various kinds over the years, but in Denver they found all that was needed to settle into the business, including a steady supply of suckers ripe for the trimming. Lou divorced his first wife, a wealthy San Francisco artist, and married his second, Nola, a young actress. He branched out from crooked card games to policy shops, a form of lottery that encouraged gamblers of meager means to play their lucky numbers with little hope of return. He also began to dabble in politics, his name surfacing in several election scandals involving ballot-stuffing and the bribing of voters.

His expanding activities put him in competition with other scam artists, including Soapy Smith and his crew. The two gangs were apparently rivals in some matters, partners in others. According to one account, Smith went on a rampage one night and walked into the Blongers' saloon to confront Sam about their territorial disputes. A police officer intercepted Smith in the nick of time, as Lou waited behind a cigar counter with a shotgun, prepared to blast Soapy into bubbles. Whether the story was true or not, the volatile Smith's influence visibly diminished as Lou Blonger's star rose. It was said that, in order to keep operating his soap racket, Smith had to pay tribute to Blonger; Van Cise heard the figure was as much as 50 percent of the take. In 1896, Smith left Colorado for good, fleeing an attempted murder rap. He died in a shootout in Skagway, Alaska, two years later. Sam soon retreated from the field, too, in favor of mining, leaving the Denver underworld in his brother's capable hands.

Lou Blonger's police record indicated more than twenty arrests. His gambling houses were raided repeatedly, usually after a complaint from a fleeced visitor. One filing accused him of operating a "systematic bunco game" that victimized "young men of tender years." In 1898, Blonger was charged with assault after beating a man with the butt of a revolver. Blonger claimed the man had swindled him out of a thousand dollars—an instance of the bunco man getting buncoed that had the police in stitches. But none of the cases resulted in a single conviction. The charges were either dismissed for lack of evidence or dropped after some private settlement was reached.

The trail of arrests stopped abruptly in 1901. By all outward appearances, Blonger was now a prosperous, respectable old gent. He kept an apartment half a block from the State Capitol for his second wife and was building a top-of-the-line bungalow near the Denver Country Club for his mistress, at a cost of thirty thousand dollars. He also had orchards on the western outskirts of town, where he grew the state's best cherries. Every year he dispatched crates of them to politicians, judges, and other prominent members of the community. (His circle of longtime friends included *Denver Post* publisher Harry Tammen and William Pinkerton, head of the famous detective agency.) A batch of cherries from Lou was a sign that you were in favor, or perhaps that you were about to get hit up for one.

Was it possible that, as Blonger claimed, he was no longer mixed up in the rackets? At least one of his gold and silver mines, the Forest Queen in Cripple Creek, had been productive enough that Blonger could be living comfortably on its proceeds alone. But Van Cise knew better. The bribe Blonger had offered him was one piece of evidence, Armstrong's account of Blonger's untouchable status another. The lack of arrests in the past twenty years merely suggested that the Fixer had become so powerful and well-insulated that arrest was now unthinkable.

There was also the matter of the company he kept. No legitimate businessman would have any reason to associate with

Adolph Duff, also known as Kid Duffy, whom Armstrong had described as the Fixer's lieutenant. Short, lean, pale, nervous and ferret-like, Duff shared offices with Blonger on the third floor of the American National Bank building downtown and claimed to be in the insurance business. But he had a history as a compulsive gambler, opium smoker, and petty promoter who used to stage crooked footraces in the Garden of the Gods, a scenic red-rocks park in Colorado Springs. Chased out of the Springs after a gambling rap, he had thrown in with Blonger and become part of the Fixer's insulation. He reportedly served as the "manager" who handled payoffs and otherwise acted as a buffer between his boss and the field operatives who ran the confidence games. But nailing down the details was difficult. When Van Cise tried to retrieve Duff's rap sheet, he was told that the Denver police file on him had been lost, including his mug shot. Searches of other jurisdictions revealed that his records had been removed from those police departments too.

The greater mystery was how Blonger and Duff had made their way from sawdust-sprinkled saloons to their spacious offices on Seventeenth Street. Not so long ago, both had been chiseling other bottom-feeders out of a few bucks here and there, slipping a crumpled bill to the cop on the beat to look the other way. Now they had nice suits, substantial real estate holdings and other investments, friends in high places, the city at their feet. After weeks of discreet inquiry, Van Cise still knew next to nothing about how their stock racket worked or the kind of money involved. But he was determined to find out.

Part of the answer, he discovered, was in his own office files: cries for justice from victims of the racket, cries that had been scrupulously ignored by his predecessor. Other pieces of the puzzle would be retrieved only by taking bold steps to ramp up his investigation, well beyond the boundaries that most prosecutors would consider prudent. Still others would drop into his lap unexpectedly, like manna from heaven, or a letter from a secret admirer.

———

BLONGER AND DUFF WERE GOOD at covering their tracks, but they couldn't keep all mention of their crimes out of the newspapers. One day a small item in the *Denver Post* caught the district attorney's attention. Albert Menaugh, a Brethren minister in Goshen, Indiana, had committed suicide after losing $12,200 in a confidence game in Denver. Van Cise wrote to the widow, seeking more details. Her attorney replied.

Menaugh had visited Denver in the summer of 1920. He was a widely respected member of his community, a former city councilman, and the assessor for the Elkhart township. The money he'd lost came from trust accounts he controlled, including a guardianship and an estate for which he was executor. How he'd been persuaded to sink those funds into a phony stock deal wasn't clear; given his reputation, he may well have been trying to increase his clients' holdings rather than steal from them. In any event, he didn't seem to have realized at first that he'd been conned. One early report stated that he'd lost the money through investments placed with the "Denver board of trade," an institution that didn't exist. By the time he caught on, the con men and the $12,200 had vanished.

Spurning his friends' efforts to spare him a prison term, the pastor insisted on pleading guilty to embezzlement. "I want to be sentenced for life," he told the prosecutor. The judge gave him one to five years in the state penitentiary. His trust clients interceded on his behalf, and Menaugh was released from prison. But the only release he found from his consuming shame and despondency was to poison himself.

Similar stories could be found in skimpy case files Van Cise inherited from Foley and in letters sent to the new DA by other victims of the con, urging him to take action on stalled investigations. Many of the incidents involved sums much greater than what Menaugh had lost; the outcomes were rarely as tragic as in that case, but they were all bad, a harrowing litany of financial ruin and disgrace. One of the first cases Van Cise came across, involving a Dallas florist named Ernst Nitsche, demonstrated how the game worked and why it was almost never prosecuted.

A prosperous German immigrant in his fifties, Nitsche had visited Colorado in the summer of 1919. While in Manitou Springs, a resort area that caters to sightseers on their way to the summit of Pikes Peak, he had fallen into conversation with a man called Crosby. The two decided to visit the luxurious Broadmoor Hotel a few miles away. While they were wandering the hotel grounds, Crosby spotted a fellow that he said was the famous Mr. Ware, a financier who'd made a splash in the newspapers for his wizardry in picking stocks. When approached, Ware seemed reluctant to admit who he was. Crosby mentioned a judge they both knew. Reassured, Ware explained that he had to keep a low profile because the syndicate of brokers who employed him didn't like all the publicity he'd been getting. He showed them a letter from the syndicate and a $75,000 security bond.

After some chit-chat about stocks and where the market was going, Crosby implored Ware to invest ten dollars on his behalf. Ware took the man's sawbuck, slipped into the Broadmoor—which, Nitsche supposed, must have contained a brokerage office—and returned a few minutes later and handed Crosby twenty dollars. More cordial conversation followed, and the stock wizard invited the two men to come with him to trade on the main exchange. They drove seventy-five miles that afternoon to a seven-story office building in downtown Denver. Ware ushered them into a room equipped with chairs, desks, and a blackboard scrawled with stock quotes, and was warmly greeted by the manager. Under Ware's tutelage, Crosby and Nitsche made several modest stock trades, doubling their money each time. Then Ware proposed that they go in with him on a $50,000 purchase of Mexican Petroleum. Within minutes they had made a killing, and Nitsche was staring in astonishment at a huge bundle of bills the manager was preparing to turn over to them.

But there was a problem. The trades had been made on credit. The manager demanded proof that they had the wherewithal to make the trades before he would release the funds. They had thirty days to deposit funds equal to the stock purchase price in a Denver bank of their choosing. After conferring with his partners about how much money they could raise—and what share of the profits each man would receive—Nitsche went back to Dallas and returned with his share: $25,000. All he had to do was show the funds on deposit in Denver, he thought, and he'd be rich.

But there was another problem. Something about the wrong initials on a purchase slip—Nitsche couldn't really follow it. The upshot was that the money had to be brought in cash to the exchange and verified before their winnings would be turned over to them. Nitsche withdrew the $25,000 from the bank and went with his partners to the exchange. Then another problem, an inconceivable blunder: While the money was being "verified," Crosby got it into his head to make one more bet on the market, apparently misinterpreting a tip Ware had given him. Just like that, it was all lost—the winnings, the cash they'd brought, everything. Furious, Ware knocked

Crosby to the ground and pulled a gun on him. He gave Nit-sche train fare to Oklahoma City and said he'd meet him there soon, after he'd put together the funds to repay his losses. But when Nitsche arrived in Oklahoma, there was a telegram wait-ing for him from Ware, saying he'd be tied up a few more days.

Realizing he'd been gulled, Nitsche returned to Denver to file a complaint. The police were of no help. Nitsche didn't give up. He circulated fliers with descriptions of the swindlers to other police departments, and a year later Crosby, whose real name was Robert Ballard, was arrested in Colorado Springs. He was shipped back to Denver to face trial for the theft of Nitsche's $25,000. But the Denver prosecutor recommended a bond of $5000, and Lou Blonger's personal lawyer, a former U.S. attorney, got it reduced to $2500. Blonger put up the bail money, a small price to pay to protect a much larger score, and Ballard disappeared.

Other cases that Van Cise reviewed followed the same script, with minor variations. The con required a team of three men, though others might play supporting roles. The one who first befriends the mark is known as the *roper* or *steerer*. It's his job to determine that the mark is a tourist, so as not to rile the police by going after locals. He then intro-duces the mark to the *spieler*—Mr. Ware, in Nitsche's case—in a manner that makes the encounter seem coincidental. The spieler takes his two new friends to the stock exchange, where the exchange manager, known as the *bookmaker*, lays down the rules and takes the mark's money. In situations where a shortage of manpower or props make it impossible to present a credible stock exchange, two grifters might attempt to man-age the whole thing, without the mark ever setting foot inside the trading room; but that version, called *playing against the wall*, was much trickier to pull off.

The Payoff—so named because the mark is "paid off" with illusory winnings before he's taken for good—was the most lucrative confidence game going. Van Cise learned its finer points and a little bit about its pedigree by consulting postal inspectors, narcotics investigators, and other federal agents. Local and federal law enforcement agencies rarely talked to each other and almost never worked together, but the district attorney figured it was time to break with convention. The feds picked up useful information about confidence rackets while tracking mail fraud and related crimes. As Van Cise saw it, the fact that they steered clear of local police made their assistance all the more welcome. Who better to school him in a complex criminal enterprise, one that Blonger's crew had fine-tuned to the point of perfection?

The Payoff, like other Big Con operations, was a twentieth-century answer to a nineteenth-century problem. Short-con games, such as three-card monte or Jefferson Smith's soap racket, required a certain amount of dexterity and hustle, but they were also quick. The main drawback was that you were dependent on the vagaries of street traffic—and sometimes, on the pliability of a passing cop. Seeking more stability, enterprising grifters began to open stores that offered legitimate merchandise up front and a friendly card game or other swindle in the back room. Around 1870, legendary con artist Benjamin Marks opened a "dollar store" in Cheyenne, Wyoming, that lured in rubes with handy household items priced at a dollar each. Marks's store is credited as the prototype, but the concept soon spread to many cities. Operators offered commissions to ropers to bring the suckers to their store and shelled out protection money to the police. A town that was well-fixed, so that the cons could be played with impunity, was known as the Big Store.

Popular as it was, the new business model had its limitations. Operating out of one location meant sacrificing mobility and anonymity; unhappy customers knew where to find you, even if the police weren't interested. And, with few exceptions, the store was still a short-con enterprise. Revenues depended on the amount of cash the mark happened to have on him when he was lured into the store. How much better it would be, the thinking went, if you could play him for all he was worth. Thus began the evolution of the Big Con, which would replace the store with an entire world of make-believe—an elegant betting parlor, an exclusive private club, a busy stock exchange—that would unfold over a matter of days or weeks, leading the mark step by artful step to his doom.

Between 1900 and 1920, increasingly elaborate versions of the Big Con emerged across the country, taking down five- and six-figure scores. In one scenario, the mark is introduced to a fake telegraph office and a disgruntled Western Union employee who knows how to beat the system; all he needs is a confederate willing to place sure bets at a local bookie joint (also fake) while the telegraph operator delays releasing the race results. Other Big Con scams involved a fixed horse race or a boxer or wrestler with deep personal reasons for wanting to strike back at his employers by throwing a match. (One racing scheme, popular in Denver for years, revolved around a can't-lose racehorse named Dineen; there was no such horse.) Each operation was different, requiring a troupe of highly skilled performers, specializing in their respective roles but also able to improvise at a moment's notice. Yet each one was built on the same basic ingredients: A roper locates a mark and determines, through casual conversation, that he has the resources to justify reeling him in. The spieler takes the mark into his confidence, explaining a surefire scheme to make money—*telling the tale*, as the grifters put it. The mark is allowed to win some money (*the convincer*). Sufficiently motivated, he is then *put on the send* for all the money he can raise. At the last moment something goes wrong, the money is lost (*taking off the touch*), and a physical altercation or other looming drama hurries the sucker out the door—and preferably out of town (*the blowoff*).

The Denver version of the Payoff was a distinct improvement over earlier models. Shifting the focus from sporting events to the stock market greatly increased the pool of willing and eager suckers; people who wouldn't dream of risking their money on a horse race, fixed or otherwise, had no qualms about playing the market. America in the 1920s was stock-crazy, a nation of shopkeepers and sales reps hoping to become Rockefellers and Vanderbilts by moving fast on a hot stock tip. A generation earlier, small-time speculators had chased their dreams of wealth in poorly regulated "bucket shops," which allowed people to bet on whether a stock was going to go up or down without actually purchasing any shares. The federal government cracked down on the shops at the same time that a growing middle class began to invest in stocks, even though many investors had only the most rudimentary understanding of how the market worked. The number of Americans owning stock more than tripled in the first two decades of the twentieth century, prompting waves of feverish speculation and outright fraud. In the summer of 1920, while Reverend Menaugh was getting conned out of trust funds in Denver, a man in Boston named Charles Ponzi was collecting millions from suckers who'd been promised a 50 percent or higher return on their money—which he delivered by paying early investors with cash deposited by later ones.

Ponzi's scheme toppled six banks. The Big Con was more discreet; all it took was the mark's life savings. Van Cise didn't believe in perfect crimes, but he had to admire the efficiency of what Blonger had built in Denver. Top confidence men from all over the country came every summer to Denver's Big Store. Blonger and Duff got a cut from every touch—how much, Van Cise still didn't know, but it had to amount to hundreds of thousands of dollars a year. If the game was played right, the sucker never realized that his money was at risk until it was gone. If the mark went to the police, the investigation would fail to locate any of the perpetrators, since the cops were part of the blowoff. Even if the complainant insisted on leading officers to the stock exchange, the place would be cleaned out before they arrived. And many of them were too mortified to report the loss.

By the fall of 1921, Van Cise had compiled a list of twelve victims swindled out of a total of $167,600 over the last four years—including six since he became DA—but he suspected that was only a fraction of the actual haul. Confidence men counted on the stigma of being a mark to keep their victims from making a fuss. As they saw it, suckers deserved scorn, not sympathy. They had tried to get something for nothing and had instead been taught a valuable lesson. "When they looked at me, they saw themselves," Joseph R. Weil, better known as the Yellow Kid, wrote about his victims in a memoir. "I only showed them their own purpose."

The Big Con operators considered themselves the elite of the underworld. Reporters tended to romanticize big-time bunco artists, depicting them as urbane, well-tailored Robin Hoods, handing greedy swells their comeuppance. But Van Cise didn't see anything noble about them. Many of them had extensive criminal records, including convictions for armed robbery and worse. Their schemes entrapped and destroyed not simply the greedy but also the trusting and naive, small-town ministers and immigrant florists. They were a wolfpack, out for blood, and to stop them would require a war chest, a team of hunters, and a plan of attack that did not involve the local police. These were things Van Cise didn't have yet, but he had an idea of how to get them.

———

FOUR MONTHS INTO THE JOB, the new district attorney sent word that he wanted to meet, informally and off the record, with anyone involved in gambling in Denver—bookies, club operators, candy-store punchboard vendors, the whole bunch. Sixty-seven members of the demimonde showed up at the westside courthouse one evening in May, curious to hear what he had to say. Van Cise's speech was brief. Colorado had strict laws against gambling, he noted, and it was his job to enforce them. The only question was whether the "boys" would voluntarily cease and desist or wait to be closed down and arrested.

For several moments there was no response, not even a guffaw. Finally, Andrew Sorenson lumbered to his feet. A large, surly Danish immigrant, Sorenson was one of the owners of the Quincy Club, which claimed to be a members-only establishment but was open to any sucker with an itch for dice or cards.

"You're the bunk," Sorenson said. "You're not the whole police department, and you can't shut me up and you know it. You can go to hell."

Sorenson walked out. So did his partner, James McAdams. But others stayed. By the end of the meeting, several had told Van Cise they were prepared to leave Denver and move to Jefferson County, outside of his jurisdiction. To speed them on their way, Van Cise began mapping out his first raid. It had to be crushing, decisive, a loud rebuke to the lot of them. And Sorenson's place was the logical target.

The Quincy Club was supposed to be an impenetrable fortress. It was located on the second floor of a five-story building downtown, and a lookout posted inside the club entrance had a view of anyone approaching by stairs or elevator. The gambling rooms were soundproofed, the exterior windows covered in sheet iron, the glass panels on the doors painted black so no one could look inside. By the time an invading police force could chop its way inside, the gambling paraphernalia would be all gone. But Van Cise enlisted the help of two men who'd lost heavily at the Quincy, both club members in good standing, as well as that of Ed Young, a massive vice squad officer who was not on the pad.

The raid was flawless. The first club member gained admission and struck up a conversation with the lookout, distracting him while Young sneaky-peted down the hall and took up a position in a corner, out of sight of the peephole. Then the second member arrived. Quincy co-owner McAdams recognized him and opened the door. Young charged in, followed moments later by Van Cise and his hand-picked squad. No one had time to flee or dispose of the evidence. The cash, dice, and cards were all seized. Van Cise couldn't resist gloating as Sorenson was hauled away.

"How about it, Sorenson?" he asked. "Do I go to hell, or do you plead guilty?"

Sorenson and McAdams pleaded guilty to keeping a gambling house and were sentenced to forty-five days in jail. The Quincy Club was out of business permanently, stripped to its bones. Van Cise's men tore out the sheet iron, the buzzers and peepholes, and donated the chairs, tables (mostly billiard tables with an overlay for craps), and cards to the city's fire houses. The raid was the first of many, and it sent the message Van Cise wanted to send: That he was not the bunk, that even the most protected operations were no longer above the law.

He began to receive letters tipping him off about other places that should be closed down, run by bootleggers and bookies and other lowlifes. Most of the letters were anonymous, some clearly from hoods looking to winnow the competition. The most intriguing by far were five letters received in the summer and fall of 1921, addressed to "Philp Van Cise," all but one postmarked in Kansas. The writer identified himself as "A. Friend," and he claimed to know a great deal about what he called "the Vice Trust in Denver."

"Now the Bunko Man from all over U.S. has made 2 Million dollars in Denver the last 2 years," he wrote. "Louie Blonger protects them. Little Duffy runs the Place. They have had 40 men working in Colo. Springs and Manitou. They bring them in and trim them in Denver."

A. Friend named several police officers and an investigator in Van Cise's office who were taking payoffs from bootleggers, gamblers, pimps, or Blonger—and, in some cases, all of the above. He broke down how the steerers, spielers, and bookmakers split the take from the confidence games. He claimed that 35 percent went to Blonger and Duff for protection; Duff was doing so well on his piece of the action that he'd recently purchased an apartment building on Broadway for $150,000. The writer also accused a particular bank of taking a cut in exchange for cashing large checks written by marks, no questions asked.

> I have been working as a Bunco steerer for Lou Blonger and Duffy for 3 years and I got double crossed this summer. The police know there is only two places in the United States we all work. That is Florida in Winter and

Denver in the summer. They are the only places that has got protection . . . Don't let them know how you got the Information But go to work on the quiet because if the police get wind of it you will never get no body. They will tell Blonger. He will wire every body to duck.

The letters stopped abruptly. The information confirmed what the postal inspectors and others had already told Van Cise, but there were new leads to investigate, too—including the business about a spy in his own office. If the man belonged to Blonger, it would be a mistake to fire him, Van Cise realized. It would be better to find a way to use him, so that Blonger would hear exactly what the DA wanted him to hear.

———

WHILE A. FRIEND EXPLAINED THE WORKINGS of the Vice Trust, another anonymous correspondent assured the people of Denver that help was on the way. An item published in the *Denver Times* on June 17, 1921, noted the arrival of an open letter to the press, announcing the formation of a patriotic club that stood ready to aid the forces of right in fighting crime. The group was referred to in some circles as the Denver Doers Club, but the letter claimed that the group had "the most sublime lineage in all history, commemorating as it does the most dauntless organization known to man."

The letter was on fancy stationery, with a Latin motto in the upper-right corner: *quod semper, quod ubique, quod ad omnibus*—a saying lifted from a fifth-century treatise by St. Vincent of Lérins, referring to that which is always, everywhere, believed by all. Printed across the face of the letter in red ink was a drawing of a knight on horseback, cloaked in a white gown and hood, brandishing a fiery cross. The letterhead indicated that the missive was from the "Imperial Palace, Invisible Empire, Knights of the Ku Klux Klan."

"The local Klan, consisting of the very best citizens of Denver, has been under course of construction for some time," the writer declared. "We are a 'law and order' organization, assisting at all times the authorities in every community in upholding law and order. Therefore, we proclaim to the lawless element of the city and county of Denver and the state of Colorado that we are not only active now, but we were here yesterday, we are here today, and we shall be here forever."

3

—

The Wire

First the money, then the team.

Getting the goods on Blonger would take a special squad of detectives, but Van Cise didn't have the funds to hire them. He couldn't put "bunco investigation" as a line item in his next budget request, either—not without alerting the enemy. So he decided to do what other promoters of worthy causes did when public funding was not available: He went looking for private donors.

He made a list of fifty prominent philanthropists in town. He quizzed lawyers and bankers he knew about which of the do-gooders could keep a secret; the responses whittled the list to thirty. They were scions of Denver's wealthiest families, the kind of people who sit on the boards of museums and universities, including banker John Evans, the grandson of one of Colorado's territorial governors; Claude Boettcher, whose father made a fortune in sugar beets, livestock, and cement; Mary Reed, the widow of a man who'd parlayed mining investments into oil leases; and Van Cise's high school classmate George

Cranmer, who'd studied under Woodrow Wilson at Princeton and was now a prosperous stockbroker.

He went to see all thirty of them, hat in hand. He brought along visual aids: a fake security bond he'd obtained from federal agents, similar to the one Mr. Ware had used to impress the florist Nitsche, along with the letters from A. Friend and victims of the scam. He explained how the Payoff worked and the need for a clandestine operation to rid Denver of this blight. He appealed to their sense of duty, their civic pride. None of them turned him down. He collected pledges totaling nearly fifteen thousand dollars—about what he thought the investigation would cost. He also managed to offend flour mill tycoon John Kernan Mullen, who hadn't been asked to contribute. When Mullen found out about the top-secret subscription fund months later, he stormed into Van Cise's office, demanded to know what was wrong with his money, and wrote a check on the spot.

The first member of Van Cise's office to be informed about the bunco probe was its star prosecutor, Kenneth Robinson. Twenty-five years old, Robinson had no trial experience prior to being hired. But he had a quick mind and was a natural at cross-examination, leading to his rapid promotion to chief deputy district attorney. Although Van Cise was a decade older than his protégé, he discovered they had a great deal in common: the war, a passion for fishing, an obsession with work. One afternoon, Van Cise summoned Robinson, briefed him on his interest in Blonger and Duff, and swore him to secrecy. Robinson agreed to take on several time-consuming aspects of the investigation, from tracking down victims and mug shots to traveling to California to meet with Los Angeles District Attorney Thomas Woolwine, one of the few prosecutors in the country to have obtained convictions against Big Con operators.

Eventually Van Cise would bring another deputy DA and

war vet, Fred Sanborn, into the inner circle. But he had to be careful not to alert the spies in his office—there were at least two, he was now convinced—that something was in the wind. He would have to import the detectives he needed, streetwise men with no ties to Denver cops, and keep them far away from City Hall. For recommendations, he turned to one of the federal agents he'd come to know—Roy Samson, regional chief of the U.S. Bureau of Investigation (renamed the Federal Bureau of Investigation in 1935). Samson suggested a former Secret Service agent, Fred Tate, who ran a private detective agency out of offices in Kansas City and St. Louis. Van Cise ended up using Tate on short-term assignments, including tailing Blonger when he took his annual winter trip to Hot Springs, Arkansas. But Tate's biggest contribution to the case was locating three detectives who were willing to move to Denver for the duration of the investigation, men who seemed to be just what Van Cise was looking for.

The first to arrive was Arch Cooper, a former Kansas City police officer. Tall, blond, shambling, Cooper came across as dissipated, self-interested, and, in Van Cise's estimation, "rather lazy." But those same qualities made him the perfect undercover man, someone who could ease into a saloon and, through a combination of amiability and indifference, blend in with the regulars. His job was to while away hours drinking and playing cards with pimps and bootleggers, then sift through the rumors and gossip to glean valuable intelligence about all the rackets in the city. If a beat cop was beefing about his cut, if a big raid was anticipated, or if a top-line spieler was expected to hit town for the summer tourist season, Cooper would hear about it.

The second man was Andrew Koehn, a short, well-dressed former St. Louis cop who impressed Van Cise as the perfect investigator—quiet, relentless, missing nothing but practically invisible himself. While Cooper established himself as a layabout in order to monitor the underworld at street level, Koehn was assigned to keep tabs on Blonger and Duff and identify the individuals who came to see them. Posing as a hosiery salesman, he rented a room on Seventeenth Street across from Blonger's office, one that afforded a view of the Fixer at his desk.

The third man showed up on Van Cise's doorstep one night. A lean, dark figure with a hat pulled low to conceal his features, he asked for "Mr. Reeves"—the surname of Van Cise's mother-in-law, which was the code name the DA had selected for use in all communications with his undercover operatives. The stranger had a letter from Tate, introducing the bearer as Robert Maiden. He had put in eight years on the Kansas City police force as sergeant and detective, served in France during the war, and worked as a federal narcotics agent. Van Cise paired Maiden with Koehn on surveillance of Blonger and Duff, an undertaking that was going to require more than one dogged stalker.

The final member of the team was another former fed— Van Cise's friend, Roy Samson, who abruptly resigned his job at the U.S. Bureau of Investigation and joined the Denver DA's office. At the time, the Bureau didn't enjoy the squeaky-clean reputation it would cultivate under the leadership of J. Edgar Hoover, and Samson was unhappy working with political appointees whose loyalties were questionable; one member of his office was known to do favors for Blonger. A childhood fire had left Samson with facial burns, making him too identifiable for undercover work. But he had a law degree and police training, and Van Cise realized he could be highly useful in assembling a prosecutable case against the con men. A cover story about a big bank fraud investigation was concocted to explain Samson's presence on his staff.

With Robinson, Sanborn, and Samson helping him in the office and Cooper, Koehn, and Maiden as field agents, Van Cise figured he had the people he needed for a first-class intelligence operation. But his experiences during the war had taught him that espionage was about more than personnel. It was about strategy, feints, observation posts—and, most of all, communications. Van Cise called on the city's chief postal inspector and obtained an order to monitor mail sent to Blonger and Duff. The mail couldn't be legally opened, but the return addresses and postmarks on the envelopes could be noted by postal employees and turned over to investigators, providing a road map to a coast-to-coast network of con men. Then he went to the telegraph and telephone companies and handed out subpoenas. He wanted a copy of every telegram Blonger and Duff sent or received, a record of every long-distance call. He also arranged for a janitor to deliver the daily contents of Blonger's wastebasket to the DA's men.

The information poured in. Much of it was trivial, but gradually a picture began to take shape, a portrait of a city on the make. Cooper heard that constable Ike Goldman was selling confiscated whiskey out of the police evidence room and that a pimp named Pinkie, whose woman had been arrested three times in one week, was being squeezed for larger payoffs. Koehn watched Blonger, in full evening dress, stroll down Seventeenth Street and duck into the back of a soft-drink parlor, where a protected game was evidently in progress. Tate reported that Blonger used his trips to Hot Springs to confer with con men operating across the South and also to see his old pal, William Pinkerton. The mob boss and the detective agency president apparently traded intel regularly, to their mutual benefit.

The surveillance revealed vulnerabilities not only in Blonger's organization but in Van Cise's own security measures. One early blunder almost crashed the whole operation. A letter from Duff to Blonger, retrieved from the trash, alerted Van Cise that Duff had gone to Kansas City to oversee a long-con operation. The details were hazy, couched in grifter argot about "getting out of the nut" and having someone "tied." Van Cise wrote to the Kansas City district attorney to warn him and ask that the elusive Kid Duffy be photographed and fingerprinted, if possible. "I do not want any inkling to go to anybody that I have given you this information, as it is the most confidential thing in my office," he wrote.

But the enemy had its own formidable intelligence network. Days after Van Cise's letter went out, Duff shot a telegram to Blonger, saying that he was leaving immediately for St. Louis: DO NOT TALK TO ANYONE UNTIL YOU HEAR FROM ME. In a subsequent letter, Duff complained that "Van Cise has all the dope" about his visit to Kansas City and wondered who tipped him off. "You had better burn this letter after reading," Duff wrote.

Blonger ignored his lieutenant's advice and tossed the letter in his wastebasket. That was lucky for Van Cise, who had ignored his own father's advice: "Better walk a thousand miles than write a letter." Van Cise's letter had gone from the Kansas City DA to the chief of police to a police captain to a bent detective, who'd handed it over to Duff. But now that Duff's letter had notified him of the leak, Van Cise could use the same unsecured line for damage control. He wrote another letter to the prosecutor, informing him of a recent budget cut: "I am so badly handicapped for funds that I have been obliged to stop all further investigation of this matter until the end of next year." A note from Duff to Blonger indicated that he'd seen that letter, too, and was reassured by it.

Van Cise took a similar approach to dealing with the suspected spies in his office. First he fed them false information about upcoming brothel raids. Their duplicity was then confirmed when undercover man Cooper reported back that constable Ike Goldman and others had been tipped off about the raids. Van Cise fired one of the spies, a young drunkard, without disclosing the real reason for his dismissal, and kept the other around so that he could continue to mislead the turncoat's friends on the police force.

By the spring of 1922, the district attorney had made extensive preparations to identify, shadow, and apprehend the operators of Denver's Big Store when they arrived that summer. His collection of mug shots of confidence men had expanded from a few dozen to several hundred. He had communications intercepts in place, relentless surveillance, undercover operatives, and a duped double agent. He knew the out-of-the-way places where police detective George Sanders met with Duff and Blonger and which nights of the week Blonger spent at his mistress's bungalow rather than heading home to the wife. But it still wasn't enough. He wanted to know what was being said in the Fixer's office. Ideally, he wanted to know what the enemy was *thinking*.

What he needed was one more addition to his team, an inside man sitting in Blonger's office. He discussed the problem with Tate, the former Secret Service agent, who had a suggestion—not a man, but something better. It was an electronic marvel, the most effective surveillance tool ever invented, a collector of whispers and smasher of secrets. One journalist had described it as "the voice of conscience made audible in speaking tones. Even experimenting with it one feels a sense of fear and danger, as if in the presence of a foe against whom there is no defense."

Hoodlums had their own name for it. They called it a Dick.

═══════

IN THE SPRING OF 1911, RODNEY J. DIEGLE dropped by the Hotel Chittenden in Columbus, Ohio, to transact a bit of business. The man he came to see had expressed an interest in getting a certain bill out of committee in the state legislature. Diegle, the sergeant-at-arms of the Ohio Senate, explained that he could deliver four votes for two hundred dollars each, plus one hundred dollars for himself. The other man produced a wad of bills and began to count out the fee. Before he took the money, Diegle checked the closet and looked under the sofa, making sure there was no one else in the room.

Diegle was sentenced to three years in prison for the bribe. The chief witness against him wasn't a third party but his own words, captured by a palm-sized transmitter hidden in the sofa and delivered by wire and earpiece to a stenographer in the next room. Diegle appealed, but the Ohio Supreme Court ruled that the evidence obtained by use of the listening device was admissible—one of several judicial decisions that would usher in a golden age of electronic snooping.

The device was the invention of Kelly Monroe Turner, an Indiana native and president of the General Acoustics Company, a leading manufacturer of hearing aids. Known as a Dictograph, it was often mistakenly referred to as a Dictaphone, but the technology was quite different. Alexander Graham Bell had pioneered the first commercial dictation machines, replacing the tinfoil recording medium of Edison's early phonographs with reusable wax cylinders. Bell's Dictaphone evolved into an entire suite of office equipment: An executive dictated into a speaking tube, making a recording on a wax cylinder, which would be played back on another machine by a typist. A "shaving machine" would then erase the cylinder so that it could be used again. Turner was pursuing the dictation market, too, but his Dictograph was a much simpler mechanism, consisting of transmitter, wires, earpiece, and battery. Its chief innovation was its highly sensitive microphone, capable of picking up and transmitting even faint sounds with remarkable clarity. Paired with an intercom system developed in Turner's laboratories, it could be used to dictate to a stenographer in a remote office or to monitor activities on a factory floor. It was soon adapted to other uses, such as allowing members of Congress to hear debates on the House floor in the comfort of their own offices. But its potential for eavesdropping made it particularly useful in criminal investigations.

A Dictograph hidden in the wall of a prison cell collected damning admissions by brothers James and John McNamara, union officials who ended up pleading guilty to a series of bombings, including the 1910 dynamiting of the *Los Angeles Times* building. A Dictograph led to the conviction of the mayor of Gary, Indiana, for bribery; sank U.S. Senator William Lorimer of Illinois for soliciting perjured testimony; and exposed a New Jersey prosecutor who was trying to extort money from a retired glass manufacturer. Novelist Edward Lyell Fox declared that the device had revolutionized crime fighting and led to the undoing of "grafters high and crooks low across the continent." Demand for the Dictograph became so great that Turner decided to offer a special "detective" version that could not be purchased, only rented, its use limited to reputable private investigators and officers of the law.

Yet at the time Tate urged Van Cise to plant a Dictograph in Blonger's place, few officers of the law had ever used one. Van Cise had never even seen one.* They were primarily

---

* In his book *Fighting the Underworld*, Van Cise refers to the device as a Dictaphone, while describing what is clearly a Dictograph. The devices he acquired had no recording capability.

employed by private detective agencies that had been hired by corporations and politicians to get dirt on union leaders and competitors. The bugging of the bunco ring would be one of the first instances on record of government agents using such a device to conduct long-term electronic surveillance of a target, a listening campaign that would remain operational for almost an entire year.

Van Cise purchased three of the devices. They were light-weight but had to be connected to wet batteries that weighed fifty pounds each. One evening while Blonger was out of town, helping a group of confidence men in Florida out of a jam, agents Cooper and Koehn visited the Fixer's office. They had a passkey, provided by a former building manager whom Van Cise knew, but they still had to dodge a night watchman while they took measurements, looking for a suitable place to put the Dick. Obvious locations, such as under a desk or behind a picture on the wall, were quickly rejected. A few nights later Koehn returned with an electrician, tools, two Dictographs, and a hundred pounds of batteries. Using a bed-spread to catch debris, they detached a chandelier hanging from the ceiling and hollowed out the cup at the top of the shaft to accommodate one of the transmitters. They placed the other device in the attic above the office, along with the batteries. It was dirty, noisy work, but they managed to elude the watchman again and erase all trace of their presence in Blonger's office by the time they left.

The president of the Mountain States Telephone and Telegraph Company had pledged to assist the DA's myste-rious investigation, and a company lineman soon strung a wire from the American National Bank attic to the building housing Koehn's stakeout room across the street. Amid the maze of other wires stretching from one telephone pole to the next, the new line didn't look out of place at all. Once all the wiring was connected, Koehn pulled down the shades, put on his earphones and waited. He heard someone blow his nose, looked across the street through a crack in the shade, and saw the old man who looked after Blonger's office in his absence, wiping his beezer. "There is a buzzing sound in the receivers, and the streetcars are heard very distinct," Koehn wrote in his first report on the bug. "The terrible noises the cars made crossing other tracks did not however drown out the talk coming over the line."

Blonger returned to town in late April. Things began to go wrong with the Dick almost immediately. The wet batteries ran down every few days and took twenty-four hours to recharge, once someone had hauled fresh water and zinc to the attic. Too much voltage fried the transmitters, which had to be replaced. Installing an amplifier was supposed to help pick up whispered remarks, but it so intensified the noise drifting through open windows—the rumble and clatter of streetcars and autos, people shouting—that it drowned out all office conversation. Sometimes the line went dead for no discernible reason at all. In addition, the young electrician who'd installed the bug and was supposed to maintain it turned out to be as temperamental as the apparatus itself, sulking and demanding that Van Cise make him a detective. And when the devices did work properly, the stenographer Koehn had hired to transcribe the conversations had trouble keeping up with the rapid-fire dialogue. Often all she captured were fragments and phrases, laced with indecipherable con-man talk about layouts and putting the bee on someone.

As if those difficulties weren't enough, real trouble surfaced just weeks into the operation. One morning Blonger walked into the office, seized his office manager by the arm, and pointed at Koehn's lookout post. "See that room across the street where the shades are down?" he asked. "The district attorney has two detectives over there. They have a tap on my telephone."

Blonger ranted about a "little fellow" who'd approached him, wanting five hundred dollars to tell him about the wires in his office. He'd told the bird to go to hell, confident he could find the bug himself. The DA had gone too far; he was going to sic the feds on him for wiretapping. "I am going to file a criminal case against him and put him where he belongs," he fumed.

Koehn ripped off his earphones and hastily called Van Cise, who told him to shut down the post and clear out immediately. The DA suspected that the tipoff came from the surly electrician, who would have to be pacified or threatened to prevent further disclosures. But they were fortunate that the tip hadn't been more specific. The first order of business was to keep the Fixer from finding the bug. Van Cise used his pull at the phone company to make sure that the technicians who were sent to check the line would accurately report that Blonger's phone wasn't tapped—while failing to mention all those wires in the attic. The techs not only agreed to keep the DA's secret, they rewired and relocated the attic setup to make it harder to detect.

Koehn found a new home for the listening post in a building south of Blonger's office, and the wires from the American National Bank were restrung. Samson discovered an ideal perch for visual surveillance in another building north of the Fixer's place, an enormous loft where rolls of wallpaper were stored. With the owner's cooperation, Van Cise hired carpenters to construct a room resembling a well-camouflaged Western Front observation post, with a small hole in what appeared to be a solid brick wall. Positioned at the opening was a powerful telescope, trained on Blonger's office. Maiden and Koehn took turns at the telescope, shooing away pigeons from an adjacent roost to get a clear view of the action across the way.

Despite the phone company's assurances, Blonger remained convinced that his phone was tapped. He complained about Van Cise to visitors and vowed to have him investigated. Even if Van Cise had been tapping Blonger's telephone as part of his criminal investigation, no federal or Colorado law in effect at the time would have prohibited the practice. But the Fixer thought the district attorney was exceeding his authority. "What business does he have to run around and arrest people, and look for whorehouses and gambling joints, and interfere with other people's business?" he demanded one day. "He should prosecute the cases the police bring him."

On another occasion, one of his visitors suggested that Blonger was looking in the wrong place. "Phone, hell," he said. "I'll bet it was a Dictaphone." For the next few minutes the members of the team stationed at the observation post watched Blonger and his guest turn over desks and chairs and peek behind pictures on the wall, in search of the Dick. They found nothing. But Duff and Blonger continued to lower their voices when sensitive subjects came up, in the event that somebody was listening.

Van Cise did his best to keep Blonger off-balance. Cooper reported that a well-known bootlegger had rented a former brothel, now owned by the Fixer, and was planning to open a beer garden. Van Cise summoned Blonger to his office and quizzed him about whether he intended to operate a house of ill repute. Blonger loudly denied it and left in a huff. "That crazy fool over there thinks I am going to open a whorehouse," he grumbled to a police officer, once he was safely back in his office. "Why, I was never in that business."

The more raids the DA staged on brothels and booze joints, the more Blonger believed the man was completely clueless about the Big Store. "That fellow don't know anything," he declared, with enough emphasis that the stenographer was able to capture every word. "He's just a big bag of wind."

═══════

THE AMERICAN TELEPHONE AND TELEGRAPH COMPANY never rested. It was too busy stringing new lines, devouring small phone companies, fending off government interference, and establishing the world's most powerful monopoly to pause in its labors. But in the summer of 1922, its president, Harry Bates Thayer, agreed to a brief interruption.

The occasion was the death of AT&T's founder, Alexander Graham Bell, from complications of diabetes, at his estate in Nova Scotia. At seventy-five, Bell had lived long enough to see his invention evolve from an oddity to a luxury to a necessity. In 1876, at the time of his first successful voice transmission, there were exactly two working telephones in the world—the one he spoke into and the receiver monitored by Thomas Watson in an adjoining room. A decade later, more than 150,000 Americans had telephones. At the time of Bell's death, AT&T ruled over a coast-to-coast network of nearly fifteen million phones, had begun to acquire radio stations, and was shoveling dividends to more than 250,000 stockholders, a figure that would double by the time of the Great Crash.

Over the years Bell lost much of his youthful enthusiasm for the telephone. He moved on to other challenges and gadgets—experiments in aviation and alternative fuels, the Dictaphone, an early metal detector, composting toilets. He also had an abiding interest in eugenics, spurred by his concern that the offspring of congenitally deaf parents have a greater likelihood of being deaf themselves. "Those who believe as I do, that the production of a defective race of human beings would be a great calamity to the world, will examine carefully the causes that lead to the intermarriages of the deaf with the object of applying a remedy," he wrote in an address to the National Academy of Sciences.

But the telephone was Bell's greatest legacy. No invention had done more to shrink the world, to demolish distance, to accelerate the pace of international commerce, to transform the way people communicated with each other. Bell's achievement had begun with efforts to penetrate the silent world of the deaf, and the grand gesture that Thayer and AT&T offered to honor his passing was to bring the silence back. On August 2, 1922, at six thirty in the evening eastern standard time, as services for Bell began, the phone system shut down across the entire continent. It was an extraordinary moment of electronic respite across millions of miles of wire, a moment that would never be repeated. For sixty seconds, the ringing in America's ears stopped.

Then the clamor resumed. People called their spouses, their sweethearts, their brokers, their bookies. They prattled, they complained, they whispered precious nothings and soul-baring secrets, heedless of who might be listening. Those on party lines could presume a certain amount of eavesdropping, and anyone who was up to anything couldn't rule out other forms of snooping, including corporate and government wiretaps. In the wake of the Volstead Act, it wasn't unusual for Prohibition agents to head down to the local phone exchange and, with the acquiescence of AT&T, plug directly into the line of a suspected bootlegger.

Bell had set out to make electronic talk possible, not to make it easier for private conversations to be monitored by a third party. But he surely recognized that the telephone was not an unqualified blessing. A few days before his death, he declared that he would not have one of the intrusive contraptions in his own study.

————

WHILE THE BUNCO INVESTIGATION SIMMERED, Van Cise's docket of other felony cases kept growing, teeming with people who needed to go to jail. Most of the cases were mundane, the usual crimes of passion and violent disputes among whiskey haulers. But the ordeal of Ward Gash was different, and the district attorney quickly took a personal interest.

On January 27, 1922, Gash, a forty-seven-year-old Black man who lived and worked as a custodian in a Denver apartment house, received a special delivery letter. It was typewritten on official Ku Klux Klan stationery and accused him of having "intimate relations with white women" and using "abusive language" in their presence. The writer gave Gash four days to get out of town and closed with a racial slur and a threat: "Do not look lightly upon this. Your hide is worth less to us than it is to you."

Gash left the city within days. His landlady asked Van Cise to help him. The DA shared the letter with reporters and vowed to protect Gash if he returned home. "We will not stand for any Ku Klux Klan monkey business in Denver," he told them. "It is my intention to try to put the Klan out of business in this city."

Racial intimidation was hardly a new phenomenon in the Mile High City. Although housing discrimination was ostensibly banned, Blacks who moved into white neighborhoods were often harassed or assaulted. Just the previous summer, three weeks after the KKK announced its presence in Denver, a bomb was tossed into the front yard of a house owned by a Black postal worker. The explosion shattered windows and gouged a large hole in the lawn. The house was on an otherwise all-white block and had been recently purchased from a Black police officer, Richard Porter, who'd resisted pressure from a committee of white residents to sell the house to them. Van Cise denounced the violence and promised that the homeowner would be protected; but he and the city's manager of safety also met privately with Porter. They urged him to undo the sale and accept an offer for the same amount from the white committee. Van Cise may have thought he was proposing a solution that would avoid further violence, but it amounted to an endorsement of the white homeowners' interest in keeping the block segregated. Porter declined the offer. Four months later, the same house, now occupied by another Black family, was bombed again. No one claimed responsibility for either incident, and the bombings remained unsolved, despite a hefty reward for information offered by the city.

His failed attempt at mediating that situation may have spurred the district attorney to take a less equivocal stand on the threat to Ward Gash. The letter was a provocation. Who were these masked vigilantes, issuing threats from the shadows on gaudy letterhead? Van Cise asked the grand jury to investigate the organization and determine if criminal charges should be filed against its leadership.

It was a taller order, perhaps, than he realized. The Klan met every Friday night at the Mining Exchange building downtown. A few members popped up unexpectedly now and then, in full-robed regalia, at funerals and church services, delivering a donation or a wreath. But the leadership had not been publicly identified; they were a bunch of ghosts in hoods. The group had only recently applied for articles of incorporation in Colorado, a move that was being opposed by the Denver and Colorado Springs chapters of the National Association for the Advancement of Colored People.

The NAACP state president, George Gross, worked as a messenger for Governor Oliver H. Shoup and had been instrumental in raising the reward money for the bombing incidents. Just as Van Cise's inquiry into the Gash letter was getting underway, Gross received a threatening KKK letter as well, telling him to leave town and warning that "we will get you if you don't." Gross was not easily intimidated—he'd once thrashed a disrespectful white man who'd showed up at the Capitol, demanding an audience with the governor—and he chose not to follow Gash's lead. He stayed at his post, the threat against him made the front page of the *New York Times*, and the Colorado attorney general promised to investigate the matter, a parallel probe to what Van Cise was doing.

After weeks of inquiries, the DA's investigators determined that the head of the Denver Klan was a homeopathic physician named John Galen Locke. Summoned by the grand jury, he proved to be an eccentric figure, short and heavy-set and sporting a Van Dyke. The examination was brief. Asked about a particular meeting of the Klan hierarchy at the Mining Exchange, Locke flatly denied any knowledge of the gathering. He denied presiding over the meeting, donning Klan robes, or even attending the event.

The jury then called Warren Given, a prominent stockbroker who was known to have been at the meeting in question. His testimony could help determine if Locke had committed perjury—but Given refused to provide it. After admitting that he attended the meeting, he declined to identify others who were present or what was discussed. He wasn't invoking his right against self-incrimination but claiming that to disclose any details would violate his "solemn oath" to a secret organization. He maintained his silence despite the possibility of jail time for refusing to answer the grand jury's questions. Judge Charles Butler found him guilty of criminal contempt of court and declared that Given had "an extremely low and dangerous conception of the duties of an American citizen."

"No person can relieve himself of his legal duties by taking an oath," Butler observed in his written ruling. "This is a government of law. No persons or associations of persons of any kind or character are above the law."

Although his attorney vowed to appeal Butler's decision to the highest court in the land, Given ended up paying a one-hundred-dollar fine and walking away from the battle. Gash was eventually persuaded to return to Denver. In its final report before its term expired, the grand jury returned no charges but recommended further investigation of the Klan. The inquiry had bogged down in a side issue—and yet, from Van Cise's perspective, perhaps it wasn't a side issue at all. What did it say about an organization if its members prized secrecy and loyalty to the cause more than the rule of law, more than the truth?

On Easter Sunday the *Denver Post* published what it claimed to be the first interview with a local Klan official since the group arrived in the state. To obtain it, the reporter went as directed to a downtown taxi stand and found a robed, hooded figure waiting in the back of a cab with curtains closed. During the subsequent ride, the Kluxer denied that his organization had threatened Gash or anybody else. The letter was a fraud, he said, written on letterhead that had been stolen from a KKK office months earlier.

The Klan felt sorry for Van Cise, he added. The DA was making a huge mistake, attacking "the only patriotic, all-American fraternal order in existence." He would be better off studying a proclamation by the group's Exalted Grand Cyclops, which the hooded one was eager to provide the reporter. It read in part: "The Knights of the Ku Klux Klan wage no war upon any race or creed. We repudiate, as false and slanderous, the vicious charges that we seek to engender racial strife and religious prejudice. Moral, law-abiding people, white or black, male or female, of whatever religious faith, have nothing to fear from our Klan. But we do warn the immoral, the undesirable, the law violator that the Klan will not tolerate their presence in our community."

The Dick captured Blonger's reaction to the grand jury investigation. He was outraged, once again, at the way the DA was stepping out of line, failing to exhibit a shred of common sense. "He makes me sick," the Fixer told Duff. "He can't keep his nose out of anything. He started something on this Ku Klux business. He better be careful, or they will get him."

4

—

The Roundup

The Fourth of July arrived, and the Big Store remained closed. Tourists crowded Denver's hotels, arranging motor trips to the mountains and picnics at Red Rocks, and no one tried to fleece them. A Wyoming stockman just off the train could stroll the length of downtown and wander into the eight-story atrium of the Brown Palace Hotel, gawking at all the filigreed wrought iron and Mexican onyx, without a single roper befriending him and offering to show him the city. By this time the previous summer, Civic Center Park had been lousy with con men, but not now. Arch Cooper reported that the downtown bunch were "all complaining that they never saw the town so dead."

From the janitor at Blonger's office, Van Cise knew that mail was piling up for several top grifters, but none of them had arrived to claim it. The telegram intercepts had turned up no messages that indicated when the Big Store might open. Instead, a roper from Chicago named Joe Perich sent a wire to Kid Duffy, asking if the firm could use a good "salesman" this summer, and received an emphatic response: DO NOT COME. DUFF.

Duff was definitely in town. So was Blonger. But they had only a trickle of visitors, and the Dick produced little of interest. Van Cise brooded. What had gone wrong? What had made them so cautious? Had the investigation sprung one final, fatal leak?

He sat down with Ken Robinson and reviewed all the past close calls. Blonger and Duff clearly suspected that they were still under some form of surveillance. But Robinson was sure they hadn't found the transmitter, despite all the whispering in the office. They might suspect it was there, but they didn't *know*. The only other possibilities the chief deputy DA could suggest was that one of the undercover men had slipped up or been bought off. Van Cise rejected both scenarios. No, this was a war of nerves between his team and the con men, a contest to see who would blink first. He doubted that the gang was prepared to wait until his term of office was up. Perhaps they were counting on something to speed him on his way.

Rumors of a campaign to recall the district attorney had been making the rounds of the pool halls for weeks. Van Cise had been expecting it. He had angered the downtown crowd with his crusades against the brothels and the gambling joints; he had alienated the mayor and the cops by preaching to the newspapers about corruption; he had stirred up the Ku Kluxers with his grand jury. But if Blonger was plotting a move against him, Van Cise reasoned, then it would be good to make the Fixer think he was on the run. It was time to blink, so the other side would relax and get back to its thievery. Then the Big Store would open, the cons would come to town, and Van Cise's men would (he fervently hoped) arrest them all before his secret investigation ran out of money.

Two weeks into July, Van Cise let it be known that he was going on vacation with his wife and children. His office had come under fire for its handling of the Orville Turley case, providing a perfect excuse for an embattled prosecutor to disappear for a few weeks. Turley, a real estate salesman, had confessed to strangling a wealthy widow in an effort to claim her Capitol Hill apartment house. The sensational crime produced one of the most breathless *Denver Post* headlines of the era—BODY JAMMED IN PIPE OF FURNACE AFTER LIFE CHOKED OUT BY NOOSE—and a desperate insanity defense mounted by Turley's lawyers. Turley was examined by two alienists hired by the state, and much to Van Cise's chagrin, they agreed with the defense's medical findings: that Turley was not responsible for his actions and was suffering from progressive paresis, a form of paralysis. The doctors expected him to live no more than two years. However, on July 18, after four hours of deliberation, a jury of laymen rejected all the eggheads' opinions and found Turley sane and fit to stand trial.* Declaring that his office would be handicapped in pursuing the prosecution of a man its experts had judged to be insane, Van Cise filed a motion seeking a special prosecutor.

Then he took Sara, Edwin, and Eleanor to a remote cabin near Mount Audubon, sixty miles northwest of Denver. Only his closest deputies, Robinson and Roy Samson, knew where he was. Robinson chatted up deputy sheriff Tom Clarke, the jail boss known to be friendly with Blonger, and let him know that he was running things until Labor Day. Without being too

* Turley would live another twenty-five years, long enough to escape from prison, go on the lam for five years, join in a nationwide scam involving tapped telegraph lines and hundreds of thousands of dollars of fake money orders, get caught in St. Louis, and expire from multiple gunshot wounds acquired during a second prison break from the Colorado State Penitentiary.

obvious, Robinson did his best to suggest that he didn't share the district attorney's zealous views and was looking forward to a few weeks of dull routine. Clarke dutifully took that nugget to Blonger, who voiced his approval in front of God, man, and the Dick. Soon Cooper was hearing saloon talk about Van Cise's departure, to the effect that the mob had paid five grand to get him out of town. The yarn made Van Cise wonder if Clarke had squeezed a bonus out of Blonger by claiming to have somehow arranged the vacation.

Whether Clarke took credit for it or not, the feint worked. The bunco men thought the Fighting DA was giving up the fight. Van Cise had hardly cleared out before the telegrams started flying: invitations to the "fishing season" from Blonger and Duff, and acceptances from "salesmen" in return. Two top earners arrived within a matter of days. A telephone number left at Blonger's office led Andy Koehn to a room at the Shirley-Savoy registered to George S. Dover of Kansas City. Poring over the voluminous archive of mug shots the detectives had assembled, Koehn identified the florid, heavy-set Dover as George "Tip" Belcher, a major operator who'd served three terms in prison and been tried and acquitted in the murder of a policeman. Then Jackie French, Duff's top bookmaker, showed up at Blonger's office, decked out in an expensive powder-blue silk suit and still glowing from trimming suckers out of a quarter-million dollars the previous winter in Florida.

"I'm going to lay low this summer and play around in the mountains," he told Duff and Blonger. "But if you need me on a big case, I'll book for you."

Koehn tailed French to a lavish apartment in Capitol Hill, where he was shacked up with Buda Godman, a dark-haired, thirty-three-year-old vamp. Godman's résumé included counterfeiting and extortion schemes as well as a stint as the mistress of Charles Stoneham, the owner of the New York Giants baseball club. Depending on the situation, Godman sometimes called herself Louise French, sometimes Mrs. Charles Stoneham—although it seems unlikely that the real Mrs. Stoneham knew or approved of the impersonation. Through Stoneham, Godman had connections with several of the most notorious gangsters on the East Coast, including Arnold Rothstein (widely credited as the mastermind who fixed the 1919 World Series) and the Cotton Club's Owney Madden. But French was her true love of the moment—and a handy fellow to have around when you needed someone to burst into a hotel room, posing as an aggrieved husband or a federal agent, and shake down some lust-crazed, thoroughly compromised rich sap.

Both French and Godman had warrants and bounties from other jurisdictions. When Samson learned that they were in town, he was eager to arrest them right away for the reward money, arguing that it would help finance the final stages of the investigation. Robinson overruled him. Nobody was to be nabbed, he said, until Van Cise gave the word.

French's comment about laying low and playing around in the mountains proved to be only half true. He was soon on his way to Estes Park, where he and Godman found time to run a badger game against an Episcopalian minister. But other grifters were pouring into town. They checked into boarding houses and hotels, met in small groups at Civic Center at night, and began to set up scores. Koehn was busier than a scout leader at a jamboree trying to keep up with them. One evening he counted no less than twenty-three confidence men on the Capitol grounds, hovering around the marks like carrion crows. He followed three of them to their hotels, noted the room numbers of the keys handed out to them, discovered that one of the innkeepers was an old acquaintance from

Missouri—and soon had the names of five more suspicious characters registered at the same hotel.

Another night Koehn followed six men from the park to the seedy Melton Hotel. After they went inside, he saw a light go on in a window at the end of the hall. He took the room next door, removed his shirt—if discovered, it would look like he was headed for the washroom—and crouched beside the door of a guest who'd signed in as J.D. Brady. He eavesdropped long enough to confirm that Van Cise's ruse was working.

BRADY: *"I bet you nothing like this ever happens again, that we have to wait for a district attorney to go out of town before we open up."*

ANOTHER MAN: *"What do you think of that fellow I had two days and he committed suicide?"*

BRADY: *"The steerers are sure getting tough breaks this year."*

Excited, Koehn went back to the files. Mr. Brady's picture was there: Arthur B. "Tex" Cooper, a top spieler. The big guns were all coming.

As the fishing season opened in earnest, the Fixer and his crews grew bolder. Blonger called up city officials every day to confirm that Van Cise was still out of town. He made several calls to Mayor Bailey and his manager of safety. Police captains came openly to Blonger's office. Blonger ordered a telephone for an office he had rented in another building on Seventeenth Street in the name of A.L. Long. In phone conversations, he referred to that office as "the Lookout." As near as the detectives could figure, it was the mob's own observation post. George Belcher spent a lot of time there, standing in the window, scanning the street below. The suckers were recruited in the parks and hotels, but at some point the steerer would bring them to Seventeenth for a seemingly chance meeting with the spieler, then a trip to the fake stock exchange. Belcher was there to signal the players into action and look out for the law. He also served as a "tailer," shadowing the mark as he went from the bank to the stock exchange, to make sure his money arrived safely.

On July 25, a Tuesday, petition collectors surfaced downtown, gathering signatures for the long-awaited recall campaign. Amid vague charges that Van Cise was "wholly incompetent" to hold office, had "violated his oath," and "willfully discriminated" in his choice of prosecutions, were the names of the recall organizers—two men and two women. The only recognizable name was that of General Sherman Bell, a former adjutant general of the Colorado Guard, who'd been Van Cise's bitter enemy ever since the young captain defied his superiors and called for court-martial proceedings against the soldiers involved in the Ludlow Massacre. It required only a day's investigation by the newspapers to discover that Bell was now spearheading a newly formed organization called the Colorado Law Enforcement League. The name evoked another disreputable klatch of "patriots," the Colorado Law Enforcement and Enactment League, which had sought to influence the 1916 Denver municipal elections by publishing the religious affiliations of candidates and urging votes for Protestants. The new group had even established offices in the same building once occupied by the CLEEL. Van Cise suspected that the real power behind the recall was the Ku Klux Klan, seeking revenge for his grand jury investigation. But for now, the group was letting Bell carry the weight. No alternative candidate for district attorney had been proposed yet.

Predictably, Blonger's people got on board at once. The first petitions were passed out at Seventeenth and Larimer, within hailing distance of Blonger's office, and those of the Fixer's associates who happened to be registered voters quickly affixed their names to the recall effort. The number of mugs on the rolls proved to be a great asset for Van Cise, who saw a way to turn the campaign to his advantage. First, he had Robinson issue a statement, noting that the district attorney was vacationing in the mountains and was expected to be gone until the middle of August. Three days later, Van Cise released a more elaborate rejoinder to the press, calling the recall "the best compliment I ever had."

"Certain people in this town," he wrote, "cannot get accustomed to the fact that the present district attorney takes orders from no one and is not in the least interested in how the underworld thinks or votes; nor does it confer any privilege with his office to be a bootlegger, prostitute, white-slaver, gambler or political fixer, as all criminals look alike to us."

Van Cise went on to recite the highlights of his first year and a half in office: the raid on the Quincy Club, the shuttering of the "notorious colored joint" known as the Rocky Mountain Club, king bookie Julius Epstein on the lam. The fingerprinting of 626 bootleggers, seven of whom had received prison sentences after a second conviction. The closing of twenty-three houses of ill repute. Dramatic reductions of the court backlog, despite the fact that his office had filed more cases in eighteen months than most Denver DAs did in four years. Convictions in thirteen out of eighteen cases Van Cise had tried himself, including ten murder cases.

He closed with a reference to his much-discussed absence: "I am going back to the mountains for my vacation—the first since I have been in office. Before going, however, I wish to thank my enemies for the compliment of invoking the recall—a two-edged sword."

Two-edged, indeed. Let Blonger and Duff think he was entirely focused on fighting the recall. Remind the entire town that he was out of action until late August. Make them all believe that he was mentally and physically elsewhere.

Then strike.

————

VAN CISE DID HIS BEST TO CONVINCE HIS CHILDREN that they really were on vacation. He took five-year-old Edwin trout fishing with him on the shore of Brainard Lake. Eleanor, almost seven, preferred short strolls in the woods, breathing the thick summer scent of lodgepole pine and scouting for deer and chipmunks. But before long her father would become lost in thought, and her mother would have to take over while he made notes and phone calls. There was so much to consider, so many loose ends to gather before the roundup could get properly underway.

Robinson called daily and showed up at the cabin a couple of times a week, in a big Packard provided by one of the wealthy donors who were financing the investigation. The donor insisted on driving, talking Robinson to exhaustion as they weaved up the mountain roads; the subject, as dusty and full of hairpin turns as their route, was whether Shakespeare's plays were the work of Francis Bacon. Visibly pleased to be liberated from the car, Robinson brought written reports from the men and plenty of questions about how the mission was going to end. Van Cise had no answers yet. It was one thing to launch a secret spy network and keep it running for months. It was quite another to safely capture scores of elusive, dangerous men and keep them confined until trial. There was no one to tell him how to finish what he had started, no model for it.

After months of turning the matter around and around, he still had not decided on the when, how, and where of the denouement. Samson was pressing to move *now*, while they had a fix on so many top con men. But Van Cise badly wanted to nail Tom Clarke, George Sanders, and the other cops on Blonger's payroll, and what he had on them so far was pretty weak: a few meetings, some friendly banter picked up by the bug. What would a jury make of that? Beneath the whole question of when to spring the trap was a gnawing fear that the evidence the team had collected over the past year—the surveillance, the victim identifications, all of it—wasn't good enough to convict. There was a case to be made for waiting. Van Cise wanted to plant a phony sucker or two, catch the gang in the act of trimming them, maybe catch Sanders or one of the other bent detectives working the blowoff. Two visitors to town, a Nebraska farmer and a lumber dealer from Houston, both friends of previous swindle victims, had volunteered to pose as wealthy lambs, ready for slaughter. They'd been directed to wander around the newsstands and hotels until they were approached. But if the fishing season ended without anyone taking the bait, most of the gang would be gone before Van Cise's team could move.

And who was to make the arrests? This, too, was a conundrum. His team consisted of six deputy DAs—three of whom had no idea an investigation was underway—and three detectives. Hardly enough manpower to round up Ali Baba, let alone forty thieves. (Koehn's latest report estimated the number of con men in town at seventy-five.) Worse, Samson was the only one of the prosecutors trained to make arrests. Using the Denver police was out of the question; the roundup would be tipped for sure. The State of Colorado had recently formed its own police force—Colorado Rangers, they were called, emulating the Texas Rangers. But they were said to be tied up in the southern Colorado coalfields. President Harding was determined to crush the mining strikes and had called on the states to work with federal authorities to suppress what the newspapers delicately termed "labor unrest."

And where would they put Blonger's bunch after they arrested them? Using Clarke's jail would be just as disastrous as asking Detective Sanders to lead the raids. The cons would be marched in the front door and spirited out the back. A temporary hoosegow would have to be found, some sturdy yet discreet location where the suspects could be held under wraps until the prosecutors could demand high bail.

None of the issues were insurmountable. Van Cise could solve them if he had enough time. But by mid-August the entire investigation was coming to a boil, whether he was ready or not. He received an urgent phone call from Robinson summoning him to Denver. Although his deputy didn't want to go into details over the wire, it was clear that something had panicked the team. Van Cise drove back that day and was shown an infuriating Dictograph transcription.

Samson had put together a list of sixty-three con men thought to be operating in Denver. It was a shorter tally than Koehn's estimate, many of them bearing only aliases or nicknames referring to physical attributes, such as "Thick Lips" and "Blind Man." Samson had sent off a copy of the list to Irvin Bruce, captain of detectives in Colorado Springs, to alert him that these men might try to recruit suckers at the city's annual rodeo. Bruce was considered trustworthy, but the list ended up posted on the bulletin board at the police station. George Sanders happened to be detailed to the rodeo patrol from Denver, got a copy of the list, and realized it came from the Denver DA. He took it straight to the Fixer's office.

"Hey, Blonger, here's something you had better look into," he said. "It's Van Cise's list."

Blonger read the paper in silence. "What of it?" he blustered. "You fellows are still with me, and that fellow can't make an arrest without using the police."

Sanders agreed. "You know us, Lou," he said.

Duff entered the room at that point, and the three huddled close together, their voices too low for the Dick to catch their words. Van Cise read the brief exchange again, with growing anger and annoyance. Blonger knew the investigation was still alive, and yet—he truly believed he was untouchable. But maybe Duff and the others wouldn't feel quite so confident. Once the word got out that their names were on a list, many grifters would be tempted to skip town, even if they still had suckers on the hook. There was no longer any time to spare. The attack had to come off in the next few days, before the enemy evaporated.

Van Cise's vacation was officially over. He went to the State Capitol, a stone's throw from the ropers working Civic Center, and asked to see Governor Shoup, a fellow Republican and former oil executive. He gave the governor a succinct account of his undercover operation and explained his need for Colorado Rangers. A strong backer of Prohibition, Shoup was eager to see his state police squad get involved in actual crimebusting. The tensions in the coalfields had eased, and Shoup said he could spare fifteen of his best men. The head of the Rangers, Colonel Patrick Hamrock, whom Van Cise knew from his days in the state militia, was instructed to have his squad dress in plainclothes and be ready to assemble at a moment's notice.

Before he could brief Hamrock, Van Cise had to address other concerns, including transportation and storage. Marked police cars would be as stupid as uniformed officers. He called up the more able-bodied donors to his secret fund and asked them to volunteer their private cars and their services as chauffeurs during the arrests. Many of them readily agreed. Denver's blue bloods had paid for the investigation, and now they were going to be in on the kill.

For a jail, Van Cise settled on a building that he knew was vacant and could be readily appropriated. He and Sara had attended the First Universalist Church, on the corner of Colfax and Lafayette, since their wedding. But at the moment the church was between ministers, and services had been suspended. Van Cise was on the church board and knew the building well. It was set back from the street, at the rear of a large lot, with a back entrance that led directly to the basement. Prisoners could be whisked out of cars in the alley without attracting a lot of attention, then down the back stairs to a large room with a high ceiling that, with the addition of bars on the windows, would make a suitable holding cell. Guards and barricades would keep the prisoners a safe distance from the door. A first-floor office could be used for processing paperwork and storing evidence, and the command center for coordinating the arrests could be located upstairs.

In a matter of hours Van Cise believed he had solved most of his problems, but other complications soon surfaced. One of the young men recruited as a driver was a bachelor who lived with his parents. He'd gone to his father to ask if he could borrow the car. Either because the son was too talkative or his father demanded an explanation, the latter soon learned that his car was going to be used in a raid on Lou Blonger's bunch. Unfortunately, the father happened to know Blonger and had signed one of the petitions demanding Van Cise's recall. He threatened to go to Blonger immediately. Van Cise had to prevail on another donor, a good friend of the fuming father, to intervene and persuade him to keep quiet.

But as the investigation slipped into its final hours, an

even greater complication presented himself. He had been in town for days, armed and on the prowl, pursuing his own independent and often reckless hunt for con men. If his press was to be believed, the very mention of this man's name would send the gang packing. Samson had alerted Van Cise the day he'd come back from the mountains, and the situation was only getting worse.

"We've got a big problem," Samson told him. "Norfleet is here."

———

SINCE THE DAYS OF THE FIRST Phoenician shell game, the art of the swindle has relied upon the complementary nature of the transaction. The deal demands a confidence man, to be sure, but it demands a sucker, too. The sucker buys into the deal not only with his hard cash but with his faith in the reality of the proceedings; the predators have, as they say, gained his confidence. But all the while the mark is convinced that it is he who has gained the confidence of the kind of men who, behind closed doors, secretly run the world.

A successful grifter must have the will to beat a man out of his family fortune, his life savings, his children's future. By the same token, a true sucker must be willing to be beaten. To play his role properly, to not crack out of turn, he has to *embrace* his defeat.

This is a critical piece of the operation that's often overlooked in discussions of the psychology of the con. Most marks are not criminals themselves; greedy or not, they have difficulty comprehending the enormous deception that has been worked on them and are likely to attribute the bad outcome to other causes. Given an exhilarating chance to stray over the line, to reap a fortune by taking one tiny step into the shadows, the sucker has an intimation that the break he's been denied his entire life is now abruptly at hand—and when it all goes wrong, the hidden scold inside him is not surprised at all. It's just his luck.

If the con is played to perfection, the mark may never realize he's been swindled. He may think that, through some wretched turn of fate, he lost his money in a legitimate business deal. Or the deal itself is so dicey, involving a rigged horse race or insider stock trades or some other forbidden fruit, that the mark doesn't dare go to the cops. In extreme cases, a sucker is kept from squawking by some final, elegant flourish, a grand blowoff that leaves him scared to death. The con men stage an argument, someone gets shot with blanks but appears to bleed real blood—thanks to a gimmick known as a cackle-bladder, a small rubber tube filled with chicken blood and secreted in the mouth—and the mark runs for cover. However, the Payoff as practiced in 1922 rarely required such melodrama. Kid Duffy and his men depended on a sucker being so utterly beaten that he was too embarrassed to admit how thoroughly he'd been conned. Shame was the ultimate weapon when it came to cooling a mark.

Or so everyone thought—until one crew came up against a mark who refused to play his part as scripted. J. Frank Norfleet had no shame and refused to be beaten. Instead, he went about broadcasting his victimization and swearing vengeance. He became the most famous sucker in the country, and thus the most dangerous one of all.

Norfleet's education in the Big Con began in the fall of 1919, when he traveled from his ranch in west Texas to Dallas to sell mules and possibly swap some land. In a hotel lobby he made the acquaintance of a chatty fellow named Miller, who claimed to be another mule man. Learning of Norfleet's interest in expanding his operation, Miller introduced him to an alleged land agent named Spencer. The next day Spencer brought in a third man by way of the old lost-pocketbook routine; he and Norfleet found a wallet loaded with money and broker's papers belonging to one J.B. Stetson. Once located, Stetson rewarded his wallet's recovery with a few stock speculations on behalf of the men who did him such a good deed.

Norfleet knew just enough about the big city and its wiles to be wary of the stock exchange, but he agreed to let Spencer trade for him, provided he didn't have to put up any cash himself. From there the con followed the same playbook as the Denver operation. Acting on juicy insider tips from Stetson, Spencer and Norfleet made $160,000 over a period of days. When the time came to collect, Norfleet discovered that he was not allowed to withdraw his share of the winnings, as he was not a member of the exchange. He was sent home to raise $20,000, to confirm he had the money to make the bids in the first place. After losing that amount in what he thought was just a stroke of bad luck, he was tapped for another $25,000 that was supposed to recoup his loss. Despite safeguards implemented by Stetson to keep everyone's bankroll safe, Norfleet's cash and his new friends soon vanished.

Norfleet was fifty-four years old. The $45,000 had been hastily scraped together from his savings, loans, and money pledged to his land deal, and its loss left him deeply in debt. But instead of going home and blowing his brains out, he became the "boomerang sucker." He vowed to track down the men who cheated him. Five had been involved in all—Miller, Spencer, Stetson, and two employees of the stock exchange. He didn't know their real names, but he had their faces burned into his memory. With his wife Mattie's blessing—"Go get those miserable crooks," she said—he visited police chiefs, country sheriffs, and private detective agencies to see if they had any means to find these men.

Over the next three years Norfleet cast his net wide—first across Texas, then across the hemisphere. He pored over hotel registers and police blotters. Posing persuasively as a hayseed, he struck up wide-eyed conversations with habitués of betting parlors and speakeasies. He traveled thousands of miles to pursue a hunch or a threadbare trail. He gave frequent interviews to newspaper reporters, providing a lurid, cautionary tale of his ruination by con men as well as detailed descriptions of the swindlers. When two of his quarries landed in jail in San Bernardino, not long after the rancher had tracked the gang to California, Norfleet emerged in the popular press as a cowboy version of Sherlock Holmes.

The manhunter's own accounts of his exploits involved frequent brandishing of the two revolvers he carried. He tracked the gang's leader, Joe Furey, who'd played Stetson, to San Francisco and Los Angeles, where Furey maintained two separate families, and promptly informed the local authorities. But instead of arresting Furey, the detectives in Los Angeles shook him down for twenty thousand dollars and allowed him to flee. Undeterred, Norfleet managed to get deputized in Texas and obtained an arrest warrant signed by the governor of Florida. He and his son Pete captured Furey in Jacksonville and hauled him back to Texas at gunpoint to face trial.

Miller was arrested in Georgia. That left Spencer. Norfleet came upon him unexpectedly on a crowded street in Montreal and wrestled him to the ground, but Spencer screamed that he was being robbed and got away in the confusion. Norfleet tracked him back to Texas, then learned he'd gone to Denver. The rancher had heard of the stock exchange there and had corresponded with the new district attorney. He took the next train to Denver, called up Van Cise's office, and was soon telling Roy Samson his troubles.

Samson begged him not to give any interviews or take any action. Something big was in the works, he hinted, and the district attorney would be back in the office shortly. Accounts of what Norfleet did with this information vary, but it's clear that he ignored Samson's plea to lay low. He went to the downtown post office and loudly called for mail in the name of Mullican. Within minutes he was offered a "drive of scenic beauty" by a man calling himself Whatley, whom Norfleet recognized from his own immersion in mug shots, as a grifter from Salt Lake City. He declined the ride and walked into the lobby of the Brown Palace, playing a Texas cotton farmer named Mullican, and was immediately befriended by one R.C. Davis. (There was something about Norfleet's face, its smooth, placid contours, that seemed to bring the con men courting.) The lean, dark-haired Davis claimed to be a Texan, too, even though he spoke of "Hooston" and "Wahkko" with an accent that sounded like it had rarely strayed west of the Hudson River. Thus began the round of pleasantries and offers of showing a fellow Texan the town that, Norfleet knew from bitter experience, would ultimately lead to the stock exchange.

Norfleet triumphantly reported back to Samson that if the DA was having trouble finding the con men, he could sure show him where they were. A meeting with Van Cise was hastily arranged that evening at Samson's house; the last thing anyone wanted was Norfleet being spotted at the district attorney's office. The lone avenger arrived at the meeting on the heels of a summer monsoon that had flooded parts of the city and peppered motorists with hail. The rain had stopped, but the skies were still blustery and unsettled, as if things could go either way.

Van Cise had expected the celebrated scourge of confidence men to be a much bigger fellow. Norfleet was five six; maybe 125 pounds soaking wet; with pale, watery blue eyes and a limp, matronly handshake. He'd made an effort to disguise himself by dying his gray hair brown, thinning and curling his mustache, and affecting a stooped-over gait that he'd observed in cotton pickers. He wore a straw-colored Palm Beach suit, spoke in a soft drawl, and exuded harmlessness.

Van Cise wondered how much of Norfleet's famous adventures could be believed. Before catching up with Furey, the rancher claimed to have ventured into a tough gambling joint in the Everglades; he barely escaped with his life after Furey sent word that their visitor was the infamous Norfleet and should be dispatched as soon as possible. He had supposedly extricated himself from this death trap by getting the drop on two desperadoes who were about to choke the life out of him, then marching them past two guards armed with carbines. Could this be the same man? It seemed unlikely, but Van Cise had known bantamweights in the army who were absolute tigers when cornered. He decided to tell Norfleet about the investigation and the impending arrests, as well as his efforts to get someone inside the stock exchange itself.

Norfleet told them about his encounters with Whatley and Davis. "I've got the runners of the stock exchange on my hip and will be into the real game in a day or two," Norfleet boasted.

The prosecutors had to admit that this was good news. Their own phony suckers hadn't generated a nibble. This might be the best hope of catching the gang in the act, Van Cise realized. Norfleet would know what to say to encourage them. But Van Cise didn't want any gunplay on his conscience. He told Norfleet he didn't want him to get picked up by the Denver police for not having a gun permit; he would have to leave his six-shooters behind when he pursued his contacts with the con men.

Reluctantly, Norfleet agreed. Van Cise's assurances that his every move would be covered by well-armed investigators didn't seem to impress him. "I have had so many dealings with crooked police and sheriffs that I am afraid of every man whose job it is to catch criminals," he said glumly.

Van Cise told him it would be different this time. But looking at the little man with the watery eyes, he saw genuine fear. Perhaps Norfleet's account of the con men trying to kill him in the Everglades was true, and it was coldblooded to give them another crack at him like this. But scared or not, armed or defenseless, Norfleet was willing, and Van Cise had decided to use him.

———

THEY SENT NORFLEET BACK TO CULTIVATE his new acquaintance at the Brown Palace on Monday evening, August 21. Van Cise knew he had to wrap everything up before Friday. Some of the cons had already let it be known that they wouldn't require their rooms past the weekend. He arranged briefings with Hamrock's men and his own three out-of-the-loop deputy prosecutors, who were astonished to discover that the investigation had reached this point without any of them having the slightest notion that it existed.

He handed out arrest assignments to the Rangers, telling them he didn't expect to encounter armed resistance. Confidence men know how to take a pinch, he explained, and rely on a fixer to get them out. But the troopers would still have to be vigilant in collecting evidence and escorting the suspects to church. "Watch your prisoner's hands all the time," he said. "Do not let them throw anything away, even a newspaper."

He demonstrated "the office," an underworld high sign that consists of opening your coat as if flashing a badge. It's the way one grifter warns another that an arrest is coming and a lawyer should be called to arrange bail. None of the prisoners should be allowed to signal each other or anyone else. "Watch out for the women," he added. "All their molls are in this racket. They are the worst grapevine we face." If a woman was present, the Rangers would have to summon another woman to guard her until the arrests were over.

He hadn't fixed the exact time of the attack yet, he told them. He was awaiting word from an undercover operative. On Tuesday evening he received a hastily scrawled letter from Norfleet, on stationery from the Hotel Metropole:

> Room 310. They are going to play me for what money they think I have—and abandon the Trip home. I will wire my wife—on the Dallas County Bank—Just as soon as I learn the exact Plans. If you get the wire to wife, you will understand. I will try and talk again. If not to late to get in. We are in Room I dont feel well.
>
> I have met the misterious man Mr. R.C. Davis my first man Mr. PJ Miller the misterious man MAB Zachery the Broker in office. We took 303,000 dollars moved to this Hotel will Finsh to morrow I may need help Room 226— Denham Bldg—I cant be at Columbia to nite I am being watched I am in Toilet now
>
> Watch after me
Mullican

The meaning was far from clear, but Van Cise had reports from Koehn and others who'd been following Norfleet around all day, and he could discern the gist of it. Norfleet had pursued his connection with R.C. Davis, the odd-accented Texan at the Brown Palace, whom Koehn quickly identified as Leon Felix, a steerer with a long rap sheet. Felix took Norfleet for a stroll downtown, bringing the conversation around to high finance and this plunger he'd seen in action in Kansas City once, hauling cash out of the stock market like it was hay. With that peculiar twist of coincidence typical of Big Con operations, Felix abruptly spotted the very man, the "mysterious stranger" from Kansas City, walking down the street, a sheaf of telegrams in his hand. Watching from a discreet distance, Koehn recognized the stranger at once—he was Tex Cooper, the champion spieler who'd registered as "Mr. Brady" at the Melton Hotel a few days earlier.

After the appropriate introductions and expressions of amazement at meeting up in Denver like this, Felix asked Cooper to invest forty dollars on behalf of himself and his friend. Cooper obliged, and soon returned with eighty dollars. Norfleet gratefully accepted his half of the windfall. Felix pressed Cooper to place more bids for them, but Cooper protested that he was too busy—and invited them to come to the exchange themselves. Norfleet accompanied them to Room 226 of the Denham Theater Building, the current location of the exchange, and proved to be a plunger himself. He applied for and received $100,000 in credit, then rolled up $300,000 trading on tips provided by Cooper. He paid back the hundred thousand advanced and was on his way to the door, with the rest of the cash cradled in his arms like a stack of logs, when Mr. Zachery, the secretary of the exchange, frantically hailed him. He used almost the exact same words Norfleet had heard in Dallas three years earlier.

"Just a minute, Mr. Mullican!" Zachery cried. "I would like to see your membership card, if you please!"

Norfleet had no such card. Alas, Zachery explained,

Mullican could not withdraw his money because he was not a member of the exchange and should never have been advanced the credit without proper authorization. He would have to leave his winnings in the vault until he could arrange to have $100,000 deposited in a Denver bank to "confirm" his bids. Outraged and sympathetic, Felix and Cooper took Norfleet to Room 310 at the Metropole and were staying with him while he arranged to get money wired to him from Mrs. Mullican, his fictitious wife back in cotton country. The letter to Van Cise had been hastily composed in the bathroom while Norfleet was supposedly taking a bath. He'd managed to post it under the guise of sending a letter to his wife—no easy feat when Felix and Cooper were sticking to him every step of the way. Their close watch of him had prevented him from making a planned rendezvous with the district attorney's men at the Columbia Hotel.

Fortunately, Van Cise and Norfleet had worked out a backup plan for this eventuality. The note's reference to not feeling well confirmed that Norfleet was following instructions. He developed a tremendous toothache after checking into the Metropole and spent much of the evening groaning on his bed, covering his face in his hands. The routine served two purposes. It helped to conceal his features from the visitors who came to see Cooper or Felix—other grifters, mostly, who might recognize Norfleet from the papers or have crossed paths with him at some point. His affliction also gave him a plausible reason for visiting a dentist the next morning. The one he selected, seemingly at random, was William Smedley, who ran the largest and most modern dental office in town—and had agreed to serve as a go-between for the district attorney. Felix and Cooper insisted on accompanying their good friend Mullican to the dentist, but they had to wait in the anteroom while Mullican went for treatment. Once alone with Smedley, Norfleet phoned Van Cise.

The call came on the district attorney's private line at an awkward moment. Police detective Sanders had waddled into his office that morning, urging the DA to modify his approach now that recall petitions were on the street. Van Cise listened politely as Sanders explained why he needed to smooth things over with the chief of police and notify the force if he was planning anything big. Clearly, the list of suspects Sanders had brought Blonger had alarmed the detective; he was smelling something like a raid. In the midst of this exhortation, the phone rang.

"This is Mullican," a faint voice said.

Keeping his face blank, Van Cise asked the caller to hold for a moment and turned back to his visitor. "George, would you mind stepping outside for a few minutes? I have some personal matters to deal with."

Once Sanders was gone, Norfleet spilled the latest. Felix and Cooper had changed plans again and were now pressing him to go to Texas on the night train to get his money. Felix would go with him part of the way, supposedly to fetch his own cash to confirm his bids. To Van Cise, this sounded like a good way of taking them down quietly, away from the other cons downtown. He told Norfleet to go ahead, that he would have the Rangers pull them off the train at the first stop—Littleton, ten miles south of Denver—and arrest Felix. Cooper would be grabbed with the rest of the group in the morning. Relieved that his ordeal was almost over, Norfleet agreed and hung up.

Sanders was still waiting in the outer office. Van Cise sent the detective on his way, promising to meet with him later in the week. Then he summoned his deputies to get the wheels in motion for a roundup in the morning. But as they discussed the coming arrests, it became apparent that sending Norfleet to Union Station that evening would be a mistake. The undercovers had information that other cons were heading out tonight by train. Some might even be on the same redeye to Texas as Norfleet. There was too great a risk that he would be recognized or the arrest observed, and a warning sent back to Denver before the dawn raids. Someone had to get word to Norfleet to stay away from the train station before it was too late.

It took most of the day, but the receptionist at Smedley's office finally got through to Room 310 of the Metropole shortly before five o'clock. Mr. Mullican was informed that the dentist was ready to finish the work on his teeth. Norfleet was back in the office in a matter of minutes; this time Felix and Cooper remained outside in a big Cadillac. Smedley handed Norfleet the phone.

"The plans are changed," Van Cise said. "You can't take that train. It is up to you to be so darn sick there won't be any question about it. Keep them with you all night."

"If they take me, it will be on a stretcher," Norfleet said.

"Everything is sitting pretty to close this deal tomorrow morning early. We will knock on your door at seven. Twice heavy and twice light."

Van Cise asked him to put Smedley back on the phone. He told the dentist to make Norfleet appear as sick as possible. "Dump everything in the shop in his mouth so you can smell it for a block," he said.

Smedley did as he was told. Norfleet staggered out to his new friends, emanating a harsh, astringent odor redolent of hospital wards, as if his head had been dipped in ether. He no longer had to fake his distress; he was genuinely ill. He vomited profusely in the back of the Cadillac and again at Union Station, persuading Felix and Cooper that a train trip was impossible. Worried that their pigeon might expire before they could complete the touch, they took him back to the hotel and spent the evening filling hot-water bottles and applying plasters.

After concluding the talk with Smedley, Van Cise turned to Robinson. The roundup was now barely twelve hours away, and he hadn't even informed the Rangers. He asked Robinson to call the drivers while he called Colonel Hamrock. Everybody was to report at the church at six in the morning.

It was time for Lou Blonger and his fellow sinners to come to Jesus.

———

Norfleet had a restless night. His handlers stayed up late, nursing him and talking about how they were going to spend their winnings once they got this misunderstanding straightened out at the stock exchange. Shortly before dawn Cooper announced he was going out for a bit. As Felix dozed, Norfleet attempted to block ready access to an open suitcase which, he'd noted earlier, contained handguns. He kept a .32 under his pillow that night, despite Van Cise's insistence that he go into the deal unarmed.

Right at seven came raps on the door—two heavy, two light. A sleepy Felix answered the summons and found two guns in his face. Robinson and a Ranger in plainclothes slipped into the room and informed him that he was under arrest. Norfleet watched from his bed, a grin spreading across his face.

"Do you know who I am?" he asked Felix.

Puzzled, Felix shook his head. "Your name isn't Mullican?"

"My name is Frank Norfleet."

Felix blanched. He was searched, handcuffed, and locked in

the bathroom. Robinson phoned Van Cise at the church. "The weather's fine," he said. "We are waiting for Number Two."

Norfleet proceeded to recount his adventures of the past forty-eight hours while Robinson went through the men's papers. Cooper waltzed back into the room at eight thirty. He was dressed for business: straw hat, blue coat, white trousers and shoes, a colorful tie with a three-carat diamond stickpin. Robinson announced that he would be searched and a receipt provided for his valuables. "First, have you met Mr. Norfleet?"

Cooper gave no reaction. He stood stoically as Robinson relieved him of his cash, papers, a platinum watch, and other jewelry. As Robinson began to compile a list of the items, Cooper said quietly, "There's no need of mentioning that stickpin. You have included plenty without it."

Robinson caught his drift. He was beginning to understand why men like Tex Cooper held the law in such contempt; they were used to buying off coppers with trinkets. "Sorry, old man," he said, "but you better take the receipt. I'll keep the jewelry so you won't offer it to some other person."

———

KID DUFFY WAS THE FIRST OF THE GANG to be brought to church. Samson staked out his apartment house on Lincoln Street in a car driven by one of Denver's leading attorneys. At eight thirty Duff emerged and began walking briskly toward his office. The car pulled ahead of him, and Samson beckoned him in. Duff thought he was being offered a ride by a friend until the guns and badges came out.

"By God," he huffed, as Samson put the cuffs on him and the car sped toward the church, "your district attorney isn't going to get away with this."

Samson told him to shut up. He went through Duff's

pockets. In his coat was a black notebook and a typewritten list—which Samson recognized at once as a copy of the confidential list of suspects he'd sent to the police in Colorado Springs. From Sanders to Blonger to Duff it had gone, all in a matter of hours, and Duff had probably flashed it all over town by now. When they reached the church, Samson turned Duff over to the Rangers and ran upstairs to show the Colonel what he'd found.

———

THE TEAM ASSIGNED TO BLONGER missed his arrival at the office. They had staked out his apartment, but he had spent the night at the home of his mistress, Iola Readon. The Dick picked up his first calls and conversations of the day, and the stenographer quickly notified Van Cise that his top-priority target was at his desk. Deputy DA Fred Sanborn burst in with a plainclothes Ranger and found Blonger huddled with a former Denver police detective named Frank Mulligan.

"The district attorney wants to see you at once, Mr. Blonger," Sanborn said. "And this other gentleman, too."

Blonger got up wordlessly and started to roll down the cover of his desk. Sanborn stopped him and demanded all his office keys. Blonger grunted. "Help yourself," he said, pulling the keys from his pocket. "You won't find anything."

The contents of Blonger's and Duff's desks were dumped into suitcases, to be examined later. Blonger was searched, along with a spare coat hanging on a rack. The coat yielded a bank deposit book in which Blonger had written the names and phone numbers of key associates. One of the names was William Arnett, a U.S. Department of Justice agent whom Samson knew well.

Raids on the Lookout and the stock exchange produced a

trove of other documents and suspects. The Lookout served not only as George Belcher's surveillance post but as a break room used by teams of spielers and steerers to prepare for action or for divvying up their loot. When Samson hit the place later that morning, he found not just Belcher, but four other men on his list, including Len Reamey, the bookmaker who'd played "Mr. Zachery" in the Norfleet scam, and Louis "Thick Lips" Mushnick, notorious for having fleeced a sugar broker in Cuba out of $245,000, said to be an all-time record for the Payoff. Samson also seized paperwork from various swindles, Reamey's complete bookmaker outfit, blackboard and all, and a con man's "boodle"—packages of currency that appeared to amount to $135,000 in hundred-dollar bills, but actually came to a mere $2108 when the packets were pried apart to reveal a core of singles.

At the stock exchange, Samson found better furniture and more paperwork, including dummy stock certificates and transfer sheets. On the top of a handsome rolltop desk sat a telephone, the same phone that had been used in so many high-finance deals and consultations over stock-exchange policy. Mr. Zachery had made use of it as recently as Norfleet's visit two days ago, to discuss with the head of the exchange the awkward matter of Norfleet's lack of a membership card.

Samson gave the phone a tug, and the bare wire came leaping out of a desk drawer. Mr. Zachery and the other employees of the exchange had been talking to higher-ups who existed only in the minds of their victims.

————

BY NIGHTFALL, THIRTY-THREE OF THE WORLD'S smoothest operators were locked up in the basement of the First Universalist Church. Van Cise estimated that there were another three dozen or so that had fled town in the last few days—mostly small-potatoes ropers, but a few major players, too, including Norfleet's man Spencer, who had left that morning. They found his suitcase at the Empire Hotel, brimming with phony identification and stock paraphernalia, and learned that he'd left instructions for it to be shipped to Salina, Kansas. Norfleet made plans to follow the suitcase that evening.

Andy Koehn and Bob Maiden swept up several steerers in the streets, while other agents knocked on hotel room doors. Most of the arrests were made without incident, although there was a hitch in taking down Elmer Mead, better known as the Christ Kid. His roommate protested that they were hauling away an important financier on the verge of completing a very important deal. The man said that he had just returned to Denver from McPherson, Kansas, with a $50,000 cashier's check, and was expected at the bank that day. No amount of explaining would persuade the boob that he'd narrowly escaped being cheated out of fifty grand. He was so convinced of the Christ Kid's good intentions that he tried to post bail for him on the spot.

At the church, the confidence men were thoroughly searched and questioned. During their examinations, they sat in little red chairs designed for children's Sunday school lessons. Some used their straw boaters to shield their faces from a *Denver Post* photographer. Forbes Parkhill, the paper's star reporter, had gotten wind of the operation early in the morning and had shown up at the church, demanding interviews and threatening to go to press immediately with his exclusive. Van Cise had called the managing editor and bought time in exchange for letting a *Post* photographer snap pictures. It was a dream assignment for a crime shutterbug. Above the heads of these notorious criminals, the wall bore quotations from Scripture:

THE WAY OF THE TRANSGRESSOR IS HARD

THE WAY OF THE UNGODLY SHALL PERISH

"This is the goddamnedest jail I've ever been in," one of the gang muttered.

Toward twilight, Van Cise descended from his command post and studied the haul from the doorway leading into the basement. Blonger sat apart from the rest, keeping his own counsel. Cool enough at the point of arrest, he had crumpled when he was brought into the strange basement rather than Tom Clarke's jail. Perhaps it was the sight of Duff and so many of his other confederates that dismayed him. In any case, the mask of bluff confidence had slipped badly. Blonger was pale and agitated. He had nothing to say to anyone, but he couldn't sit still. The old jackal was worried, Van Cise realized, with a sudden flush of exultation.

Lou Blonger had made a fortune being on the other side of these arrangements. He was the one who fixed the low bail when his buddies took a pinch. Now he was in the dock with the rest of them. He was of no earthly use to them anymore. He couldn't save them.

The larger question darkening his brow was whether he could save himself.

5

—

Unfixed

The church was no place to hold the confidence men overnight. Van Cise arranged to ship them to jails in the neighboring towns of Golden and Brighton, where they could be properly booked and supervised. During the processing, many of the suspects provided false names. Several struggled with their keepers as they were fingerprinted and photographed, trying to blur the record and preserve their prized anonymity. Duff was one of them; having gone to so much trouble to deep-six his old rap sheets, he wasn't about to start a new one without a fight.

The next morning the suspects were brought back to the church. Van Cise made a big production of summoning Captain Washington Rinker and several police detectives under his command to inspect the prisoners prior to taking charge of them. It was Van Cise's way of letting Rinker know that he and his men would be held responsible if any of the gang happened to disappear before their bail hearings. Then the whole crew was taken to the Denver jail, except for three men who'd been picked up by mistake by Bob Maiden, the DA's most head-strong investigator. Rousted as suspected ropers from benches outside the Capitol, the trio turned out to have nothing to do with the bunco operation and were released.*

One prominent target of the dragnet was still at large: Jackie French, the bookmaker Samson had wanted to arrest well ahead of the others because of the five-thousand-dollar bounty on his head, stemming from back-to-back six-figure scores he'd engineered in Florida. French had spent much of the summer in the mountains with Buda Godman, his lover and badger-game partner. But he'd played stock-exchange manager in Denver many times over the past few years, and Van Cise regarded him as one of the most important operators in Duff's network. Shortly after the first reports of the bunco ring roundup made the newspapers, a tipster alerted the Rangers that French was staying at the fashionable Stanley Hotel in Estes Park. Van Cise asked the town marshal to detain him there, then drove up with Samson that night to personally escort him to jail.

In contrast to his less-refined colleagues, John Homer French—alias J.H. Fitfield, John Finch, J.R. Clark, John Fillmore, J.H. Fultis, J.H. Francis, and J.H. Fairmont, but known to his friends as Dapper Jackie—was personable, handsome, and oddly talkative. The local cops assigned to guard him reported that they found a pipe and a jar of opium in his suite. French told the visitors he didn't know what this was all about, but he was sure it could be straightened out. Left alone with Van Cise, he mentioned that he had a new Studebaker and several thousand dollars in cash and jewelry that might be of interest to the

---

* One of the three men, an out-of-work salesman, resisted the collar, and Maiden struck him in the head with his revolver. The man later obtained a modest settlement for false arrest.

right fellow. Van Cise then introduced himself as the district attorney and decidedly the wrong fellow.

"Oh, hell," French said. "No hard feelings, are there?"

"Not at all."

The hopped-up French was handcuffed and driven back to Denver. Godman fled to New York to seek comfort in the arms of her sugar daddy, Giants owner Charles Stoneham, while pondering how to spring her boyfriend. The other defendants and their allies weren't idle either; hours after the arrests, attorneys waving writs of habeas corpus descended on the courthouse, demanding the release of their clients. Haggard from lack of sleep, Van Cise was able to head them off by filing a "blanket information," charging all the suspects with conspiracy to commit a confidence game. Bail was set at $25,000 each. Blonger and Duff posted bond immediately, but the price was too dear for the rest—high living and incessant gambling left many confidence men with an acute shortage of funds between scores. William A. Bryans, an attorney representing several of the defendants, pushed to have the bonds reduced, leading to an explosive court hearing that set the tone for the acrimonious, bare-knuckle legal battle that lay ahead.

Van Cise was an hour late to the Monday afternoon hearing. He complained that he hadn't received proper notice of the proceeding. Bryans responded that a statement he'd made in court Saturday morning, announcing his intention of seeking bond reductions, was sufficient notice, even though Van Cise hadn't been present at that session. Bryans then demanded the release of Jackie French, who'd not yet been charged. Citing the indictment issued against French by a Miami grand jury and his involvement in Denver's Big Store, Van Cise asked the judge, Clarence J. Morley, to set French's bond at fifty thousand dollars. Bryans objected strenuously, accusing Van Cise of lying about his lack of notice and his reasons for detaining French. Van Cise denied it.

Bryans repeated his claims. "I don't want to be disputed," he said.

"You are disputed," Van Cise said, drawing closer to Bryans.

Bryans called him a liar again.

"Don't say that again," Van Cise said.

Bryans did.

Van Cise swung on him. According to one observer, the blow struck Bryans in the neck; another says it was a sock in the eye. Bryans flailed back. The two attorneys exchanged punches for several seconds before others could separate them. After things calmed down, a swollen-faced Bryans stood and apologized to Judge Morley. An apology followed from Van Cise, his tie and starched collar in disarray. Morley lectured them both but declined to take harsher action.

The tussle made headlines. The *Denver Post* described the DA's "thrashing" of Bryans—a former county clerk, assistant city attorney, and veteran criminal defense lawyer—as "the most commendable act of his official career." That the *Post* was now eager to jump on the Van Cise bandwagon represented a major shift for the city's largest newspaper, which had omitted Blonger's name from its reports on the bunco arrests for two days because of his friendship with publisher Harry Tammen. But the paper's editors couldn't ignore public sentiment, and Van Cise was undeniably the man of the hour. Once mocked as a killjoy because of his raids on booze houses and brothels, he was now fawned over as the Fighting DA, the city's fearless gangbuster.

The wave of positive press effectively scuttled the Klan-backed recall campaign against him. The recall organizers claimed to have collected almost twenty-two thousand signatures on their petitions—a dubious figure, given how low-key and almost invisible the entire effort had been. But just days after the bunco roundup, and hours before the signatures were supposed to be submitted to election officials, the documents disappeared in a mysterious burglary of the Law Enforcement League offices. D. D. Davidson, the LEL official and Klan member who reported the theft, tried to blame Van Cise or his supporters. But Davidson left town before investigators could interview him. The more likely scenario was that the "burglary" was the organizers' way of extricating themselves from a doomed venture.

The bunco raid sent a tremor through the entire city administration. People wondered why the Denver police had been left so conspicuously out of the action, why the DA had to go to private donors to fund the investigation, how so many criminals could operate so freely in the city for so long. Mayor Bailey had peculiar answers to those questions. A former federal marshal himself, he criticized Van Cise's operation as highly irregular—and suggested that the bankers and stockbrokers who funded the investigation had selfish motives for doing so. Perhaps, he told reporters, this was a case of the "big fellow" squeezing out competition from the "little fellow." Sounding a theme that the grifters' lawyers would adopt in their defense, he maintained that investing in stocks wasn't much different from playing a confidence game: "We have taken a chance with our money and must know it. If we lose, are we suckers? If we win, are we con men in the making?"

The Denver police faced an even more embarrassing situation. It was rumored that the notebooks seized from Duff and Blonger contained names of several officers and pay-off amounts. Chief Rugg Williams promised to take "drastic action" against any bad apples on the force, if the district

attorney would only share his findings. But Van Cise was keeping his cards close to the vest. He didn't have enough to charge
any detectives yet, and he was hopeful that a grand-jury probe
into police corruption, spurred by the arrests, would produce
more hard evidence. In the meantime, a jittery George Sanders
went to see Van Cise at his home.

Big-bellied, with hair thinning on his large head, Detective
Sanders had been a familiar figure to the surveillance teams dog-
ging the con men. He was no sooner admitted to Van Cise's den
than he burst into histrionics. He fell on his knees and sobbed
his innocence. He knew Blonger and Duff, sure, everybody in
town did, but he wasn't involved in protecting them, he insisted.

Van Cise was unmoved. What about the list of suspects,
the DA asked, that Sanders had obtained in Colorado Springs
and taken to Blonger? Sanders replied that he'd met Blonger
by chance that day and had shown him the list because Blonger was curious about it.

Van Cise scoffed. He didn't want to reveal the existence of
the Dictograph, which was still active in Blonger's office, but
he couldn't resist calling Sanders on his lie. "That is not what
you said," he replied. "You told him you had my list. Then
Duff came in, and you talked it over with both of them. You
are one of the gang, and you are going to the pen with the rest
of them."

Visibly shaken, Sanders seemed ready to crack. But then
Van Cise made what he would later regard as one of the worst
tactical errors of his entire campaign. He asked a question
that revealed how little he knew about Blonger's protection
arrangements.

"How did Blonger pay you fellows, George?"

Sanders composed himself. He stood up, said he must be
going, and was quickly out the door.

━━━━━

PUTTING THE BUNCO MEN BEHIND BARS had required thousands of hours of planning, sleuthing, and surveillance. Keeping them there would prove to be even harder.

The bail battles were only the beginning. The fistfight hadn't cowed Bryans, who brought in reinforcements. Van Cise and his men were soon dealing with a barrage of motions, maneuvers, and distractions orchestrated by a cadre of eight defense attorneys. Heading the group, as lead counsel and top strategist, was the dreaded dean of Denver's criminal defenders, Horace Hawkins.

Passionate, bombastic, and incorrigible, Hawkins was no mere provocateur; he was more like a flame thrower or an incendiary device, something designed to blacken and shrivel whatever got in its way. He had represented the United Mine Workers of America during the Ludlow violence and managed to get a trumped-up murder conviction of UMWA leader John Lawson overturned on appeal. He had also defended stockbroker Warren Given during his contempt proceeding for failing to answer questions about the KKK put to him by Van Cise and his grand jury. His politics were hard left, but in the courtroom, Hawkins was a strident advocate for whatever cause he represented. He could muster just as much thunderous indignation over efforts to deprive a pickpocket of his liberty as he could over a railroaded union official or a clubman's sacred right to join secret organizations. And in the plight of Lou Blonger, Kid Duffy and their compatriots, the attorney found a great deal to be indignant about.

Hawkins believed that the best defense of the bunco men was a bellowing offense. He denounced the district attorney as a power-mad "whipper snapper" who deprived free-born, liberty-loving people of their constitutional rights and their property, for no good reason at all. He referred to the First Universalist Church basement as a dungeon and accused the prosecution of "blaspheming the holy sanctum" by holding his clients there a few hours. "Van Cise should have been shot in his tracks for using such high-handed and outrageous methods," he declared.

Behind the inflammatory rhetoric was a concerted effort to delay the trial and find out exactly what the DA had on each of the defendants. Judge Charles Butler agreed to hold preliminary hearings to determine if Van Cise had probable cause to make the arrests, a drawn-out process that gave the defense early access to many of the state's witnesses and exhibits. Affidavits supporting the charges filed had been signed by detective Andrew Koehn; the defense took the position that no such person existed, forcing Van Cise to put his best undercover agent on the stand. Koehn had no trouble proving that he was a real person, but his appearance in open court ended his usefulness as the mob's shadow.

Van Cise won the battle over severance—that is, whether to try the defendants individually or en masse. Both sides knew that the conspiracy case would be stronger if there was only one trial, regardless of the number of shysters packed around the defense table, and the prosecution successfully argued that such an approach was legally justified and efficient. But Hawkins kept pressing. If he couldn't get the case thrown out or broken into pieces, then he wanted Van Cise disqualified as prosecutor.

The defense claimed that Van Cise had a conflict of interest. After the arrests, civil suits had been filed against several of the defendants by victims of the scam. One pigeon, seeking to recover fifty thousand dollars taken off him by spieler Tex Cooper, was represented by an attorney named Harold

Webster. Van Cise had shared a suite of offices with Webster and another lawyer, Clyde Barker, prior to becoming district attorney, but they had never worked on any cases together or shared any fees. Yet filings in the civil suit listed the plaintiff's law firm as Barker, Van Cise & Webster. At a marathon hearing, Van Cise argued exhaustively that he had no involvement in the civil case and that his name on the complaint was a clerical error. But Judge Butler was sufficiently troubled by the matter to rule in favor of the DA's ouster. Butler named two special prosecutors to handle the trial: S. Harrison White, a former Colorado Supreme Court justice, and Harry C. Riddle, a former district judge.

As it turned out, the disqualification was a boon to the prosecution. White and Riddle were accomplished and respected jurists, fully capable of standing up to the blustering Hawkins. Although he wouldn't set foot in the courtroom until the trial was over, Van Cise was now freed up to work on the case behind the scenes. And his removal meant little in practical terms; the judge appointed to preside over the trial, George Dunklee, ruled that members of the district attorney's staff could attend the proceedings, consult with the prosecutors, and even supply them with questions. The defense maneuver had backfired.

Regardless of who the real winner or loser was, each legal battle pushed back the trial date. The confidence men used the time well. A few managed to get their bail reduced and fled. Some worked at changing their appearance, growing scruffy beards and wild hair and dressing like hobos for their court appearances, making it harder for their victims to identify them. And Jackie French and his friends were determined to squelch other witness identifications with cash.

Van Cise was tipped to the scheme by the bug in Blonger's office. Blonger was heard complaining about Walter "Sox"

Byland, a top steerer who, like French, had recently made bail. "He's got everything ready to fix those witnesses," Blonger groused. "He's got the dough in his pocket, and yet here he is in Denver."

Byland and French were buying off marks. Their women, Gladys Byland and Buda Godman, embarked on a grand sucker tour of the greater Midwest, dropping in on victims and offering to reimburse a portion of what they had lost—in some cases, as much as 80 percent of what had been taken from them, payable in installments. All the recipients had to do in return was keep out of Colorado until the trial was over. Van Cise could hand out as many subpoenas as he liked, but under existing laws, the prosecution had no way to compel witnesses from other states—and the marks were all from other states— to come to Denver to testify. It was a clever plan; if anyone hollered about witness tampering, the argument could be made that Godman and Mrs. Byland were simply trying to settle civil suits that had already been filed or were anticipated.

Van Cise sent Robinson in the vamp squad's wake to try to salvage his witness list. Robinson was able to persuade several victims of the con to stay the course, but he couldn't fault those who took the money; there was no guarantee that convictions would lead to any kind of restitution. Yet some of the most aggrieved victims rejected the bribe outright. Robinson found George Kanavuts, a Greek immigrant who owned a movie theater in Sapulpa, Oklahoma, still steaming after French's emissaries came to see him and offered to repay $20,000 of the $25,000 he'd lost in Denver in '21. "I ran them out of my movie," Kanavuts boasted. "I would not want that $20,000 as bad as I would them men go to jail."

Byland and French had only so much money to spread around. They might have fared better by distributing some of it closer to home. While they were trying to cool a few marks, one of their own was getting hotter by the day. Forgotten by his chums, abandoned by Blonger and Duff, he would become Van Cise's star witness, his inside man. What he knew, what he could provide on the stand, was better than what even a Dictograph could offer. He knew things Blonger and Duff wouldn't talk about, even in the privacy of the Fixer's office.

════

As THE WIFE OF A PUBLIC MAN, Sara Van Cise often found herself competing for her husband's time against an implacable foe: his sense of duty to his office and his profession. His work frequently took him away from her and the children, away from family dinners and outings downtown and walks in Cheesman Park, the whole cycle of domestic life. It had been like that ever since his service in the militia, when the Ludlow tragedy and its aftermath had cast a shadow over their wedding. Then had come a couple of years of respite, followed by the war. And the hectic race for district attorney. And now the all-consuming bunco investigation and the looming trial. She tried to face it all with a show of cheerful resignation. What she had not expected, though, was the way that world of work and duty would come crashing into her home, or how that intrusion would provide opportunities to join in her husband's battle, bringing them closer together rather than driving them apart.

Long before he disclosed his investigation to his deputies, the district attorney told his wife what he was doing and what he hoped to accomplish. The more he learned about the confidence men and their corrosive influence, the more he shared his findings with her. The case became a kind of intimacy between them. As the undercover operation progressed, their house on Race Street became a mail drop and way station; Sara fielded phone calls, messages, and odd visitors who appeared on the doorstep at odd hours. When Norfleet sent his secret dispatch from a bathroom at the Hotel Metropole, indicating he had the con men on the hook, it was Sara who received the letter and took it to her husband.

After the arrests, her role expanded. The defendants' wives and girlfriends were frantic to get their men out of jail. California Kate, the wife of Elmer "The Christ Kid" Mead, was heard on the Dictograph storming into Blonger's office, grabbing the Fixer by his giant honker, and threatening to bite his ear if Elmer wasn't bonded out immediately. (He was.) Others besieged the district attorney with tearful phone calls and perfumed notes, begging for leniency and promising that their men would cooperate in prosecuting their fellow conspirators. Fearing entrapment, Van Cise wasn't about to accept the invitations to discuss the matter in a hotel room or some out-of-the-way dive, and he couldn't bring the women to his office without exposing them to possible retribution. So he sent Sara and Robinson to screen them. Having his wife there as chaperone would squash any sexual intrigues, he figured, and he valued her read of the supplicant's character as much as any legal appraisal that Robinson could offer.

Almost all the meetings were dead ends. The women were working an angle, or their men turned out to be small-time scufflers who had little new information to offer; they weren't high enough in the pecking order to have anything to trade. But one evening, Sara and Robinson brought back to the house a woman whose story sounded more promising than most, a woman Van Cise was eager to meet. Nina Hansen was a demure, well-mannered brunette. Nothing about her suggested an impoverished upbringing or struggles with morphine addiction, although she spoke frankly about both. She explained that she not only wanted to save her man's neck, but to do it in a way that would rupture all his ties to his criminal past, so that the two of them could embark on a new life together.

Hansen was the common-law wife of Len Reamey, the bookmaker who'd introduced himself to Norfleet as "Mr. Zachery" at the stock exchange. Van Cise remembered him: a small, thin-voiced man in his early thirties, with the build of a jockey, a receding chin, and delicate, girlish hands. Three days after the roundup, Reamey had pleaded for a private meeting with the district attorney. He was brought from the jail to the prosecutor's office on a Sunday morning, his body shaking and teeth chattering with the agonies of opium withdrawal. He indicated he was ready to make a statement, but then changed his mind after a court reporter was summoned.

At the time, Van Cise had not appreciated the importance of this 114-pound wonder in Blonger's organization. Hansen set him straight. The Denver operation required many steerers and spielers, but only one bookmaker. Jackie French had booked most of the scores in previous seasons, but Reamey had been his protégé and taken over as bookmaker this past season. He was essentially the fourth-highest man in the gang, after Blonger, Duff, and French, and had direct dealings with each of them. He was the link Van Cise had been looking for, the one that tied the Fixer to what went on in the stock exchange.

Van Cise couldn't visit Reamey in jail without alerting the rest of the gang. He gave Hansen a list of questions to ask her man; if the answers were satisfactory, a deal for immunity might be arranged. Hansen made several trips to the jail over the next two weeks. Then Van Cise had Reamey brought to his office for the first in a series of interviews. Hours before, Hansen had been sent quietly out of town for the duration of the trial, so that the other defendants' wives couldn't find her.

No longer jonesing for the pipe, Reamey told the story of his life and crimes calmly and without hesitation. Born in Arkansas, he'd gone to work in a sawmill at age eleven, right after the death of his father. He later became a waiter, working concessions at racetracks and fairs from Tijuana to Canada. In Calgary he became involved in crooked coin-matching games and other petty crimes and teamed up with Hansen. He drifted into Denver in 1918 and was introduced to Duff, who put him to work as a steerer. He was so successful that Duff offered him a chance at playing the bookmaker, explaining that French was being promoted to oversee a similar operation in Kansas City. Trained by French, Reamey ran the stock exchange for the latter part of 1921 and throughout the 1922 season. By his count, the gang had been taking down close to half a million a year in Denver, and Van Cise's roundup had prevented them from completing more than a dozen touches, worth $338,000. The standard split for each score was 42 percent to the steerer, 15 percent to the spieler, and 5 percent to the bookmaker. The remaining 38 percent went to Duff and Blonger, for protection and permission to operate.

Reamey had been good at his job, as cool as a croupier while hustling dazed marks out the door, moments after they'd lost their bundle. It was no prick of conscience that sent him to Van Cise. No, it was the way Blonger, Duff, and French gave him the high hat when he pleaded for bail. All that stuff about being great fixers, that was all hooey. They got themselves out and left him to suffer the tortures of the damned. Even when he begged them, threatened to turn state's evidence, they brushed him off. Duff said Blonger wouldn't allow him to post bond for the little bookmaker, for fear everyone else would demand it too. Blonger blamed Duff. They treated him like a sucker. They thought he didn't have the guts to turn on them. The hell with them.

Van Cise was impressed with Reamey. He was risking his life talking to the DA, yet he had Norfleet's imperturbability and then some. The con men's supposed code of honor wasn't as sterling as the newspapers made it out to be—most of them would chisel each other and their own mothers if they could get away with it—but they did take exception to squealers. Everyone in the game had heard about what happened to Willard Powell, also known as the Waco Kid, after he turned informant against the infamous Mabray Gang, promoters of fixed sporting events based out of Council Bluffs, Iowa. In 1921, Powell had been gunned down by multiple shooters in the dining room of the Ponce de León Hotel in Saint Augustine, Florida; his slayers were still at large. To protect his witness, Van Cise arranged for Reamey to be housed in a cell far apart from the rest of the confidence men, a cell reserved for condemned prisoners on their way to the gallows at the state penitentiary. French visited him there one evening, a few days after news of Reamey's deal for immunity made the newspapers. Reamey provided an account of the conversation to the district attorney.

"Looks like you are going to send everybody to the pen," French said. "Would you consider going out on bond?"

"When I wanted bond, you wouldn't give it to me," Reamey replied. "Now I would not go out if the back door was open."

"You know Duff can frame up a sucker and get you brought back to Omaha, and the fixers can bury you there," French said. "If he can't do it in Omaha, Joe Rush and I can do it in Chicago."

Reamey told him to do what he liked. He was tired and ready to turn in. French took his parting shot.

"You will never live to testify, Len," he said.

The condemned man went to bed.

═════════

BETWEEN THOSE WHO SKIPPED BAIL and those Van Cise agreed to turn over to other jurisdictions for prosecution, the number of defendants in the dock had dwindled to twenty by the time the case went to trial in early 1923. The group still included the principal players Van Cise wanted most badly to send away: Blonger, Duff, French, Tex Cooper, Tip Belcher, Sox Byland, Leon Felix, and Louis Mushnick, as well as a dozen other veteran ropers and spielers. Reporters dubbed them the Tricky Twenty.

It was the longest and costliest trial the state had ever seen. Despite the dull bits—long days of jury selection, a stupefying ten hours of opening statements—it held the city in thrall for nine weeks. The courtroom was packed to capacity each day, the testimony recounted at length beneath blaring headlines in the evening papers. The prosecution called eighty-three witnesses and introduced more than five hundred exhibits, a freight train of evidence chugging slowly toward its inevitable destination.

The defense team couldn't derail the train. All it could do was toss debris in its path and try to slow it down. Objection followed objection, with an occasional insinuation of prosecutorial misconduct thrown in for good measure. At one point Hawkins and special prosecutor Harrison heatedly called each other liars and seemed ready to reenact the Bryans–Van Cise bout. But the bunco men's lawyers had to rein in their approach after Judge Dunklee harshly reprimanded one of them, Mike Waldron, telling him to quit badgering witnesses or get off the case. The dressing-down triggered such a raucous outpouring of whistles and applause from the gallery that Dunklee ordered the courtroom cleared.

The defense had a brief moment of triumph when a

witness mistakenly identified attorney Hawkins as one of the confidence men who had cheated him. But it was just about the only stumble in the state's case. One victim after another took the stand and pointed out the members of the Tricky Twenty who had stolen from them. On cross-examination, the defense attorneys couldn't shake the feistier witnesses, such as the dauntless Norfleet and Kanavuts, the Greek who'd angrily rejected French's bribe and now delighted in identifying him as "dat crook" at the stock exchange. And they had to proceed gingerly with the frailer, more pathetic victims—an old man with trembling hands, a bewildered widower who'd come to Colorado to escape his grief and been fleeced instead, a broken-down harness maker who'd lost his life savings—for fear of alienating the jury entirely.

Effective as it was, the victim testimony was only one element in the prosecution's arsenal. Harrison and Riddle introduced a flood of telegrams, linking the defendants to each other and the recent "fishing seasons," as well as wires sent to the marks as part of the blowoff. They invited the jury to inspect the numerous props seized in the raids, the phony stock certificates and fake membership cards and the con man's boodle of dollar bills, made to look like stacks worth hundreds of thousands of dollars. They brought in moving company employees who identified Duff as the man who furnished the Lookout, a carpet cleaner who fingered Belcher as the main occupant of the Lookout, a secretary at a real estate company who remembered Tex Cooper as the man who leased the office used for the 1921 stock exchange. A handwriting expert testified that Duff had deposited checks written by members of the gang and that notations in Blonger's bank book, listing several phone numbers associated with the operation, were in the Fixer's own hand. Maiden described his surveillance of the con men as they went hunting for marks and the sightings of Duff and Blonger in the company of Sanders and other cops.

But it was Reamey who tied it all together and provided the trial's most sensational revelations. When he finally took the witness stand, six weeks in, hundreds turned out to hear him or at least catch a glimpse of him, pressing into the dwindling pockets of standing room until the latecomers had to be turned away. Embedded in the crowd were several plainclothes special deputies, charged with guarding the little bookmaker's life; at least one gun-toting Blonger associate was intercepted at the door and ejected.

Reamey was on the stand for the better part of four days. Speaking rapidly, he recounted his role as steerer and bookmaker on dozens of occasions. He explained who was involved in each transaction, who said what, how much money was taken and how it was divided—so many scores, the scripts so similar in each one, that Hawkins complained that the witness sounded like a phonograph record. But his account implicated one after another of the defendants, until it finally led to the bosses of the whole operation. Reamey described encountering Duff and Blonger in Hot Springs last winter and being invited to book for them for the '22 season, a meeting that had been observed by Van Cise's operative, Fred Tate. He described how Duff had brought "Van Cise's bunco list" to the Lookout one afternoon, saying that Sanders had provided it and boasting that the DA couldn't move on them because of their "ironclad" protection. He recalled a meeting with Blonger on the street outside his office, during which the Fixer handed him five hundred dollars in ones to use in constructing his boodle. He told a riveting story about an elderly mark who'd returned to the stock exchange with

Christmas, 1897: Philip Van Cise at age thirteen, with sister, Ethel, and father, Edwin.
Courtesy of the Van Cise Family

"The captain with a beard": Van Cise denounced the Colorado National Guard's investigation into the 1914 Ludlow Massacre as a whitewash.
Courtesy of the Van Cise Family

Philip S. Van Cise

REPUBLICAN CANDIDATE
FOR
DISTRICT ATTORNEY

"A Fighting Man for a Fighting Job."

Van Cise pushed his war record in the 1920 race to become Denver's district attorney.
Courtesy of the Van Cise Family

Lou "The Fixer" Blonger offered protection to confidence men working in Denver's Big Store.
Robert R. Maiden Papers/Call # C MSS WH 229/Western History Collection/Denver Public Library

Adolph Duff, Blonger's right-hand man, served as the "manager" of Denver's Big Store.
Robert. R. Maiden Papers/Call # C MSS WH 229/Western History/Denver Public Library

"A", Bunk Headquarters,-Blonger's office; "B", Observation Post.

A trial exhibit reveals the location of the "Western Front observation post"
constructed across the street from Blonger's office.
Courtesy of the Van Cise Family

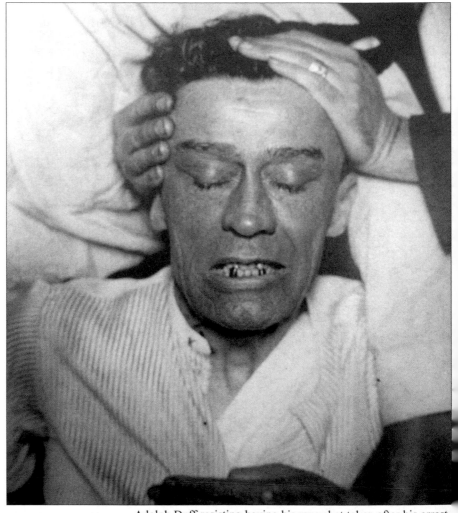

Adolph Duff resisting having his mug shot taken after his arrest.
Robert. R. Maiden Papers/Call # C MSS WH 229/Western History/Denver Public Library

"Dapper" Jackie French tried to buy off marks to keep them from testifying at trial.
Robert. R. Maiden Papers/ Call # C MSS WH 229/ Western History/Denver Public Library

Despite threats to his life, bookmaker Len Reamey agreed to testify against his fellow buncs.
Courtesy of the Van Cise Family

Van Cise was formally awarded a Distinguished Service Medal in a 1922 ceremony, while his wife, Sara, and children Eleanor and Edwin looked on.
Courtesy of the Van Cise family

John Galen Locke, the eccentric Grand Dragon of the Colorado Realm of the Ku Klux Klan,
was described by one reporter as "living in the Middle Ages."
Denver Post Collection/History Colorado /Accession No 86.296.2998

In 1924, thousands flocked to Klan meetings and cross-burning ceremonies
on top of South Table Mountain in Golden.
Special Collections/Call # Z-1875/Denver Public Library

Top: Colorado Klan women preparing Thanksgiving food baskets in 1925.
Bottom: "Master Richard," a baby adopted by the Klan women, dressed in his own robe and hood.
Special Collections/Call #X-21540/Denver Public Library

June 13, 1925: Accompanied by attorney Ben Laska, Locke reports to the Denver jail
to start serving a sentence for contempt in his federal tax case.
Denver Post Collection/History Colorado/Accession No. 86.296.3010

Clarence J. Morley, a former district judge and high-ranking Klansman, became Colorado's governor.
Special Collection/Call #RH236/Denver Public Library

Locke poses in his Minute Man uniform.
History Colorado/Accession No. FFF398 Box 3

Klan members staged a Memorial Day parade in downtown Denver on May 31, 1926.
Tens of thousands were expected to attend; fewer than five hundred showed up.
History Colorado/Accession No. PH.PROP.1734

After leaving the DA's office in 1925, Van Cise continued to practice law well into the 1960s.
Courtesy of the Van Cise family

a gun and had to be hustled out of town by the police, a special service that cost the gang eight thousand dollars out of a nineteen-thousand-dollar take.

Reporters hung on Reamey's every word. The defendants put up a show of disinterest. French refused to meet Reamey's gaze and spent breaks flirting with female admirers. Blonger stared off into space. Duff had worn tinted goggles during much of the trial; now he dispensed with them but sat impassively, masticating an undetermined substance. (Comments overheard by the Dick indicated a rift had developed between Blonger and Duff, with each blaming the other's carelessness for their predicament.) When it was finally time to cross-examine the witness, the interrogation didn't even touch on Reamey's most devastating claims. It was largely an attack on his character, an attempt to paint him as a liar and a dope fiend.

Reamey was unflappable. Yes, he had lied throughout his criminal career. But not today. Yes, he had been an opium addict, but not anymore. Asked about opium found in his safe deposit box after his arrest, he responded that it didn't belong to him. "I got it from Duff and French, in French's apartment," he said. "They were both smoking the pipe. Duff says to me, 'Will you take this junk and put it in your box?' I did."

His inquisitor, defense attorney Sam Crump, managed to shake his composure only once, when he referred to the witness's common-law wife as a "common prostitute." Fists clenched, Reamey leaned forward in his chair.

"She never was that, and don't you say she was!" he roared.

Crump retreated behind his lectern. The cross fizzled. If the case had depended solely on Reamey's word, the word of a confidence man, perhaps the assault could have gone somewhere. But the case was Reamey *and* the testimony of the marks *and* the undercover operation *and* that trainload of other documents and details, and they all corroborated each other. By the time Reamey left the stand, Van Cise was feeling confident enough that he didn't see any need to introduce what had once seemed his most powerful weapon of all—the evidence gathered by the Dictograph.

The existence of the Dick had never been disclosed to the defense. Van Cise had no doubt that his use of it had been within the law, but its admissibility in court was another matter. The prosecution would face an uphill battle if it tried to introduce fragmentary transcripts. Even if Judge Dunklee permitted them, that decision could well be reversed on appeal, dragging the whole case down with it. After some discussion, the team decided on a more oblique approach.

Andy Koehn was the state's last witness. He gave a meticulous account of his months-long surveillance of Blonger's office. Asked point-blank about Dictographs, he described their placement and announced that they were still in operation. At that point, Samson left the courtroom and contacted Van Cise, who called Maiden, who was awaiting the boss's signal to remove the devices. They were brought to court that afternoon, and Koehn was able to show them off to the jury while Blonger and Duff did a slow burn. No one at the defense table knew what the transmitters had heard, and that was the point—the bugs were a looming threat, not-yet-evidence that might (or might not) have to be dealt with later. If the principal defendants chose to take the stand, they couldn't be sure they wouldn't be tripped up with words they'd uttered in Blonger's office months ago.

The special prosecutors rested their case and braced for a ferocious counterattack. To their astonishment, none was forthcoming. Hawkins announced that the defense declined to present a single witness. He also proposed that both sides skip closing arguments and proceed directly to handing the case over to the jury. It was tempting to think that disclosing the existence of the Dictograph had influenced that decision, but Van Cise suspected something else was at work.

Maybe Hawkins and the other defense lawyers had convinced their clients that they could win the case on appeal. Or maybe the defendants had other reasons to feel confident. Bookies around town were reportedly offering 2–1 odds in favor of a not guilty verdict, a proposition that suggested the kind of inside knowledge essential to handicapping a fixed race. The buncs had tried to buy off witnesses. They had tried to buy off Reamey.

Why wouldn't they try to fix the jury?

WHEN THE LAWYERS ASKED HIM QUESTIONS during jury selection, Herman Okuly gave them straight answers. He was thirty-one years old. He had moved to Colorado from Indiana two years ago. He worked as a machinist at a Denver lumber company. He had a wife and daughter at home, and yes, serving on a jury would be a hardship for him.

They told him he was Juror Number One. He sat through the selection of Jurors Two through Thirteen—the last one an unlucky alternate—and then the opening statements. One night in February, after the first long day of actual testimony, he was roused from bed by the ringing of his doorbell. In the darkness of his unlit front porch stood a man dressed in dark clothes, with cap pulled down and coat collar turned up. Not particularly tall or short, not distinguishable at all, this fellow.

The man asked if he was Okuly. When Okuly said he was, the man put five hundred-dollar bills in his hand, explaining this was payment in advance for a verdict of not guilty.

For an honest mechanic, Okuly displayed exceptional guile. He took the bills inside so he could look at them in the light. He invited his visitor to come in, too, but the man stayed on the porch. Okuly gave him back the bills, saying that a favorable verdict ought to be worth a lot more. How about five hundred for his vote, he suggested, and another two thousand if he could get the whole jury to vote for acquittal? If this was acceptable, Blonger should scratch his right ear in court tomorrow while looking at Okuly.

The man left. Okuly contacted his employer, William McPhee, and told him about the attempted bribe. McPhee, one of the donors who had helped finance Van Cise's bunco investigation, called the district attorney early the next morning and reported the incident. Van Cise explained that legal procedure barred him from speaking with Okuly, but he would take appropriate steps. He informed the special prosecutors of the attempted bribe, who informed Judge Dunklee. He also made sure Samson was in the courtroom that morning, watching discreetly as Blonger glanced at the jury and scratched his right ear.

Months earlier, in conversation with the wife of another defendant, Blonger had predicted that it would take a year to try all the charges against the group—and that not one of the gang would be found guilty. "Cheer up," he told her and the Dictograph. "They will have a hung jury in every one of them. They will never get a conviction any place."

It would take only one crooked juror to hang the entire panel. Blonger was too smart to leave his fate in the hands of one man; chances were good that at least two or three others had been approached besides Okuly. But how could you prove it? The jury was in an inviolable bubble for the duration of the trial. Investigators couldn't question any of them without risking a mistrial, and Van Cise didn't want a mistrial. He assigned men to follow jurors he suspected might be bought. The tails were done at great distance, so as not to alarm the targets, and revealed little of value other than that two of them were regulars at the same speakeasy. There was little else he could do but wait.

Rumors circulated throughout the trial that members of the panel had been offered five thousand dollars or even ten thousand dollars for acquittal on all counts, and that at least three of them were on the take. The case was finally handed over to the jury on a Saturday morning. That evening a courthouse reporter pawed through a custodian's trash collection and found that the jury's first ballot was 9–3 in favor of conviction. The tally seemed to confirm the rumors and was extremely encouraging news for the defense. Three holdouts were more than enough to crash Van Cise's locomotive.

At the conclusion of the trial, all the defendants were supposed to have their bail revoked and be returned to jail to wait for the verdict. But jailer Tom Clarke was feeling so ebullient about the prospects for a hung jury that he arranged for a Saturday night party in the grand jury room for his friends Blonger, Duff, and French, featuring contraband pints of hooch. Reporters and members of the con men's entourage joined in, and the soiree deteriorated into a drunken debauch. Dapper Jackie was observed in what one reporter described as a "prolonged osculatory exchange" with a young widow. By midnight the grand jury room was an aromatic wreckage of empty bottles and vomit. A well-oiled Clarke escorted his prisoners to bed and then went in search of Van Cise. He found the district attorney in his office, where he was waiting in idle hope of a late-breaking verdict. Clarke began to berate him, telling him that it would take a bigger man than Van Cise to put Blonger and Duff away. The Fighting DA confiscated the deputy's pint and told him to go home.

On Sunday morning news of the "booze orgy" made the newspapers. The press acted suitably scandalized. The jury spent all day in deliberations, surfacing only for meals.

On Monday, Clarke resigned as chief deputy sheriff. The jury continued its discussions well into the evening.

On Tuesday, Judge Dunklee gave the jurors what is known as an Allen charge, urging the holdout jurors to reconsider their position and try to reach an understanding with the majority. Raised voices could be heard emanating from the jury room, but the impasse continued.

On Wednesday, with the deliberations now approaching a record-breaking hundred hours, the foreman called for another ballot. Sensing that the holdouts were wavering, Okuly decided to give them a push. "The difference between me and you three sons of bitches," he said, "is that I turned my five hundred dollars over to the judge, and you've still got yours."

Other jurors joined in the harangue. The next vote showed the panel leaning 10–2 in favor of conviction. Noon arrived, and so did another ballot. Now the count was 11–1.

Late in the afternoon, the jury sent word that it had reached a verdict. The defendants, the attorneys, and the crowds poured back into the courtroom. The clerk read the verdict: All twenty guilty on all counts. Guilty of conspiracy to defraud, guilty of defrauding through a confidence game, guilty of grand theft. Each man faced up to thirty years in prison.

Blonger slumped in his chair. Duff didn't flinch. Hawkins asked that the jurors be polled. Starting with Okuly, one after another confirmed that this was their verdict. But Juror Number Ten, George Sharp, struggled with the question. Sharp had been the last holdout, and he wanted everyone to know he had capitulated under duress. He muttered something about being sick. The clerk put the question to him again, and he equivocated once more. Judge Dunklee took over.

"Is or is not this your verdict?" the judge asked.

"Yes," Sharp said.

"Does the juror desire further time to deliberate?"

"No. I want to get out of this."

Dunklee thanked the jurors for their service and discharged them. As they stepped out of the box, Samson handed them subpoenas. They were summoned to testify before the grand jury, which would be investigating Okuly's allegations of attempted bribery.

Now that he could show his face in the courtroom, Van Cise was mobbed by reporters. He had many people to thank. Without Reamey, without his undercover team, without Okuly and the other honest jurors, the outcome might have been quite different. Yet it was the Fighting DA, the Bugaboo of Buncs, who was all over the front pages now, while his home and office were inundated with congratulatory calls, letters, and telegrams. Seldom had the city's scribes adopted as optimistic a tone as in the sunny editorials that celebrated his victory.

"The underworld has been dealt a crushing blow," one proclaimed, "and those who live by their wits have at last learned the lesson that the law is to be respected in Denver."

PART TWO

HOODS

Where the wolves are killed off, the foxes increase.

—HERMAN MELVILLE,
The Confidence-Man: His Masquerade

If you can convince the lowest white man he's better than the best colored man, he won't notice you're picking his pocket.

—LYNDON B. JOHNSON
(to Bill Moyers, 1960)

6

—

The Klandestine Candidate

On the evening of November 25, 1915, while most Georgians were at home digesting their Thanksgiving dinners, sixteen pilgrims traveled by hired bus from an Atlanta hotel to the base of Stone Mountain, a giant dome of igneous rock twenty-five miles east of the city. Using flashlights, they ascended the mile-long trail to the summit, where they piled small boulders to create a makeshift altar. A Bible and an American flag were placed on the altar. Then the leader of the group, William Joseph Simmons, lit a match and ignited a sixteen-foot wooden cross that he'd hauled up the mountain earlier that day and doused with kerosene. While the cross blazed, Simmons guided the others through the recital of a creed he'd written himself, an oath of allegiance to their country, their faith, their race, and their new secret society—a rebirth of the Ku Klux Klan.

The original Klan had been a short-lived and highly unstable venture. It began as a social club with a tinge of mystical hooha, launched by young Confederate veterans in Pulaski,

Tennessee, nearly a year after the end of the Civil War. (The name evoked the Greek word for circle, *kyklos*, and the tribalism of Scottish clans.) The members dressed up in white gowns and conical headpieces and engaged in nocturnal sorties intended to prank, amuse, and alarm their neighbors. But in 1867 the Klan reorganized as a vigilante force, bent on thwarting Reconstruction efforts by terrorizing freed Blacks, carpetbaggers, radical Republicans, and their supporters. Operating primarily in rural areas in several states, the night riders were responsible for hundreds of lynchings, floggings, beatings, and other crimes until a federal crackdown suppressed the organization in the early 1870s. The subsequent withdrawal of federal troops and return to power of southern Democrats made the group superfluous; with Blacks systematically stripped of voting rights and barred from most jobs and educational opportunities, the Klan was no longer needed.

The ceremony on Stone Mountain was attended by two elderly members of the first KKK. Yet the organization christened in fire that night was not a revival of the old Klan but a reimagining of it. Simmons had studied the protocols and organizational structure of the original, and he readily embraced its central tenet of white supremacy—as well as its love of arcane jargon and theatrical rituals. He borrowed heavily from its Halloweenish nomenclature, designating himself as the group's Imperial Wizard, the national leader over other officers known as Goblins, Titans, Terrors, and such. But what Simmons had in mind was something far more marketable than the 1860s Klan. It was a nationwide call to white Protestants to unite and defend their women, their homes, and their communities from a seemingly endless array of threats posed by Blacks, Jews, Catholics, immigrants, and others who were not, could never be, "100% American." A true American's duty, Simmons wrote, is to "keep Anglo-Saxon American civilization, institutions, politics, and society pure, and thereby . . . transmit it with clean hands and pure hearts to generations yet unborn."

Fifty years after the South's defeat, Simmons was not the only one to recognize that there was money to be made by waxing nostalgic over slavery and the terrorist exploits of the Ku Klux Klan. That had already been amply demonstrated by the success of *The Birth of a Nation*, the first full-length motion picture in cinematic history and the cultural phenomenon of the year, which was released eight months before Simmons's trip to Stone Mountain. Director D. W. Griffith's three-hour epic transfixed audiences with its use of panning shots, close-ups, iris effects, night photography, and other technical innovations, showing that movies could be art. But it was also a highly inflammatory piece of racist propaganda, portraying the Klan as white knights riding to the rescue of delicate maidens menaced by brutish, rapacious blacks (many played by white actors in blackface). The movie was based on *The Clansman*, a best-selling novel by influential Baptist minister Thomas Dixon, who preached against "creeping negroidism" and had gone to graduate school with Woodrow Wilson. Dixon managed to arrange a screening of *The Birth of a Nation* at the White House. The President of the United States was supposedly so captivated by the film, which quoted from his own writings in several title cards, that he provided Dixon and Griffith with an enthusiastic blurb: "It is like writing history with lightning, and my only regret is that it is all so terribly true."

The oft-cited line is of suspicious origin, even for an unabashed segregationist like Wilson. If he did indeed say that, he disavowed his endorsement a few months later, after the movie triggered protests from the NAACP and riots in several cities. At a Boston theater, Black activists who'd been refused admission forced their way inside and hurled eggs at the screen. In the South, random attacks on Black men surged in the wake of screenings. Kansas censors banned the film for promoting racism and historical inaccuracies. In Denver, protesters persuaded city officials to cancel the premiere, only to see that decision overruled by a judge. The controversy stoked ticket sales. *The Birth of a Nation* cost more than $100,000 to make, an unheard-of figure for the era, but it's estimated that it earned $18 million in its first few years of release—a sum which, adjusted for inflation, makes the film one of the highest-grossing blockbusters of all time.

Simmons would later claim that he'd been dreaming about resuscitating the Ku Klux Klan years before the movie came out. Perhaps so, but having Griffith's spectacle available as a recruiting tool did speed things along. The ceremony on Stone Mountain was hastily arranged just one week before *The Birth of a Nation* was set to open in Atlanta. (The cross-burning was a nod to similar scenes in Dixon's novel and the film; the first KKK didn't engage in such pyrotechnics.) The day of the premiere, a contingent of hooded initiates rode horses past the lines of moviegoers outside the Atlanta Theatre to announce the arrival of the new order. Soon Simmons was swearing in dozens of new members and planning similar publicity stunts in other cities.

The organization grew slowly at first, but its Imperial Wizard found any degree of progress gratifying after decades of disappointment. Born in Alabama, Joseph Simmons had enlisted in the army at age eighteen and served during the Spanish-American War, but never rose higher than private. He aspired to be a doctor, like his father—who might have been a Klansman as well. Short of funds, young Joe went into the ministry instead, but failed to attract the kind of notice and adulation accorded to a firebrand like Thomas Dixon. In 1912 he was suspended by the Methodist hierarchy for inefficiency. After a grim period as a garter salesman, he became a well-compensated district manager in the Woodmen of the World, a fraternal organization with 750,000 members. Simmons was a heavy drinker who belonged to numerous lodges, churches, veteran associations, and fraternal groups. While there is scant evidence that he had any intention of creating the political powerhouse the new Klan would become, he did recognize that a secret fraternal order drenched in the mythology of the Old South had commercial potential.

From the Elks to the Rotarians to the Knights of Pythias, hundreds of fraternal organizations beckoned to small businessmen and working-class Americans in the early part of the twentieth century. Between 1900 and 1925 their membership almost doubled, to more than ten million. They provided camaraderie, community building, and networking opportunities for people who couldn't afford to join snooty country clubs— yet like private clubs, the fraternal groups often restricted membership on the basis of faith or race. Some, like the Woodmen, were organized as "mutual benefit societies" that offered insurance, burials, or medical assistance to their members. Others, including the Masons and the Odd Fellows, stressed charitable projects. Learning the secret signs and greetings and collecting lodge pins was part of the fun, as was being involved in something you weren't supposed to discuss with outsiders. But while it recruited heavily from other groups, especially the Masons, Simmons's Klan would take the familiar concepts of fraternalism and exclusivity in a startling new direction.

Simmons devised an extensive rule book for the new organization and copyrighted it. The terminology relied heavily on "kl" sounds. The rule book was known as the *Kloran*; a local lodge was a *klavern*; the administrator of a klavern was a *kligrapp*; a recruiter was a *kleagle*, who worked under another administrator, the *King Kleagle*; an initiation ceremony was a *klonversation*; the initiation fee was a *klecktoken*; and so on. Members encountering each other on the street were expected to communicate in tortuous acronyms: "Ayak?" (Are you a Klansman?) "Akia!" (A Klansman I am!) "Sanbog!" (Strangers are near, be on guard.) Those who joined the Klan were said to be "naturalized," while outsiders were known as "aliens." And there were a lot of aliens. More than any other fraternal order, being a Klansman was sharply defined by all the people who couldn't possibly be members. Only native-born white male Protestants need apply.

For five years the Klan attracted scant public attention, its membership confined to a few cities in the Deep South. During World War I, Simmons attempted to promote the group as patriotic watchdogs, quick to parade in support of American troops or against foreign agitators infiltrating the labor movement, but the effort failed to make much of an impression amid so many other jingoistic, flag-waving displays. By 1920, the KKK consisted of a few thousand members, far fewer than the dues-paying hordes Simmons had envisioned, and the Imperial Wizard was having trouble paying his bills. Then he made the deal that would transform the Klan into a force to be reckoned with. He put the odd couple of Edward Clarke and Elizabeth Tyler in charge of publicity and recruiting efforts.

Clarke and Tyler ran an advertising agency in Atlanta and had handled promotional campaigns for the Salvation Army, the YMCA, and the Red Cross. Ambitious and unconventional—it was whispered that Tyler, a widow, and Clarke, a married man, were romantic as well as business partners and had once been arrested together in a brothel raid—they were also savvy pioneers in the emerging field of public relations. The contract with Simmons put them in charge of the "Propagation Department" of the Klan, with Clarke designated as Imperial Kleagle, and allowed them to claim 80 percent of the initiation fees they generated. It sounds like an outlandish amount, but Clarke and Tyler had to cover commissions and other expenses of the recruitment drive, which were substantial. For every new Klansman the Propagation Department brought in, the frontline recruiter was paid four dollars out of the ten-dollar initiation fee. The rest was sent up the chain of command: a buck to the King Kleagle, $.50 to the Goblin who oversaw that sales district, $2.50 to Clarke and Tyler—and the remaining $2.00 to the national Klan's treasury.

The propagators assembled an army of more than a thousand kleagles spread across the country. They were a professional sales force, eager for their cut, not all that different from Kid Duffy's ropers. Clarke and Tyler aided the membership drive with ads, flyers, and pitches to newspaper reporters; the resulting articles often tilted more toward ridicule than adoration, but they helped to raise the visibility of the Invisible Empire. To some degree, the recruiting message was customized to reflect the particular circumstances of the community the Klan was courting, stressing race troubles in the Deep South; patriotism and anti-immigrant fervor in the industrial Midwest; a moral crusade against bootleggers, loose women, and Catholics in the Bible Belt—bugaboos tailored to fit long-simmering local prejudices.

This dog-whistle approach, shifting the pitch to match the audience, allowed the Klan to capitalize on a host of resentments rather than rely on a single issue to attract members. The enemy was a moving target: Blacks rising above their "station," godless Bolsheviks, Jewish bankers and movie moguls,

disease-spreading immigrants, flappers having sex in automobiles, you name it. Whatever the problem, the Klan was
the answer. A typical flyer touting "What the Ku Klux Klan
Stands For" offered a grab-bag of racial, cultural, and political
grievances:

> It stands for White Supremacy, do you?
>
> It stands for the sanctity of the home.
> I know you do.
>
> It stands against the married man who deserts
> wife and babe to bask in the sensual splendor of
> the depraved bawd, do you?
>
> It stands against the conscienceless bootlegger
> who cares not whether he take the life of his
> neighbor with poisoned booze . . .

Ben Lindsey, a trailblazing Denver juvenile court judge who
became one of the Colorado Klan's bitterest enemies, believed
that the core of the group's appeal was the license it gave its
members to scapegoat just about anybody for anything. "They
paid ten dollars each to hate somebody," Lindsey observed,
"and they were determined to get their money's worth."

The war had stirred up fear and hatred of foreigners, particularly German immigrants. When the war ended, much of
that animosity was redirected at the fourteen million immigrants, largely from southern and eastern Europe, who'd
arrived in the United States since 1900. The postwar prosper-
ity had not been doled out equally, particularly in the Midwest and intermountain West, where miners and farmers were
struggling; the shaky economy fueled fears that native-born
Americans were losing ground to the new arrivals. The rapid
pace of technological change, the emergence of women as

a force in the workplace and in the voting booth, the rising crime associated with Prohibition, and other cultural upheavals of the Jazz Age left many white males fuming—and looking for somebody to blame. The Klan provided convenient culprits for their rage. Housing values not what they should be? Blame the foreign-looking family that just moved in down the block. Don't like what bootlegging is doing to your town? Blame the Italians, with their homemade wine and fabled ties to crime families—and, by extension, blame the Catholics for any number of social ills, with their arcane rites in a dead language and immigrant parishioners and legions of children indoctrinated in parochial schools. Catholics, the Klan taught, were not true Americans because they owed their allegiance to the Pope. As for the Jews—the Klan was hardly alone in dredging up ancient calumnies to portray them as a tribe apart, and thus un-American. The same year that Clarke and Tyler launched their recruitment effort, auto tycoon Henry Ford began publishing a ninety-one-part series of articles based on *The Protocols of the Elders of Zion*—a bogus document, fostered by anti-Semites in czarist Russia, that claimed to reveal Jewish plans for global domination.

Clarke and Tyler had figured out how to market hate as a brand, and their efforts proved to be wildly successful. In the fall of 1921, a congressional inquiry into the activities of the Klan revealed that the Propagation Department had signed up more than eighty-five thousand new members in the previous sixteen months, a tenfold surge in the total size of the group. The emerging klaverns stretched from Miami, Florida, to Portland, Oregon, to Portland, Maine. Much of the $850,000 raised went back to the sales force, but Clarke and Tyler did well for themselves, and a significant amount of the 20 percent cut ($170,000) that went to Klan headquarters in Atlanta was used to purchase a house for Simmons and award him $25,000 in back pay. Taking into account other sources of income—five bucks per member for annual dues, a couple more dollars in the form of a tax from headquarters, additional donations required to receive impressive-sounding honorifics and "degrees" in the organization, several dollars more for Klan robes (only official robes, made by the Klan's own factory, would do) and other paraphernalia, from Klan holy water to fiery-cross jewelry to life insurance—the Klan's annual revenue stream had gone from next to nothing to close to two million dollars a year, with thousands of new members coming on board every week.

Simmons maintained that the group had not yet embarked on "any definite activity" and was still getting organized. But the national leadership's control over local klaverns was severely tested by the rapid growth. Reports of murders, floggings, beatings, tar-and-feather parties, and other eruptions of violence, mostly directed against Blacks but in some cases targeting European immigrants or suspected "race traitors," trickled in from states that had been among the first to organize Klan chapters, including Texas and Florida. Testifying before the U.S. House Committee on Rules, Simmons denied that such actions were sanctioned by the KKK. Confronted with a tally of sixty crimes committed by masked men in recent months, he insisted that the perpetrators were not his men.

"The Klan does not countenance, nor will it tolerate any lawless acts by its members," he said. "We teach respect for the law, love of country, and a closer fellowship of service."

The Klan was not about racial hatred but racial pride, he said. He had dear friends who were Catholics and Jews, and in his youth he had taught the alphabet to "many old Negro men." The term "white supremacy" as used in Klan literature "means the supremacy of the white man's mind as evidenced by the achievements of our civilization." He indignantly rejected the suggestion that he had conceived of the Klan as some kind of "grafter's game," but his responses to questions about where all the money was going were vague. He had been ill, he said, and hadn't had as much time to review his books as he would have liked.

The evasions in Simmons's testimony were roundly mocked by a generally hostile press, yet in many respects his appearance before the lawmakers was a triumph. He presented the Klan as a benevolent gathering of law-abiding men who loved their country. He likened himself to a persecuted, misunderstood Christ, with no personal interest in wealth or power. And he concluded his presentation with a dramatic swoon, reinforcing the claim that he'd left his sick bed to defend his cause. Bolstered by the publicity, the membership rolls of the KKK swelled at a furious pace. Simmons and his top lieutenants routinely exaggerated the size of the Klan, but soon they could legitimately claim a following that numbered, not in tens or even hundreds of thousands, but in millions.

Success altered the mission. Within a few months Tyler, Clarke, and then Simmons himself would be out of the picture, and the Klan's political ambitions would be impossible to ignore.

———

IN THE SPRING OF 1923, THE POLITICAL TALK among Denver's leading citizens tended to revolve around one consuming question: Who was going to run the city? The Blonger trial had exposed the stench of corruption permeating Dewey Bailey's administration. A reckoning seemed to be at hand, an opportunity to clean house, to break with Denver's tradition of phony reforms and pliable leaders and restore confidence in local government. But Bailey was forging ahead with plans to pursue a second term, and the mayoral election was only six weeks away, touching off a scramble to find a reform candidate who could beat him and his well-funded machine.

The obvious choice was the Fighting DA. Calls for Van Cise to declare his candidacy began even before the Blonger trial was over. A clip-out "membership application" appeared in newspapers, inviting readers to join the Van Cise for Mayor Club. On the evening of March 30, scarcely forty-eight hours after the jury returned its guilty verdict, Van Cise hosted a gathering of fifty friends and supporters, many of them prepared to get the campaign in motion as soon as he gave the word.

But Van Cise had other ideas. A cartoon on the front page of the next day's *Denver Post* depicted the DA being offered a ticket to the mayor's office on a golden platter; the caption read, IT DIDN'T TEMPT HIM VERY LONG. Van Cise released a statement declaring that not only was he not running for mayor, "I will not be a candidate to succeed myself in my present office." He had unfinished business as district attorney and a four-year "contract" with the voters that he intended to honor. But after that he was done. Unsaid but implicit in his remarks was a commitment he'd made to Sara to serve only one term, so that he could get back to the more regular hours and better pay of a private law practice while Edwin and Eleanor were still young. He wouldn't rule out a run for higher office someday—in fact, he would briefly flirt with the idea of running for a U.S. Senate seat in 1924, against Klan-backed incumbent Lawrence Phipps, before withdrawing his candidacy—but the mayor's job wasn't for him.

Unlike the district attorney race, Denver's mayoral elections were nonpartisan; a person needed only a hundred signatures on a petition to run for mayor, and no candidate could rely on party affiliation to carry the day. Calling the Bailey administration "a disgrace to American government," Van Cise urged the five challengers already in contention to "select one of their number to make the race and definitely concentrate the opposition to Bailey into one real army. If all they want is cheap notoriety, they will all stay in the race and go down to an inglorious defeat."

A few days later, a caustic report released by the grand jury investigating police corruption offered additional arguments for Bailey's removal. The grand jury failed to issue any indictments, but the report blasted eight city employees as "totally unfit to hold any office" and called for their immediate dismissal. The roll of shame included Detective Sanders, Constable Goldman, and Manager of Safety Frank Downer, who was accused of failing to keep track of seized booze and being drunk while on duty. Sanders and Goldman soon resigned, but other targets of the corruption probe slipped the net. Van Cise suspected that Billy Arnett, Blonger's pal in the Justice Department, had been involved in protecting the bunco ring, but he couldn't prove anything to the satisfaction of Arnett's superiors. To shore up his case against Sanders and the city cops, Van Cise had tracked down A. Friend, the writer of the anonymous letters, an admitted expert on graft in Denver; but the man was now running a protected gambling house in Kansas City and couldn't come forward without jeopardizing his own arrangements with the law. The investigation into jury tampering during the bunco trial went nowhere, too, although Van Cise didn't doubt that Blonger was behind it.

In response to the report, Downer threatened to sue the grand jury for libel. Bailey hedged and pledged to study the matter. Bailey's opponents seized the report as a cudgel. Each of the challengers claimed to be just the man to clean up the town. Van Cise threw his support to Mark Skinner, a Democrat and former state senator who was being touted as the "fusion candidate," capable of uniting business, labor, and reform interests. Skinner also had the backing of Governor William Sweet, who despised Bailey. But Skinner's campaign lasted only two weeks before he was forced to withdraw. The city charter required that a mayoral candidate must have lived and paid taxes in Denver for five years; Skinner, formerly of Colorado Springs, had been an official resident of the Mile High City for only four years. With the petition deadline for new candidates only hours away, Skinner's backers hustled to find a suitable replacement.

The new fusion candidate was George Carlson, a man after Van Cise's own heart. He had been a district attorney in Fort Collins, known for cracking down on gambling and graft. He had also been Colorado's first dry governor, overseeing the implementation of the state's early Prohibition law in 1915–16. With less than three weeks to go before the election, Van Cise went on the stump for Carlson, praising him as a fighter, a doer of deeds, "a he-man who knows how to enforce the law." And he attacked Bailey and the bibulous Downer at every turn.

"The present mayor called in Black Jack Jerome to break a strike and then surrendered the sovereignty of the city to federal troops to restore order," he observed. "Under his administration Blonger flourished for half a million a year; was entertained at a booze party in the courthouse; and still enjoys special privileges in the county jail. Bootleggers flourish, and a wobbly man with a jellyfish disposition administers the Department of Safety."

But some elements of the anti-Bailey forces did not warm to Carlson, a Republican known for his hostility to the labor movement. Progressives, union leaders, and Governor Sweet (a Democrat) drifted toward the other major contender in the race, Benjamin Franklin Stapleton. Fifty-three years old, bland and pragmatic, Stapleton was nobody's idea of a he-man, but he was well-connected in Denver political circles. He had allies in the Democratic machine as well as among the bankers on Seventeenth Street and the leaders of the city's ethnic neighborhoods. Born in Kentucky, he'd moved to Denver as a young man and served in the Spanish-American War. He never quite got his law practice off the ground, but he'd held various city jobs under Boss Speer, including justice of the peace and police magistrate—sometimes more than one job simultaneously. In 1915 he'd been appointed as Denver postmaster, a much-coveted federal sinecure. After six years in that position, he became an oil executive. In the mayoral campaign he stressed his knowledge of police operations and city government in general. He promised to put together a businesslike, efficient, nonpartisan administration.

"He was a nonentity," recalled Charles Ginsberg, a politically active Denver attorney who initially supported Stapleton, in an oral history given many years later. "He was a police judge that nobody knew or cared about. He was just a name. There was nothing against him and nothing for him."

Yet Ginsberg and a few other reformers feared that Stapleton wasn't quite as nonpartisan as he claimed to be. He was a joiner and a Mason, and there was talk that in his youth he'd joined the American Protective Association, an anti-Catholic secret society, and that he might be tied to the Ku Klux Klan. Crime and corruption were undeniably the top issues in the election, but the growing influence of the Klan across the state was also a concern—so much so that Ginsberg and Phil Hornbein, another prominent Jewish attorney, urged Stapleton to issue a statement denouncing racial bigotry. The candidate complied. Although the statement didn't mention the Klan, everybody knew what group he was talking about.

"True Americanism needs no mask or disguise," Stapleton declared. "Any attempt to stir up racial or religious prejudices or religious intolerance is contrary to our constitution and therefore un-American."

The race was a close one. The city had a ranked-choice voting system that allowed voters to select their first, second, and third choices among the eight mayoral candidates on the ballot. Bailey drew the most first-choice votes, but Stapleton fared better in total votes, pulling ahead of Bailey by six thousand votes out of nearly seventy thousand votes cast. Carlson finished a distant third.

Among contemporary observers, Stapleton's narrow victory was largely credited to his ties to the Democratic machine, but other forces were at work, too. The deciding factor may have been the grassroots, get-out-the-vote campaigning on his behalf by an organization the candidate never acknowledged. The concerns about what Stapleton really stood for were well-founded. He was a longtime friend of John Galen Locke, the Grand Dragon of Colorado's Ku Klux Klan, and Stapleton had been issued Klan membership No. 1128—a number low enough to suggest that his KKK initiation had occurred long before he declared his candidacy. Nor was he the only closeted Klansman in the mayor's race. Although Van Cise didn't know it, the man he'd supported at the outset, Mark Skinner, held membership No. 1108, his name entered just a page ahead of Stapleton's in the official Klan roster.

Formally, the Colorado Klan hadn't endorsed any candidate, recognizing that its public support could be a liability for the office seeker. It was still operating from the shadows. But that was about to change. Days after the election, a single

Klansman in robe and hood posed on the steps of Denver's City Hall, one arm raised in salute. The photo ran in the KKK's national magazine, *The Imperial Night-Hawk*, and there was no mistaking its meaning. The Klan had arrived at the seat of Denver government, and it was settling in nicely.

———

STAPLETON'S ELECTION AS MAYOR CAME just over two years after the Klan had established its first foothold in the state. In 1921, Imperial Wizard Simmons came to Denver at the invitation of Leo Kennedy, a former American Protective Association leader, to meet with like-minded businessmen who were interested in starting a local klavern. Simmons gave his pitch in a private gathering at the Brown Palace and ended up enrolling several enthusiasts on the spot.

By most measures, Colorado was an unlikely venue for what Simmons was peddling. The state had no deep-rooted history of racial violence—nothing that approached the systematic oppression in the South, certainly, or the 1921 race massacre in Tulsa, which left hundreds dead and leveled an entire Black neighborhood. Blacks represented less than 2 percent of Colorado's population, and they tended to be better-educated and have a higher degree of home ownership than Blacks in the Northeast or the South. Denver's population was overwhelmingly white and born in America, yet fully half of the residents had at least one parent who was born in another country. Roughly one out of seven Denverites was Catholic, and thriving Catholic parishes could be found across the state.

But Colorado proved to be surprisingly fertile ground for the Klan. The Centennial State didn't have the South's legacy of slavery, but its own brief on race relations was hardly bloodless, from the 1864 slaughter of hundreds of Arapaho and Cheyenne women and children, an atrocity that became known as the Sand Creek Massacre, to an 1880 anti-Chinese riot in Denver, to the scores of people executed without benefit of trial by frontier lynch mobs. (The "court of Judge Lynch" remained open decades after the frontier closed; one of the most repugnant murders occurred in 1905, when Preston Porter Jr., a fifteen-year-old Black railroad worker accused of raping and killing a twelve-year-old white girl, was chained to an iron stake outside the eastern plains town of Limon and burned alive in front of a crowd of three hundred, including numerous newspaper reporters.) Denver's white citizens may have considered themselves less prejudiced than their benighted relatives in the Jim Crow South, but a color line ran through the town, segregating housing and schools, theaters and swimming pools, restaurants and parks. Discrimination against Catholics and Jews was less pervasive but still significant, keeping them clustered in ethnic neighborhoods and almost completely absent from the ranks of judges, councilmen, or other positions of authority.

The fault lines of racism and religious bigotry were already there, waiting to be exploited. Yet it's doubtful that the Colorado Klan would have amounted to much without the canny and opportunistic leadership of its chief, John Galen Locke. Over the course of three years, Locke transformed the Colorado KKK into one of the most politically powerful Klan organizations in the country, second only to the Indiana KKK in per capita support—and second to none in the degree to which it controlled state government.

Accounts differ as to whether Locke attended that first meeting with Simmons. He was an early convert, in any case, and firmly in charge of the Denver klavern by the time he appeared before Van Cise's grand jury in 1922 and denied being a Klansman. On May 14, 1923, he was appointed Grand

Dragon of the Colorado Realm. Pompous, melodramatic, a showman-*cum*-dealmaker in the tradition of Phineas T. Barnum and Niccolò Macchiavelli, he was the perfect choice to head an organization that relied on theatrics, lies, and misdirection to further its aims. The two rose and fell together. The Klan's meteoric success in Colorado was stamped with Locke's boundless self-confidence and brilliant organizing skills; its failure reflected his hubris and capacity for self-destruction.

Born in 1871 in New York City, Locke was the oldest son of a surgeon, Charles Earl Locke, who'd fought for the Union during the Civil War. The family claimed a lineage in America stretching back to the arrival of the *Mayflower*; Locke's great-grandfather had served in the Revolutionary War. In 1888, Charles Locke moved his family and his practice to Denver. Both father and son enlisted in the Colorado Volunteers during the Spanish-American War; Charles was wounded in battle in Manila, while his son never saw combat.

J. G. Locke studied medicine at various schools and finally received his medical degree in 1904. He chose to pursue homeopathy at a time when so-called natural remedies were falling out of favor with the medical establishment. For the rest of his career he remained an outsider in Denver professional circles—scorned by the local medical society as a borderline quack, adored with almost cultlike fervor by his patients for his homemade potions, compassion, and modest fees.

His rogue medical practice was probably the least exotic thing about Locke. Even among the dime-store demagogues and tin Napoleons attracted to the Klan, he stood out. Short, round, tipping the scale at 250 pounds, he had the physique of a bullfrog but a shrill squawk for a voice, supposedly the result of damage to his larynx from a brawl in his youth. His fans considered him a mesmerizing orator just the same. He had a fondness for well-tailored suits that hid his rotundity, for diamond jewelry, and military regalia. He rode around town in a red Pierce Arrow that had a family coat of arms emblazoned on its doors, like a generalissimo's staff car. He loved to hunt, was arrested once for shooting a pheasant from the comfort of his car, toted a .44 most of the time, and was reputed to be a champion knife thrower.

In 1906, he divorced his wife of fifteen years after the death of their seven-year-old son. The couple married again a decade later, then separated again. Locke had an office and surgery downtown on Glenarm Place, just across the street from the Denver Press Club and next door to the Denver Athletic Club, that also served as his residence and Klan headquarters. The place was like something out of a Lon Chaney horror movie, decorated with displays of armor, antique weapons, and animal heads. Locke kept more than two dozen guns and several crates of ammunition in a vault in the basement and more firearms in a chest upstairs. Behind a hidden door was a throne room where, flanked by hooded flunkies and his dogs—a dalmatian and two Great Danes—he met with Klan supplicants. One reporter who visited him had the impression that Dr. Locke "was living in the Middle Ages, that he was sort of a romantic man."

Like Simmons and Stapleton, like many Klan adherents, Locke had ties to the American Protective Association, Spanish-American War veteran groups, and the Masons and other fraternal organizations. A 1918 biographical sketch describes him as an Elk, an Episcopalian, and "a prominent figure in Masonic circles." Yet whether he ever believed in the teachings of the Kloran remains an open question. His personal conduct was greatly at odds with the Klan's anti-Catholic stance. No matter how volubly he might denounce Catholics at meetings or dress down subordinates for fraternizing with them, he had many Italian Americans as patients, and he employed two Catholic women, sisters Mary and Anna Kossler, to assist with secretarial and nursing duties in his practice. (By some accounts, Locke's ex-wife was Catholic, too.) After his death, stories would surface that he had dissuaded his more rabid followers from acts of violence against Catholic targets, including a scheme to blow up the Cathedral of the Immaculate Conception, the Denver diocese's lavish French Gothic mother church in the heart of the city. Locke told the plotters that the diocese would simply collect insurance on the loss and build an even grander temple.

In his writings, Locke described Jews, Catholics, and Blacks—or, as he put it, "the exploiter, the moral tyrant and the usurper," respectively—as the enemies of white civilization. Yet he also urged a certain degree of moderation in battling those enemies. He had seen what had happened in other states, such as Texas and California, where Klan vigilante actions quickly spiraled out of control, leading to raids and indictments and pariah status for the organization. Locke was interested in broadening the Colorado Klan's reach and its power, not marginalizing it by catering to its most militant true believers. His plans aligned neatly with those of several members of the Klan hierarchy in Atlanta, who were in the process of wresting control of the national organization from Joe Simmons.

The Imperial Wizard's heavy drinking and his increasing reliance on the public relations team of Tyler and Clarke didn't sit well with some of the faithful. There were complaints about the hefty commissions Tyler and Clarke were pocketing and their rumored moral turpitude, as well as Simmons's inability to keep a lid on vigilante yahoos. Led by Hiram Evans, a Dallas dentist, the dissidents sought to rein

in the more rambunctious klaverns and ditch the sentimental slop about hooded knights riding to the rescue while the
magnolias bloom. Once known for participating in vigilante
actions himself, Evans was now keen on attracting higher-
quality applicants and building a classier Klan. He wanted
to transform the organization into a political and economic
force, one that could deliver votes to compliant candidates
and boost the sales of receptive businesses. By the spring of
1923, Evans's group had eased Simmons into a "promotion"
to Emperor, a ceremonial post that held no power, and dispensed with the services of Clarke and Tyler. Imperial Wizard
Evans moved his base of operations to Washington, D.C., and
began paying recruiters salaries rather than commissions.

In Denver, Locke focused on recruitment and feel-good
media events. The local klavern outgrew one meeting place
after another, while other chapters began to find traction in
Boulder, Pueblo, Canon City, and Grand Junction. Klansmen
teased the press with bits of theater, showing up unexpectedly
in their finest robes at funerals or church services and offering a donation. When a prominent Denver restaurateur died,
a plane dropped white carnations on the funeral procession,
each one affixed to a red ribbon bearing the words KU KLUX
KLAN. When famed evangelist Aimee Semple McPherson
came to Denver on a lecture tour, the Klan "kidnapped" her
and pledged its protection. When they came to light, acts of
intimidation, such as the threatening letters sent to Ward
Gash and NAACP leader George Gross, were disavowed—
blamed on stolen stationery or some other handy excuse.
These were all preliminaries, signs that the Klan was biding
its time and awaiting its moment.

Six weeks after the election of Mayor Stapleton, handbills
appeared around town announcing an upcoming lecture at the

City Auditorium that would explain what the Ku Klux Klan was all about. The speaker, George C. Minor, was a paid apologist for the Klan, one of several Protestant ministers who went around the country defending the organization. The news caused an uproar. Not only had the new administration seen fit to rent out a city facility to the Klan, but placards announcing the event had been affixed to the doors of the Cathedral of the Immaculate Conception, as well as to the doors of several other churches and synagogues, a clear provocation.

The day before the lecture, Stapleton met with one delegation of concerned citizens after another, demanding that he cancel the event. They included Catholic and Jewish leaders, representatives of the NAACP, and attorney Phil Hornbein, who reminded Stapleton of his campaign pledge renouncing bigotry and secret organizations. Governor Sweet sent a telegram: "No possible good and much harm will result from this meeting." Stapleton waffled but ultimately insisted that the show must go on. The Klan was entitled to present its views, he said, as long as it didn't attack any other race or creed.

The free lecture was slated to start at eight thirty in the evening on June 27. The auditorium quickly filled with an estimated four thousand people, a mix of Kluxers, anti-Kluxers, and the curious. After a brief organ recital, Minor took the stage. He began by daring the crowd to send him packing: "If there is a single man in the audience who does not wish to hear what I have to say, let him rise to his feet, and I will withdraw."

Several people stood up: a Black minister, a little girl, two Catholic priests from the cathedral. The priests had been chaplains during the war and were dressed in their army uniforms. One of them, Father Francis Walsh, began to explain that he objected to the "invitation" he'd received, plastered on his church door. Applause broke out; others jeered and hissed.

Minor tried to quiet down the hecklers. Rice Means, Stapleton's newly appointed manager of safety, announced that the meeting was over and ordered the audience to disperse. Amid grumblings and boos, the place quickly emptied. The Invisible Empire had tried to emerge from the shadows, but the moment wasn't right yet; the best the group could hope for was to be seen as free-speech martyrs, muzzled by intolerant papists. But the wheel was about to turn. A few months later it would be the other side struggling to make itself heard, drowned out by a mob of Klansmen, under the direction of Grand Dragon Locke.

===

THE FLAP AT THE AUDITORIUM did not go unnoticed at the district attorney's office. The Klan was part of the unfinished business Van Cise was determined to clear away in his last eighteen months in office. So far, he had been able to convict only one Klansman of a single offense, and a pretty minor one at that: Warren Given's contempt-of-court conviction for refusing to admit that Locke was the Klan leader. But he could see more trouble looming, now that Stapleton had revealed his Klan sympathies. Who knew how many cops, city officials, judges, and state legislators were secretly Klan members too?

In his darker moments, Van Cise wondered if he had cleared out a rat's nest at City Hall, only to see it replaced with something much worse. He talked to his confidant Robinson about ways of investigating the Klan, or at least getting a handle on the identities of its leaders. As the group grew larger, it might become more vulnerable to infiltration. He knew some newspaper reporters who were thinking along the same lines, trying to finagle Klan memberships so they could expose what went on in the meetings. Perhaps it was time to launch a full-scale undercover operation, similar to what he had done to smash the bunco ring. But what crime was the Klan committing, specifically? Sedition? Inciting violence against immigrants and minorities? Defrauding its own members?

Van Cise began collecting Klan fliers and pamphlets and looking into what other prosecutors had done to fight the organization. Before he got too far down that road, he had other unfinished business to address. In June, Judge Dunklee handed down the sentences in the bunco case: seven years in prison for Blonger, Duff, French, Belcher, Cooper, and six other defendants; a mere three years for the Christ Kid and seven others. The twentieth defendant was deemed to be insane and was spared prison entirely. Van Cise considered the terms quite light. He was surprised when the Fixer reached out to him from the jail, begging for a final meeting before he was sent to the penitentiary in Canon City. Van Cise had the old man brought to his office.

Blonger had lost weight. His clothes hung on him. He was all wheezes and groans. He pleaded for mercy with trembling hands.

"All my insides are gone," he said. "Seven years, three years, one year is death. Surely you don't want me to die down there."

As always, the man had a proposition: Send him to the pen for two months, then ask the governor to pardon him. Let him die a free man. It was the least the Colonel could do.

Van Cise said nothing. He thought about the Reverend Menaugh, who'd lost the funds his clients had entrusted to him and then ended his life with poison. He thought about another victim of Blonger's operation who had spent his last months in grinding poverty, his life savings gone, devoured by wolves. When he finally spoke, it was with surprising vehemence.

"What leniency have you shown to others?" he asked.

"I will fight to the last any attempt to give you leniency of any kind."

Blonger saw no point in arguing. There was no fix to be had. He shuffled off to his doom, a badly defeated man.

He died six months later in the prison infirmary, at the age of seventy-four, of kidney trouble and what was described as "a general organic breakdown." Hundreds turned out for his requiem mass at the Cathedral of the Immaculate Conception. Former deputy sheriff Tom Clarke helped carry the flag-wrapped casket. Jackie French sent a wreath of a hundred Easter lilies. It was one of the grandest funerals Denver had ever seen, underwritten by Blonger's widow, Nola. She had managed to retain a chunk of his fortune despite the legal bills, the lawsuits, the government liens, and the humiliation she'd endured after the trial, when news broke of the "double life" her husband had led for decades, dividing his time between her and his mistress.

The newspapers eulogized him as a picturesque character, generous to a fault, always ready with a few bucks or a Christmas turkey for the needy. "Lou Blonger stuck to his friends," declared the *Denver Post*. "He had them in all walks of life."

7

—

The Star Chamber

They snatched Patrick Walker two blocks from his shop. A twenty-five-year-old optician and active member of the Knights of Columbus, the Catholic fraternal organization, Walker had seen men loitering outside his eyewear store for the better part of a Saturday evening. They were gone when he locked up and walked south on Glenarm Place. But as he approached Twenty-First Street, five men poured out of a car, guns drawn, and hustled him into the vehicle.

They drove north, past Riverside Cemetery, into sparsely populated farmland on the edge of the city. They took him into an isolated shack and asked him questions about his religion. Evidently not happy with the answers, they beat him with the butts of their revolvers, inflicting deep cuts and bruises on his head and shoulders, and told him to leave town. One of the men told Walker that they were KKK and were "looking for a man who had been doing some rotten stuff around town." They were "going down the line with all the men like him."

Before he lost consciousness, Walker managed to tell the men that he had done nothing wrong.

The police declared themselves baffled by Walker's story. He could not identify any of his assailants, even though only one of them wore a mask. No identification, no arrest.

———

THEY SNATCHED BEN LASKA OUTSIDE HIS HOUSE. The son of Russian Jewish immigrants, the forty-nine-year-old defense attorney was a former vaudeville artist, known for performing magic in and out of the courtroom. Laska amused juries and annoyed judges with his sleight-of-hand routines, but his greatest trick was making the charges against his bootlegger clients disappear. One Friday evening, hours after Laska had gotten yet another rumrunner off with a small fine, he received a phone call at his home. A man who lived a block away on Cook Street was dying, the caller said, and needed a lawyer.

Laska agreed to a deathbed consultation. He was barely out the door when two men approached him. One grabbed him by the throat and slapped a hand over his mouth. The other seized his legs. They carried him to two other men waiting in a car. All four wore masks.

They drove north, past Riverside Cemetery. They dragged him out on a country road and beat him with blackjacks. They told him to stop defending bootleggers, or they would be back. Then they drove off.

Laska told reporters that he believed his attackers were Klansmen, in cahoots with "certain officers of the bootleg squad and officials of Magistrate Henry Bray's court." A few months earlier, Laska had been accused of bribing witnesses to keep them from testifying against his clients. Grand Dragon Locke had taken a personal interest in the matter, accompanying Denver police chief Rugg Williams when the chief set out to arrest the attorney. Laska had been acquitted at trial, frustrating the Klan and its allies on the police force. The assault on him was payback, he insisted, for being a zealous advocate for his clients.

Chief Williams scoffed at Laska's charges. So did Sergeant Fred Reed, head of the bootleg squad—and, like most of the squad, a Klansman on the sly. The actions of his men on the night in question were all accounted for, Reed insisted, and they were "too high-principled" to try to enforce the Prohibition law with blackjacks.

The investigation went nowhere. Laska eventually made his own peace with the Klan, a feat as amazing as any of his magic tricks. By 1925, he had become the Grand Dragon's personal attorney.

＝＝＝

THE BEATINGS WERE ANOMALIES. Locke understood that the threat of violence was often more effective than actual bloodshed. Get physical, and your foes may feel the need to respond in kind, while your more squeamish followers jump ship. But a well-placed threat, emanating from the unassailable depths of the Invisible Empire, could work wonders. It could instill fear in your enemies and inspire awe in your supporters at the same time.

The intimidation campaign was like the Empire itself, elusive yet ubiquitous. On the night of November 10, 1923, less than two weeks after the assault on Walker, eleven crosses were ignited at locations across the city. One was on the steps of the Capitol building; another, on the threshold of the Black neighborhood known as Five Points; others at parks and green spaces across the metro area. The crosses were supposedly a patriotic gesture, commemorating Armistice Day, the eleventh day of the eleventh month. Alarmed city council members demanded an investigation. Mayor Stapleton and police officials downplayed the incident. They said they weren't convinced there had been any crosses, much less arson, and didn't see anything to investigate. A few weeks later, a string of crosses blazed in the foothills west of Denver, visible for miles.

Caravans of Kluxers drove through west Denver neighborhoods on Friday nights, hooting and honking, mocking Jewish residents and their Sabbath. Klansmen teamed up with hellfire Protestant ministers to host lectures on the Catholic menace. The speakers were often charlatans who claimed to be ex-nuns or ex-priests and to have firsthand knowledge of the secret horrors and lusts of the convent and the sacristy. The Knights of Columbus were vilified as the advance guard in the Pope's master plan to take over America; a fake Knights of Columbus oath, which bound the initiate to wage war on "all heretics, Protestants and Masons" to the point of annihilation, circulated widely among the credulous.

Possibly because they were more numerous, the harassment seemed to be directed at Catholics more than other groups. A savage KKK missive to the *Denver Catholic Register* declared that while Blacks, socialists, and Jews were bad enough, "the Romanist is worst of all." The newspaper's young editor, Father Matthew Smith, reported that cars swerved toward him on several occasions during his daily walks to his office, trying to scare him or injure him.

For the most part, though, the Klan's bullying tended to be more subtle than trying to run down padres on the street. Under the rule of the new Imperial Wizard, Hiram Evans, the national KKK was moving away from street skirmishes to political and economic warfare. The new approach, which

Locke strongly endorsed, emphasized "klannishness"—the concept that Klansmen must support each other in all endeavors. That meant voting for the "right" candidates, regardless of their party affiliation, and patronizing Klan businesses. It also meant shunning businesses that employed or catered to Blacks, Catholics, Jews, and other "wrong" types until they knuckled under or were driven out of business.

In Colorado, Klansmen were encouraged to advertise their businesses at KKK meetings, paying two dollars for the privilege of having a slide with a company logo projected on a screen for a few moments every week for three months. Members also let each other know their shops were Klan-approved by putting signs in the window that proclaimed they were 100 percent American or TWK (Trade With Klansmen)—or simply by announcing that they offered "Klean Klothes for Kiddies," "Kwik Kar Kare," or some other KKK-branded service. Extensive lists were drawn up of businesses to be boycotted, including the Neusteter's department store, owned by Jews. The Klan leadership even concocted a bogus roster of businesses that Catholics were supposedly required to patronize, to bolster their claim that the groups they were boycotting were doing the same thing.

Klannishness was readily embraced by many prominent businessmen, including Gano Senter, owner of several restaurants downtown and a Grand Titan of the KKK. Born in Nebraska, Senter had gone to sea as a youth. His memoir of his adventures reads like a Jack London novel: He was shanghaied at fourteen, jumped ship, was recaptured and put in irons, then escaped again, only to be captured by the Tlingit tribe in Alaska and adopted by another tribe before eventually working his way back to Denver. A virulent anti-Catholic, Senter posted signs in his Radio Café announcing, "We serve fish every day—except Friday," and welcoming those in the know to a "Kool Kozy Kafé." His wife, Lorena, was the founder and imperial commander of the Women of the Ku Klux Klan of Colorado, a ladies' auxiliary devoted mainly to charity work. The Senters' café quickly became a gathering place for prominent Kluxers, including several members of Locke's inner circle, who proudly smoked the special Cyana cigars promoted by Dale Deane, a Denver court clerk. Cyana was another acronym: "Catholics, you are not Americans." Father Smith wandered into the place one day, seeking a meal, and was handed a tract on the Catholic menace by Senter, who struck the priest as a "thoroughly sincere jackass."

The boycotts typically hurt small businesses more than larger ones. Some were only tepidly supported and weren't effective at all. Yet klannishness tended to boost membership. There may not have been many true believers like Senter, passionate enough about their racism or religious paranoia to flaunt it publicly. But the inducements and pressures to join the Klan went far beyond ideological appeal. Some joined in the expectation that it would improve business, or at least keep them from showing up on a do-not-trade list. Some were told they had to get rid of certain employees, Blacks or Catholics or whatever, in order to truly thrive. For every rabid nativist or racist, there were others who joined under duress, afraid of being left at a disadvantage or targeted themselves. Fear wasn't just a weapon to train on the enemy. It was the glue that held the group together.

———

VAN CISE KEPT COUNT. Over the course of three years he was approached thirteen times about joining the Klan—cajoled, urged, pressed, told it was the smart thing to do. The final invitation came from the Grand Dragon himself, and then all hell broke loose.

That the Kluxers tried to enlist the district attorney, after failing to recall him, may say something about the cynicism of the organization. But it was also an acknowledgment that he was fundamentally different from the other outspoken foes of the KKK, people like the NAACP's Gross or Father Smith or attorney Charles Ginsberg, who regularly spent his lunch hour denouncing the Klan from the bed of a pickup truck parked at Sixteenth and Champa downtown, like a deranged prophet. Van Cise was a WASP, a Mason, and a Republican, and from a certain perspective his views on race and immigration could be considered Klan-friendly. That's not to say that he believed in white supremacy; he took his oath to uphold the Constitution seriously, and he had been strongly influenced by his father's admiration for the Black soldiers he'd encountered during the Civil War. ("They have more politeness, more intelligence, more piety than the whites," Edwin declared in one 1864 diary entry. "They are generally the most intelligent men we [have].") But he didn't go out of his way to challenge the established order and prevailing prejudices of his time, either; even in defending Ward Gash, the janitor the Klan had threatened, Van Cise had reportedly referred to Gash—a Black man ten years his senior—as a "good boy." In a speech to a Kiwanis gathering in Fort Collins, he lashed out at Governor Sweet as a "millionaire Bolshevik" who had recklessly pardoned dangerous criminals, a law-and-order theme sounded by the Klan as well. He also declared that "southern Italians, southeastern Europeans, and Turks made poor citizens." His experiences at Ludlow had taught him respect for the immigrant miners he met, but he believed the country was having trouble assimilating so many foreigners from different cultures. "This is our country," he told the Kiwanis, "and no one has a right to come here or live here unless we want him."

At the same time, he was repelled by just about every aspect of the Klan. Its teachings were ridiculous—a hash of conspiracy theories, cornpone Christianity, and racial fears that only the dimmest of its members seemed to take seriously. The rank and file weren't as gullible, but they were spineless enough to go along with it anyway, hoping to get something in return. The leadership consisted of thugs and con men, hiding under hoods and working a scam. The organization was ruining businesses, dividing people, and profiting off their misery. It was a menace to democracy. "It is injecting into the political and social life of this country a religious issue which has no place in either," he wrote in a draft of a speech that he hoped to deliver someday to an audience much larger than the Kiwanis Club. "It may call itself Klan, but in reality it is a mob."

He knew how to prosecute a criminal conspiracy involving bootlegging or confidence games. But in those cases, the primary goal had always been profit. The Klan's objectives were much more complex—money, yes, but also power, and the suppression of anyone and anything the group didn't consider to be 100 percent American. In its first year, the Stapleton administration had promoted klannishness in one city agency after another. The result wasn't pretty. It resembled the work of an army of carpenter ants, burrowing its way inside the bole of a maple tree and hollowing it out, leaving behind a pile of sawdust and a stately husk, ready to collapse. How do you stamp out a conspiracy that eats away at the police, the courts, and representative government, the very institutions you count on to put things right?

Klannishness was surely the reason Stapleton had appointed Rice Means as manager of safety. Means had squelched the

Klan lecture at the auditorium, but it was likely he'd done so on the orders of Locke or Stapleton. All three were part of the same cabal of Spanish-American War veterans with American Protective Association connections that seemed to form the nucleus of the Colorado Klan. An impressive orator who'd failed in several runs for office, Means denied being a Klansman. But Van Cise learned that he had been initiated into the Klan in a ceremony in Pueblo shortly after Stapleton's election and was being groomed for higher things by Locke. Stapleton soon named Means as city attorney, filling the manager of safety post with another Klansman, Reuben Hershey.

Over at the police department, Stapleton retained the services of Bailey's chief, Rugg Williams, for several months, despite mounting pressure from Locke to replace him with someone of the Grand Dragon's choosing. Williams was a placeholder at best; word was that he'd been a reluctant conscript into the Klan and that key decisions about assignments and promotions were being made by subordinates, including a sergeant who boasted that he was the "real" chief. Whoever was in charge, the police seemed to investigate only those crimes that the Klan wanted investigated. The cross burnings remained a bit of unsolved mischief. The police maintained that they had no leads, despite the discovery of a KKK communiqué, dated a few days before the event, that directed the recipients to report to one of fourteen named leaders for an unspecified mission. After the Capitol Hill neighborhood was papered with Klan posters one night, including some hurled into a Knights of Columbus lodge, a street fight erupted between the lodge members and Klansmen; police managed to arrest several of the Knights of Columbus brawlers, while the Klan provocateurs somehow slipped away.

Disturbing as the police takeover was, it was the spread of

klannishness in the courts that most alarmed Van Cise. He had heard about a Klan justice of the peace and the Klan ties of the police magistrate that Laska had complained about, Henry Bray. A much greater threat was the Honorable Clarence J. Morley. A former public administrator and school board member, Morley had been elected to a six-year term as a district court judge in 1918. He was a slight man, bespectacled and owlish, who came across more as a taciturn, humorless accountant than a dynamic jurist. In his first two years as DA, Van Cise had dealt with the judge rarely—notably, the time he got into a fistfight with William Bryans in Morley's courtroom during the bunco bail hearings. On that occasion, Morley had deplored Van Cise's behavior and had even harsher words for his deputy, Robinson, whom he accused of striking Bryans while others were restraining the lawyer. In 1924 Morley was assigned full-time to the criminal division, and he and Van Cise were soon at war with each other.

One of Morley's first moves in his new post was to hire Frank Mulligan as a bailiff. Mulligan was a former police detective who had served time in prison after participating in an armed robbery at a roadhouse. He had been sitting in Blonger's office the day the bunco raid went down. Now here he was, disgraced cop, ex-con, and friend of fixers, drawing a paycheck from the courts and supervising jury selection. As for Morley himself, Van Cise knew that he was Klan, and pretty high-level Klan at that. The district attorney had five operatives—a mix of volunteers and trained investigators, none of them known to each other—keeping tabs on Klan meetings. They staked out meeting halls and wrote down license plates, tried to infiltrate the meetings when possible. Morley spoke regularly at those gatherings. He was a Klokan, one of three top advisers to the Grand Dragon. Despite the title, Morley was usually on the receiving end of the advice; he seemed to relish being in Locke's inner circle and doing his bidding. One of Locke's admirers described Morley as a "charwoman" who followed orders and never had an independent thought.

It was customary to empanel a new grand jury in the criminal division at the start of the year. Morley took a klannish approach to the process. He rejected ten of the twelve names that had been randomly selected for jury duty and issued subpoenas, summoning a Klan-approved squad of replacements. Packed with Kluxers, the grand jury declined to sit for the usual group photograph. Morley instructed them that they could seek the district attorney's counsel if they wanted to, or they could banish him if they chose: "It is your right and privilege . . . to request the district attorney at any time to retire from the jury room during any of your proceedings."

When Van Cise learned of Morley's instruction, he was livid. Colorado law clearly stated that district attorneys "shall appear in their respective districts at any and all sessions of all grand juries," and that it was their duty to advise the jury and examine witnesses. He went to the grand jury room to explain this to the panel. He had just started to talk when a juror interrupted him.

"We don't need your advice, and you can get out," he said.

Van Cise replied that if it was up to him, he'd be glad to part company with the bunch right now, but the law required his presence. The law expected him or his deputy to question witnesses, not them.

"What do you think about Sergeant Reed?" another juror demanded.

Reed, the head of the bootleg squad, had reportedly fallen out of favor with Locke. Reed had arrested a bootlegger with Klan ties, then refused a demand from the Grand Dragon to drop the charges. Van Cise responded that he thought Reed was an able officer.

"We don't think so," the second juror snapped. "We're going to indict him."

Out of the mouths of idiots . . . In a flash, Van Cise saw what Morley was doing. He had assembled a star chamber of inquisitors, prepared to unleash the powers of the grand jury against the Klan's enemies, alien or internal. To hell with the rule of law, to hell with due process.

"Any such indictment," Van Cise said, "will be attacked by the district attorney, and any action of this grand jury will be investigated."

Before departing, he warned the group not to call any witnesses in his absence. For several weeks, he was too busy to bother with Morley's grand jury, preparing for the biggest murder trial of his career. Joe Brindisi, an Italian immigrant and former streetcar conductor, was charged with killing Mrs. Lillian McGlone and Miss Emma Vascovie in McGlone's Denver apartment. Police theorized that McGlone pulled a pistol on Brindisi during a quarrel over romance or money or both, and that Brindisi pried the weapon from her and shot both women in the head. Brindisi claimed that McGlone shot Vascovie, for reasons unknown, then tried to kill him, forcing him to shoot her. Fearing a lynch mob, Brindisi fled to Mexico. He was arrested in Detroit months later. Anti-immigrant feeling was running high—the newspapers referred to Brandisi's "swarthy" good looks and dubbed him the "sleek sheik of north Denver's Little Italy"—but Van Cise was determined to get a conviction based on evidence, not hysteria.

The courtroom was packed. Extra guards roamed the halls and kept close watch on the gallery and the defendant. Judge Morley presided. During one of the recesses Morley summoned

Van Cise to his chambers. He showed the district attorney a note from the grand jury. The group had been meeting without Van Cise's knowledge and, since the DA was busy with a murder trial, requested that a special prosecutor be appointed. Morley already had a certain Klan lawyer in mind for the job.

"Morley demanded that this be done and cursed me when I refused to accede to this request," Van Cise wrote in an account of the conversation. "Morley told me that he was doing this to protect me, and I told him that I needed no protection from him or from anyone else, and that he or anyone else, if they desired to make charges against me, could go into open court and do it, and for them to cut out all this secret and childish stuff."

Van Cise's closing argument in the Brindisi case was a memorable one. He arranged the bloodstained clothes of the two women to show the positions in which their bodies were found and walked the jury through a step-by-step reenactment, the state's version of what happened in the McGlone apartment the day of the murders. It was "a seemingly perfect chain of circumstantial evidence—with every link well formed," one reporter observed. The jury was out thirteen hours, quibbling about whether it was first-degree or second-degree murder. They decided on first-degree. Since the prosecution had not sought the death penalty, that meant life in prison for Brindisi.

The accolades for the district attorney poured in. Van Cise hadn't heard so many atta-boys since the bunco convictions. The most unusual plaudit came by Western Union to his home. "Congratulations on your splendid address to the jury and your wonderful victory," the telegram read. "Dr. J. G. Locke."

He had never received such a nice note before from someone he hoped to put behind bars.

Two days later, Dr. Locke presented himself at the district attorney's office. He wore a well-cut suit, not the robes he favored for more festive occasions. He once again praised Van Cise for his handling of the Brindisi case. Then he urged the prosecutor to consider running for governor in the fall—with, of course, the backing of a certain group, a group so well-known that there was no need to mention its name. "You know that we have a very strong and influential organization," he said. "And we want to back a man of your type and caliber."

Van Cise had been here before, with Blonger—another corpulent devil who offered him all the kingdoms of the world, if he would only play along. Once again, he declined.

The next day, Mayor Stapleton named a new chief of police, William Candlish. A former state senator and assayer, Candlish had no background in law enforcement and a pile of debts from a failed radium-processing venture. Stapleton and Manager of Safety Hershey offered differing accounts of how Candlish happened to be selected, but it soon became obvious that he was Locke's man. Candlish got busy with promotions and reassignments, rewarding Klan members on the force with plum positions and banishing Irish Catholic cops to remote beats and night shifts. He devised a chief's uniform that was heavy on gold braid. Noting that the chief seemed to spend a lot of time in soda parlors, which often served as fronts for bootlegging operations, Ray Humphreys of the *Denver Post* dubbed him Coca-Cola Candlish.

For former Stapleton supporters who'd cheered his promises to reform the police department, the Candlish appointment was a stark betrayal. It gave impetus and urgency to a campaign to recall the mayor, launched by attorney Hornbein. The petition didn't mention the Klan influence directly, but among the grounds for the mayor's removal it stated that the police force had become so demoralized that "crime runs rampant in our midst."

Van Cise was no fan of recall elections; he thought it was too easy to get them on the ballot, and he'd almost had to face one himself. But he also recognized that the recall process might be the best chance of stopping the Klan in its takeover of city government. A successful criminal prosecution of the group was unlikely—not in Morley's courtroom, surely, and not on Candlish's watch. He had to find a way to take the intel he'd gathered on the Klan leadership and deliver it, all neatly tied in a bow, to a higher court: the citizens of Denver.

A PUBLIC OFFICIAL LOOKING TO SPILL SECRETS in Denver had many niche publications to choose from, including a Black weekly, a Jewish weekly, and a Catholic weekly. But of the four major dailies in town, only one had shown any appetite for going after the Klan. The *Rocky Mountain News* and the *Denver Times*, both owned by the same company, had Kluxers in management and were largely mute about the organization. The *Denver Post* blew hot and cold; at Klan meetings, Locke bragged of having taken one of the paper's owners, Harry Tammen, for a ride one night and "made him a Christian." Another insider account had it that Locke had ordered Tammen's partner, Frederick Bonfils, to retract an unflattering story and run another one praising the Klan—or else his newspaper building would become "the flattest place on Champa Street."

With the other newspapers so compromised, that left the runt of the litter, the *Denver Express*. Owned by the Scripps-Howard chain, the paper had a puny circulation and no showcase Sunday edition. It lured working-class readers with celebrity gossip, puzzles, and contests. But led by editor Sidney B. Whipple—a short, skinny Dartmouth grad in his mid-thirties, who'd been a foreign correspondent in prewar London in his youth and found journalism too exciting a vice to give up—the *Express* and its meager staff did more serious reporting on the Klan than anybody else. Initially a loud supporter of Stapleton, Whipple had spent considerable time and ink repenting his decision and tracing the mayor's unsavory connections.

On March 27, 1924, the *Express* dropped a bomb on City Hall—the first installment of a weeklong series titled "Invisible Government." The exposé peeked under the sheets and named names. Outed as Kluxers: Mayor Stapleton. Manager of Safety Hershey. City Attorney Means. Chief Candlish. Judge Morley. Police magistrates Albert Orahood and Henry Bray. Carl Milliken, Colorado's Secretary of State. "At least" seven police sergeants and twenty-one patrol officers. And "nearly all, if not all, of the present county grand jury now in session."

"With the openly expressed tenets of the Ku Klux Klan, the *Denver Express* will not attempt to raise an issue," the newspaper declared. "But it does challenge, and will continue to challenge, the rights, morals, and ethics of any organization which attempts to dominate an American community through intimidation of its officers, through the seizure of public functions, or through the fear inspired by its own secret tribunals."

The report didn't identify its sources, but Van Cise's fingerprints were all over the piece. Among other giveaways, the article mentioned that Dr. Locke was planning to put a Klansman in the governor's office, and that the district attorney had been approached about the job and turned Locke down. By nightfall the series was the talk of the town—and an emerging crisis for the Klan. If this was the opening salvo, what was in store for the next seven days?

That evening, Locke's office had a steady stream of visitors—mostly men huddled in overcoats with their hats pulled low. At ten o'clock, an *Express* reporter confronted Judge Morley as he emerged from the building. Why was a district judge paying a call on the Grand Dragon at such a late hour? Morley said that he'd been feeling ill and decided to consult his physician.

The next morning two men barged into the *Express* office and demanded to see the editor. They showed Whipple an arrest warrant and told him he was summoned to appear before the grand jury. The panel had been dormant for weeks, but the *Express* series had brought it back to life, for the sole purpose of investigating how Whipple had obtained the information he was publishing. Before they took him away, Whipple told an assistant to call Van Cise and let him know he was being arrested.

Van Cise was waiting at the courthouse when Whipple and his escort arrived. He followed them as they went upstairs to the grand jury room and went inside. Two Klansmen stationed at the door tried to bar the district attorney from entering. He pushed past them and went in. He was succinct. The grand jury, he informed the panel, has no power to arrest anyone. Whipple could sue them all for damages. They couldn't question him unless Van Cise was present. And he was putting an end to this "travesty" right now.

He grabbed the diminutive editor by the arm and walked out. No one followed them.

That was on Friday morning. Over the weekend Morley held more secret sessions with the grand jury while the *Express* series continued to stir the pot. KU KLUX KLAN BOASTS RULE OVER CITY HALL, read one headline. CHIEF CANDLISH GIVES KLUXERS INSIDE JOBS, read another. And this: EXPRESS EDITOR HALED BEFORE GRAND JURY.

On Monday, Morley directed the district attorney to appear in his courtroom, in the presence of the grand jury, so that he could hear the judge's instructions to the panel and cease his interference. Van Cise came prepared with a motion of his own, asking the judge to correct his instructions and tell the grand jury that the DA must be present at all sessions, other than the jury's actual deliberations. As Van Cise read his motion aloud, delineating the judge's illegal acts, Morley's face reddened with rage.

"There is nothing in that motion," he said. "It's simply a cheap play for notoriety on your part."

Morley embarked on a long tirade. That was fortunate, as Van Cise was stalling for time. Just as the judge seemed to be winding down, deputy DA Robinson arrived with a bundle of documents—one for each juror and one for the judge. Van Cise stood up.

"Notwithstanding what this court has now said," he began, "and notwithstanding the additional erroneous instructions to this hand-picked, so-called grand jury, I now have the pleasure of serving both the court and all the jurors with writs of mandamus* from the Supreme Court of Colorado, ordering you to hold no further sessions of this jury without the presence of the district attorney, and giving you five days in which to show cause why the alternative writ should not be made permanent."

The writs were handed out in dead silence. Morley read his copy and turned to his grand jury. "Gentleman of the jury, you are excused for one week," he said. "The court will be in recess."

The case was argued in the Supreme Court at the end of the week. The law was on Van Cise's side, the decision unanimous in his favor. By that point, the grand jury's term had

---

* Writs of mandamus are court orders directing government officials or entities to fulfill their public duties.

expired, with no indictments issued against anyone. Van Cise savored the victory. It showed that the Klan could be beaten; its influence had not yet reached the highest court in the state. But the prosecutor also knew that the most important battles ahead were the recall and the statewide elections in November—battles that would be fought in the streets and the voting booth, not in court.

In the wake of the *Express* series, eleven of the newspaper's largest advertisers were told to stop doing business with the paper or face a Klan boycott. Several complied, costing the newspaper substantial revenue. But Whipple kept sticking his nose in the Klan's business and pushing for the mayor's recall, drawing heavily on information provided by a well-informed anonymous source. His dogged coverage made him and his small paper finalists in the reporting category for the 1925 Pulitzer Prize.

8

—

The Dangerous Summer

It started out as a surveillance job. Robert Maiden, special investigator for the district attorney, hung around outside Klan meetings and scribbled down license plate numbers. He hid in bushes, behind corners and in dark doorways, and tried to identify the bigwigs as they arrived or left. It was not all that different from shadowing Blonger and his friends— except that the number of persons of interest seemed to double every few weeks.

The Klan was spreading faster than a flu bug. Membership surged so rapidly in 1923–24 that the organization was in a perpetual hunt for larger meeting spaces. They had started out at a mortuary operated by one of their members, then relocated to a series of fraternal meeting halls downtown, each of them a short walk from Locke's office. Then, as summer approached, they began to gather *al fresco* on top of Ruby Hill, a popular sledding area in southwest Denver, and South Table Mountain outside of Golden, a mesa at the edge of the foothills west of the city. Locals called it Castle Mountain because of a blockish butte at the mesa's northwest end.

The downtown meetings had typically drawn a few hundred people. Monday nights on Castle Mountain were attended by as many as eight thousand people, their cars clogging West Colfax between Denver and Golden and jamming the exit road to the mesa for hours. Just a few months earlier, the Klan had been content to boast that it was "10,000 strong in Denver." Now it claimed to have fifty thousand members across Colorado, half of them in Denver. Those figures were inflated, but thousands of Kluxers on a plateau every week called for further investigation. Van Cise was eager to place men inside those meetings, and Maiden volunteered to be one of them.

Joining the Klan was easier than Maiden expected. He dropped in on the new chief of police, introduced himself, and paid twenty dollars for his initiation fee and related costs. Chief Candlish called Locke, who gave his approval. Locke had first met Maiden two years earlier, when the detective was new in town and looking for a physician for his ailing young daughter. Locke had treated her over the course of several office visits, until she was well again.

Locke knew that Maiden worked for Van Cise. Maybe he hoped to turn him, like so many other cops, to the cause of the Invisible Empire. Maybe he simply didn't care. The Klan still attempted to impose hush-hush security at its meetings, posting guards at the entrance, demanding membership cards or secret handshakes. When a reporter from the *Express* was spotted staking out the Knights of Pythias Hall, studying Klansmen as they emerged, a Denver police officer was dispatched to run him off. But the Klan was outgrowing its anonymity. The *Express* series had outed several of the leaders, and the group's increasingly high-profile gatherings outed many more. A special ceremony on May 13, 1924, marking the first anniversary of the charter granted to the Realm of Colorado, featured remarks by Locke, Candlish, Rice Means, Gano Senter, Judge Morley, and several others, all identified in the program by name and some by title as well, including the Grand Dragon, the Exalted Cyclops, the Grand Kludd, the Grand Klokard, and the "Klaliff-elect Klan No. 1," who happened to be Morley. When put on the spot in public forums, Means and Morley still denied being Klansmen, while Mayor Stapleton avoided answering questions about the Klan altogether. Yet here they were—in the official program, on the speakers' platform, shuffling to and from Locke's office, exhorting the multitudes from the mountaintop. The Klan wasn't hiding in the shadows anymore.

The gatherings on Castle Mountain were grand spectacles. A Klan marching band played patriotic tunes and religious ballads. Preachers gave hellfire speeches while crosses blazed. An honor guard on horseback fired guns into the air. The white-robed throngs, which skewed young and boisterous, whistled and cheered and sang along. His squeaky voice amplified electronically, Locke played ringmaster, introducing one speaker after another, cracking jokes, fulsomely praising generous donors and berating the Klan's enemies, updating his knights on the Empire's progress in its relentless march to power. The Grand Dragon was an emotional, effective speaker, but Maiden thought the crowd reaction was less spontaneous than it seemed, right down to the prolonged outbursts of applause that seemed to originate somewhere near the platform and surge through the crowd like an electric current. Locke always seemed to be on the verge of a startling announcement, hinting about some looming, game-changing development that never came to fruition but sent the faithful into a frenzy anyway.

From what Maiden could see, it was just rabble-rousing, plain and simple.

═══════════════════

EXCERPTS FROM SPY REPORT SUBMITTED TO
District Attorney Van Cise, Ku Klux Klan meeting,
Pythian Building, April 28, 1924:

Lodge called to order by Dr. A.L. Douglas, E.C. [Exalted Cyclops], and prayer followed. Petitions of about 30 [applicants] were passed on third reading, 50 on second, and about 75 on first. Three men were rejected by unanimous vote, objection being their evident affiliation and contamination with the C [Catholic] religion. Slides were then flashed on the screen showing the business of men in the order . . .

At this point the Grand Dragon, Dr. Locke, appeared in characteristic [illegible] pose and was given a tremendous ovation. When the applause subsided, he exclaimed in a rather thin voice to his secretary, "Telephone to Mayor Stapleton, and tell him to come here immediately." Roars of applause . . . The telephone call to the Mayor evidently was not satisfactory, and Dr. Locke appointed a committee of two to call upon the Mayor and bring him to the meeting. The members were then cautioned that upon the entrance of the Mayor, no applause was to be given. He evidently was and is in bad standing. The committee returned and reported that the Mayor was confined to his bed, unable to appear, but would answer the summons a week from last night. The committee reported [that] while they were engaged in talking the Mayor sought the bathroom several times. All of which was received with scornful hoots . . .

All members were instructed to call Joslins [department store] and tell the firm that unless they withdrew their ads from the Express they would be boycotted . . .

Present between 800 and 1000. Judge Morley was present behind a little desk, telling the members how to investigate application.

EXCERPTS FROM SPY REPORT, Ku Klux Klan meeting, Pythian Building, May 5, 1924:

Each member upon entering was furnished [a] robe, which made identification very difficult. Robes were worn in honor of Brown Harwood, Imperial Gazeek* from Atlanta, Ga., who stopped enroute to Wyoming . . . [Harwood] spoke about the membership not being large enough, and stated there should be at least 40,000 members in Denver, and that Denver needed the organization as much as any state in the union . . .

The work in listing C firms [to boycott] has not progressed far enough yet. Members were called down for not attending to this important duty.

Dr. Locke's secretary, Strickland, then explained that he had been trying all week to get in touch with Mayor S without avail. He finally got him on Monday and the Mayor explained that he had a dinner

---

* Harwood was the Imperial Klazik, or vice president, of the national KKK and was at one point the Grand Dragon of the Texas Klan.

engagement . . . and would not be able to attend. Strickland promised to have him at the hall next Monday, or break a leg. A large chair was then shown, with a seat cut out, and a chamber [pot] and the members were told that it was being reserved for the Mayor. This was received with great delight.

―――――――

THE GATHERINGS TOOK UNEXPECTED TURNS. Some nights the Grand Dragon brimmed with good feeling and talked about the importance of preaching love and not hate. Other times he seemed intent on venting his wrath. He called wayward Klansmen to the altar and castigated them for their sins against klannishness. Why were they trading with Jews, fraternizing with Catholics, skimping on donations? He reserved his greatest scorn for those who were reportedly messing around with other Klansmen's wives. Adulterers were expelled, tarred and feathered, sometimes ordered to leave town. But even those who committed minor infractions came to dread Locke's disapproval. "He could look at you with those beady eyes, and you would feel that he was boring a hole right through you," recalled Adolph Hecker, a Klan enforcer who was in and out of the Grand Dragon's favor.

Locke's harangues against Mayor Stapleton were a regular feature of the meetings for many weeks. The Faustian bargain Stapleton struck with the Klan had soured shortly after his election. Stapleton balked at taking orders like one of the Grand Dragon's flunkies. He bristled at Locke's escalating demands to place Klan members in key city posts, and he had appointed Candlish as police chief only after considerable arm-twisting. Now he was avoiding Locke entirely, making excuses for his absence from Klan rallies. Locke deemed the man insufficiently grateful for all that had been done for him. But with the recall campaign underway, Stapleton was going to need the Klan vote once more. He would have to come around. To make sure of it, Locke boasted that he had recall petitions of his own, containing thousands of signatures and ready to be filed, if it became necessary for the Klan to replace the mayor.

Whether Stapleton survived the recall or not, the Colorado Realm had its sights on higher office. City attorney Rice Means was expected to run for a short-term seat in the U.S. Senate, a seat made available by the death of its former occupant, Sam Nicholson, with two years left in his term. Locke planned to make his good friend Judge Morley the Republican nominee for governor. A gaggle of other Klan candidates running for state office found their way to the meetings on Castle Mountain, too, eager to introduce themselves.

To push through a solid Klan ticket statewide, Locke announced a plan to hire fleets of recruiters—"assistant kleagles," each of whom would be paid four hundred dollars a month to bring in at least fifty new members a week. He wanted to see the membership in Denver alone reach fifty thousand, maybe sixty thousand. "He realized, he said, that the organization was not powerful enough to swing the entire fall election," one of Van Cise's spies reported, "but if it were composed of fifty thousand in Denver, no matter what the District Attorney said or did, they would be able to sweep all opposition aside."

The recruiting drive was readily endorsed by the assembly. Anything Locke proposed sailed through the crowd without protest, as if predestined for approval. The real decisions were being made off-stage, by Locke and his inner circle, a group the spies couldn't penetrate. But Van Cise suspected that all was not well at the top. He had obtained a copy of an open letter to Colorado Klan members, accusing Locke of fraud and embezzlement. The writer was a supporter of Imperial Wizard (now Emperor) Simmons, and he claimed that Locke had banished members without cause, initiated others without proper approval, skimmed Klan funds that should have gone to headquarters, and made under-the-table deals with the usurper, Imperial Wizard Evans, to their mutual benefit. He also took Locke to task for the "ridiculous farce" of the Van Cise recall campaign, "the faked-up letters purporting to come from the Knights of Columbus," and other failures and deceptions.

"How long, fellow Klansmen, can he keep you befuddled?" the writer asked. "How long will you permit him to think and act for you?"

Van Cise didn't know if the writer's complaints were widely shared or a solitary crusade. But the letter was evidence of a rift that could possibly be exploited down the line—not only between the Simmons and Evans factions within the Klan, but between Colorado's Grand Dragon and the national KKK. Locke's attempts to bully Stapleton, his delight in administering punishment himself, his imperious attitude toward anyone who dared question his authority—these were all intriguing developments, the wobbles of a hooded Humpty-Dumpty, teetering on top of a high wall.

———————————

EXCERPTS FROM SPY REPORT, Ku Klux Klan meeting, Castle Mountain, June 23, 1924:

Motion was made that routine business be dispensed with owing to the large number of new citizens to be naturalized . . . Petitions were circulated for signatures to abolish the state civil service, on the grounds that 70% of the office holders of the state, protected by civil service, were Catholic . . .

Over 1000 cars were on the hill and I estimated 1800 present, beside the 550 new members. It took over one hour to get to the Golden Road. Owing to the robes and darkness it was impossible to get any names only those that were heard in conversation.

EXCERPT FROM SUPPLEMENTAL SPY REPORT,
Castle Mountain, June 23, 1924:

Gathered from talks with members about occurrences of the past three weeks:

Mayor Stapleton finally came to a meeting in Denver and was called to the altar. He took an oath that if the Klan stayed back of him in the recall election and he was elected, he would clean out all the Catholics in the city of Denver. This is being considered by the Klan and a decision will be reached soon.

That Dr. Locke had a detective watching R.R. Maiden, who was seen with a party who had his credentials taken away from him on the mountain and made to walk to Denver. Maiden and this other party was seen coming from the District Attorney's office, and all their moves watched. Dr. Locke enjoys telling anything he can put over on the D.A.

The Golden Klan had voted to take in Sheriff Kerr and this was stopped by Locke on the ground that Kerr was protecting the bootleggers in general and one Jack Standard in particular.

EXCERPTS FROM SPY REPORT,
Castle Mountain, July 14, 1924:

The meeting was called to order at 8:25 p.m. by
Dr. Oeschger, who lectured a few moments on the
policy of klannishness . . . Locke then called for a few
remarks from Klansman Stapleton, erstwhile mayor.
Stapleton explained that he had nothing to say but
that "he would work with the Klan and for the Klan in
the coming election, heart and soul" and if re-elected
would give the Klan the kind of administration they
wanted. This was his entire remarks. Dr. Locke then
called for a vote to see whether or not the Klan would
back Bennie in his desire. The vote was unanimous
that they would help re-elect Stapleton. Roars of
applause . . .

Locke then called for a few remarks from the "next
Governor of Colorado," C.J. Morley. Morley responded
and said that a few days ago several men had taken
his hat from him and tossed it in the ring . . . Not for
himself, mind you, did he wish to run, but only for the
benefit of the Klan, so that he could clean up the state
and place only Americans on guard . . .

The next distinguished gentleman to be called
was Rice W. Means. This party stated that he had just
come from the Arkansas Valley, where the Americans
were organizing in great shape, but that they all were
looking to the Denver Klan for guidance . . .

The next on the program was Chief Candlish . . . [who] told what a wonderful man Stapleton
was, and that while he and the mayor did not worship at the same political shrine, he wanted to see

him re-elected . . . He stated that another term with the Mayor, and the red necks and slimy Jews would crawl in their holes and pull their holes in after them. This about let him out, with the exception of praising Locke, as they all do in winding up . . .

[Locke] then called Klansman Bogard to the altar. He asked Klansman Bogard if he had recently gotten a divorce from his wife, which Bogard said he had, and if he had signed a confession of infidelity, which he stated he had not, also if he had any illicit relations with a girl at the House of the Good Shepherd, which he stated he had not. He was then told to sit down.

Everyone seemed disappointed that nothing was done to Bogard.

New members: between 550–600
Total attendance: " 2000–2150

———

ACROSS AMERICA, THE RISE OF THE KU KLUX KLAN was a major issue, if not *the* issue, of the 1924 election season. From the Deep South to the Northwest, in Colorado, Texas, Oregon, Indiana, Georgia, Kansas, and Ohio, virtually every race for an important state office was a referendum on whether the Klan and its collaborators would be embraced or repudiated. Yet any meaningful debate about the Klan threat was oddly missing from the national political scene. It was as if Congress and the executive branch were pretending that the Invisible Empire was truly invisible.

Despite the concerns raised in the House hearings three years earlier, federal law enforcement agencies were largely content to view Klan violence and intimidation as state issues. Local authorities could decide for themselves if they wanted to prosecute vigilante actions—or ban masks from being worn at public gatherings, as California and Louisiana had done. Politicians seeking national office were reluctant to attack the Klan, not wanting to alienate the Evangelicals, temperance groups, and populist movements aligned with the organization. Even those willing to deplore Klan vigilantism usually took pains to make it clear that they were not criticizing the group's beliefs (never mind that the Klan's version of Jesus hated Jews and Catholics, waved an American flag, and preached white supremacy). When national leaders did speak out against the Klan—as President Calvin Coolidge eventually did, through a spokesman—the reproof was usually couched in words of mild disapproval, not emphatic condemnation.

The timidity was a sign, perhaps, of how ill-prepared America's leaders were to deal with the Klan and what it represented, and the gulf between the way the nation presented itself to the world—as a bastion of equality and tolerance— and the realities of its race relations. You couldn't squarely confront the Klan without acknowledging, to some extent, the soil from which it had sprung. You couldn't condemn its espousal of white supremacy without calling into question the Jim Crow laws or shining an unwelcome light on deep-rooted biases and notions of superiority that even many liberal whites held dear. "Until 1925 I was one of those mildly amused by the KKK," W. E. B. Du Bois observed. "It seemed to me incredible that such a movement could attract any number of people or become serious. And then at first hand and at second I saw the Klan and its workings in widely different places . . . the Ku Klux Klan attempted to do a job which the American people, or certainly a considerable portion of them, wanted done; and they wanted it done because as a nation they had fear of the Jew, the immigrant, the Negro. They realize that the

American of English descent is not holding his own in this country; that America survives and flourishes because of the alien immigrant with his strong arm, his simple life, his faith and hope. They realize that no group in the United States is working harder to push themselves forward and upward than the Negroes; and over all this rises the Shape of Fear."

Spirited struggles over any mention of the KKK were waged at both the 1924 Republican and Democratic national conventions. The Klan had a presence in both parties, primarily among Democratic delegates from the South and Republicans in the West and Midwest. At the GOP gathering in Cleveland, a proposed anti-Klan plank in the platform, denouncing racism and secret societies that take the law into their own hands, was whittled into a bland declaration of allegiance to the Constitution. Imperial Wizard Evans, who came to Cleveland with a staff of sixty and directed the behind-the-scenes fight against the plank, made the cover of *Time* magazine for his efforts. As expected, Coolidge breezed to the nomination against scant opposition, and any criticism of the Klan remained muted.

A livelier time was had at the Democratic convention in New York City two weeks later. A proposed plank that specifically repudiated the Klan touched off hours of strident debate. It was finally defeated by a mere four votes out of more than a thousand cast. The split reflected the polarization of the party, torn between the Klan-backed presidential candidate, William McAdoo, and Al Smith, the Catholic governor of New York. Fifteen days of bitter infighting and more than a hundred ballots failed to resolve the stalemate. The exhausted delegates ultimately settled on an obscure compromise candidate, John W. Davis, a conservative Wall Street lawyer guaranteed to upset no one—and to lose to Silent Cal by a wide margin.

The skirmishes at the conventions were reminders that the Klan leadership still had to be cautious in their power brokering. A public endorsement by the group was considered the kiss of death by many politicians. Others welcomed Klan support, as long as it wasn't noised about. Grand Dragon Locke was particularly adept at making discreet deals with unlikely allies. Shortly after the conventions, he met privately with Colorado Senator Lawrence Cowle Phipps at the Drake Hotel in Chicago. Phipps was a multimillionaire steel magnate from Pennsylvania; his critics joked that he'd moved to Colorado because a Senate seat would be much cheaper to buy there than one back East. He was seeking reelection in the fall but had failed to generate much enthusiasm among the voters, presenting himself as a somewhat vague but reassuringly Republican presence. His campaign slogan: "A vote for Lawrence C. Phipps is another vote for Coolidge."

Phipps was no Klansman. He and Locke had almost nothing in common. But the senator needed voters, and Locke had them. According to accounts of the meeting provided by Locke insiders during a subsequent investigation into election fraud, Locke agreed to throw the Klan's support to Phipps's reelection in exchange for a cash payment. One version states that Locke demanded $75,000 and settled for $40,000. Others say the final figure was $50,000 or $60,000. Locke boasted of being offered $100,000. Whatever the actual amount, it never made it to Klan coffers. Locke preferred to deal in cash, avoided banks whenever possible, and had ordered one of his most trusted associates to build a watertight, rustproof chest that he could bury on rural property he owned. To his minions, Locke explained that supporting Phipps was one of those "strange bedfellow" arrangements the organization had to accept to get Means elected to Colorado's other Senate seat and make Morley the governor.

In subsequent months Locke met frequently with Phipps at the latter's office in downtown Denver. The meetings lasted between twenty minutes and two hours. Locke told his chauffeur that "he could do anything he wanted to with Phipps." He declared that the election of Phipps, Morley, and Means was a sure thing, that he would bet $100,000 on it.

While Locke made new friends and extended his influence, the anti-Klan forces in Denver were having a rough time of it. The recall campaign against Stapleton survived a burglary of its offices and a legal battle, challenging the legitimacy of the petition signatures; a recall election was scheduled for August 12. But the only serious contender among those seeking to replace Stapleton was the most divisive candidate imaginable: Dewey Bailey, the man Stapleton had ousted from the mayor's chair barely a year ago. Bailey was anti-Klan, but he carried a lot of baggage from his own scandal-rocked administration. The voters were being offered a choice between a Klan stooge and a corrupt machine boss.

Several of the anti-Klan leaders, including *Express* editor Sidney Whipple and recall attorney Phil Hornbein, came out in support of Bailey as the lesser of evils. So did the *Denver Post*. But others couldn't muster any enthusiasm. Van Cise, for one, declined to campaign for the same grafter he'd helped chase from office in the first place. He would not run for mayor himself, but he would be damned before he went on the stump for Dewey Bailey.

———

FROM A DISTANCE, THEY CAME ACROSS as two young couples sitting in a car at dusk. It was late July, and they were parked by the side of the road, watching the thousands of cars headed to Castle Mountain for the cross-burning festivities. Deputy

District Attorney Otto Moore and *Denver Post* court reporter Joe Cooke took turns calling out the license plate numbers of cars as they turned off Colfax and headed up the road to the mesa. The two women, both secretaries in the district attorney's office, alternated writing down the numbers.

They had been at it a while when a motorcycle pulled up behind them. The man called himself a "special officer" but gave no name. He demanded to know what they were doing. He flashed a badge. So did Moore.

Moore was the newest hire among the city's prosecutors, eager to try cases and take bad guys off the street. He had learned self-reliance at an early age. He was five years old when his family moved from an Indiana farm to Denver, hoping the thin, dry air would help his mother's tuberculosis. He was ten when his mother died. By the time he entered high school he had left home and was supporting himself with three paper routes. Drafted into the army, he spent twenty-seven months in France. After returning to Denver, he married, earned a law degree at the University of Denver, and was promptly hired by Van Cise. Now he was twenty-eight, and his real education in the law was just starting.

Other cars pulled over. They asked the motorcycle driver what was going on. They heaped abuse on Moore and his passengers, calling them traitors and rednecks. Hands reached into Moore's car and snatched the yellow tablets full of numbers out of the women's hands. Moore was outraged. This was a public road. What gave these clowns the right—

Moore's Model T touring car was swarmed by Klansmen. They lifted it entirely off the ground, its human cargo still inside, and toted it seventy-five yards to a spur road. Then a Stutz Bearcat drove up behind them, nosed into the Ford's flimsy rear bumper, and began pushing the car up the road toward the hogback south of Golden. Moore steered as best he could, the powerful roadster propelling them at speeds in excess of what the Ford was used to. After they'd been pushed far from the Castle Mountain traffic, the Stutz disengaged and whipped alongside them.

"You'll be damn sorry if you try to come back this way," a man in the Stutz said. Then the roadster rumbled off.

Moore didn't try. At that evening's rally, Locke triumphantly announced the seizure of the tablets, one more example of how the Klan was beating the pants off the DA. The crowd was delighted. But throughout the summer, reporters and Van Cise's undercover operatives continued to test the Klan's patience and its security arrangements. Forbes Parkhill, the *Post* newshound who had broken the story of the bunco raid, scored another exclusive when he infiltrated a state KKK leadership strategy meeting. Parkhill had discovered that the secret handshake of the moment involved pressure from a forefinger on the greeter's wrist. The correct grip got him into the room long enough to hear Rice Means tell the others to order all their followers to vote for the Klan candidates, regardless of party affiliation. Then the district attorney of Canon City, a solid Klan town, recognized Parkhill and had him ejected.

The *Post*'s Joe Cooke, who'd been with Moore the night of the Bearcat encounter, kept trying to find a way into the meetings on Castle Mountain. One night he was detained at gunpoint by more "special officers." Cooke was told he was under arrest. When he asked what the charge was, no answer was forthcoming. After an hour he was released. That decision didn't sit well with Locke, who demanded that Cooke come to the altar that night. When Cooke didn't respond, the Grand Dragon called for two volunteers to bring Cooke to the next meeting. Van Cise's agents alerted Cooke that he might be the surprise entertainment come Monday night. Instead of going into hiding, Cooke made his usual court rounds that Monday. Late in the afternoon, he was talking to Van Cise on the steps of the westside courthouse when he saw two men lurking nearby. He pointed them out to Van Cise before heading for the *Post* building.

The two men followed him as he crossed Speer Boulevard and walked up Stout Street. A limousine appeared alongside the reporter, then pulled to the curb further up the street. Cooke could see it coming: the men would rush him from behind and hustle him into the limo. But then another vehicle pulled up beside him and honked. It was Van Cise's men. Cooke got in. They took off and left the limo purring at the curb.

The cat-and-mouse games involving the Klan, the press, and Van Cise's team made good stories down at the Press Club. But Otto Moore considered the jousting on the roads a minor irritation compared to what was happening in the police department and the courts. From what he could see, the integrity of the justice system itself was in peril.

A few weeks after being shoved around by the Bearcat, Moore was assigned to one of the most brazen rape cases he would ever prosecute. The victim, who was in her early twenties, had been approached by a local businessman on the street and offered a job. She had gone to his office with him, ostensibly to meet his partner. She emerged covered with bruises, eyes blackened, clothing torn. She went to the police and explained that the man, Oscar Samples, had demanded sex, then attacked her when she refused. A doctor examined her and confirmed sexual assault. Moore filed rape charges against Samples, who had a prior conviction for distributing obscene literature to high school students. But the complainant was having second thoughts, once she learned what the trial process involved; in those days, defense attorneys routinely impugned the character of rape victims, and newspapers often made their names and their ordeals quite public.

Moore arranged for the woman to meet with Judge Morley so that she could express her concerns. The judge spoke with her for forty-five minutes. "Morley counseled her like a father," Moore recalled many years later. "He urged her to protect womanhood against monsters of that kind."

The woman agreed to testify. But shortly before the trial, Morley learned that the defendant Samples, Klan membership #13709, was a prominent recruiter in the Denver klavern. The judge summoned Moore to his chambers, said he felt bad about pressuring the woman to proceed, and proposed dismissing the case. By this point, though, the victim was intent on testifying against her attacker.

At trial, Morley granted every defense objection and overruled every objection Moore made. The jury still convicted Samples of rape. He was facing one to fourteen years in prison. Morley threw out the verdict and granted a defense motion for a new trial, declaring that he had serious doubts about the truth of the victim's story; after all, hadn't she gone willingly to the man's office? Moore took the case to trial again. He ended up with a hung jury—because, he suspected, Morley had packed the jury with Klansmen. A third trial also ended in a hung jury, at which point the victim declined to testify again.

Moore, who would later serve two decades on Colorado's Supreme Court, never forgot the hot shame of the case. Whatever fuss the Kluxers made about protecting womanhood, they were happy to let a predator like Samples go free when he was useful to them. And the judge who fixed the whole sorry business, who violated a young woman's trust and protected a rapist, was the Klan's choice to be Colorado's governor.

EXCERPTS FROM SPY REPORT,
Castle Mountain, August 12, 1924:

[Secretary of State Carl] Milliken said that he felt wonderful this night and that all Klansmen ought to feel the same for uniting to put over Stapleton . . . He said that no longer would the 15 percent of Jews and Catholics dictate to the 85% white people . . .

Locke then made a talk about Col. Van Cise, that the Colonel was a Catholic at heart, and was forming a businessmen's anti-Klan society, with an office in the Equitable Building . . . He stated that he had a record of the first meeting held and intended to get them all . . .

Attendance all—about 3000.

THE KLAN CAME INTO ITS OWN THAT AUGUST, stunning the state's political establishment with its grassroots organizing, its coordination, its unexpected numbers. At the Republican county assembly held at the Denver Auditorium, representatives from neighborhood caucuses gathered to select delegates to the state convention and designate primary candidates. Roughly two-thirds of the assembled representatives were Klansmen, recognizable to each other by the white carnations they wore in their lapels. Klan police officers stationed at the doors tried to bar reporters and non-delegates, including several veteran party leaders. Locke directed the proceedings from the mayor's box while Rice Means acted as floor leader. They effortlessly pushed through an all-Klan ticket of candidates, led by Morley, Means, and Phipps. To cap it all off, Means then obtained overwhelming approval of his hand-picked list of delegates to the state convention without bothering to reveal who any of them were. Most of those present had no idea who would be representing them at the convention.

Van Cise made several attempts to protest the hijacking of his party. "If we don't get fair play, it's going to split the party wide open," he said.

He was hissed and shouted down.

At the state convention two days later, the Klan failed to secure the top spot on the statewide ballot for its candidates. The organization didn't have the same kind of influence in GOP circles elsewhere in the state as it did in Denver and a few nearby counties. But Morley, Means, and the rest of the Klan ticket still made it on the ballot, with a month to go before the Republican primary.

A week after that, nearly eighty thousand Denverites voted in the mayoral recall election, the largest turnout in the city's history. Stapleton trounced Bailey by thirty-one thousand votes, five times the margin of Bailey's defeat in the mayoral election of 1923. The incumbent had carried every district in the city; Bailey's only show of strength was in the Jewish neighborhoods on the west side. It had been a low-blow race even by Denver standards. Stapleton's backers had kept the opposition from using city venues for campaign events and spread rumors that Bailey was a Klansman. The rumors weren't true, but Locke wasn't above nominating his enemies for KKK membership, without their knowledge, to discredit them. Stapleton released a terse statement saying that he felt "inspired" that the citizens of Denver had twice shown their confidence in him. Locke gave his first substantial interview to the *Denver Post*, gloating over the returns and leaving no doubt about the mayor's true affiliations: "The Klan had charge of the campaign and election of Mayor Stapleton, and is entitled to credit for his overwhelming victory."

The Grand Dragon likened his humming machine to the crackerjack efficiency and discipline of the U.S. Army. He spoke disdainfully of the district attorney, who had leaked spy reports to the *Express* right before the recall election, in a last-ditch effort to expose Stapleton's kowtowing to the Klan. It hadn't made any difference.

"We know—that is, I know—that today, Phil Van Cise is trying to organize a committee of one hundred prominent or near-prominent men to fight the Klan in the coming campaign," Locke told the reporter. "I know the name of each man who is taken into Phil's organization. I know he peddled the Klan stuff to a newspaper, and I know he is very foolish to hate the Klan . . . I'd just like Van Cise to know that we know what he is doing."

Locke was well-informed. After watching the Klan steamroll the opposition at the county assembly, Van Cise was scrambling to organize an alternative slate of Republican candidates before the primary election. He had enlisted a hundred business leaders and attorneys to sponsor the effort and was hastily recruiting candidates. Reporter Forbes Parkhill, who was one of those persuaded to run for a seat in the state legislature, dubbed it the Visible Government ticket—a slate of public-minded citizens whose intentions and affiliations were clearly known, unlike the clandestine candidates of the Invisible Empire.

Van Cise organized a strategy meeting with his backers one evening at the westside courthouse. He invited fifty people to attend. Fearful that some might be scared off if their names were disclosed too soon, he avoided any public announcement of the meeting. But Locke's spy network was at least as good, if not better, than the one Van Cise had keeping tabs on the Grand Dragon. The night of the meeting, approximately three hundred Klansmen gathered on the lawn outside the courthouse. They formed a line on both sides of the sidewalk. They called out the names of the arriving guests and discouraged several from entering the building. A hearty two dozen of Van Cise's supporters ignored the taunts and attended the meeting. The group adjourned around ten, after deciding that the Visible Government ticket would hold several public rallies in the days leading up to the primary, including a major presentation at the City Auditorium.

Van Cise emerged from the courthouse around midnight. A scatter of Kluxers still lingered on the lawn, evidently waiting for him. His path to his car took him through a gauntlet of them. They bumped and shoved him, cursed him, swatted at him. That they didn't do more was probably because of the brightly lit fire station next door. The fire department had not fallen to the Klan as completely as the police, and that night the station was staffed by Catholics and other anti-Klan employees.

Van Cise made it to his Ford. The Klansmen piled into their cars, waited for him to pull away, then followed. Van Cise felt like a grand marshal leading a parade. Instead of driving home, through the relatively empty streets of Capitol Hill, he headed downtown, the Kluxers in hot pursuit.

He had not gone far when he saw a water truck ahead, lumbering toward a hydrant. He slammed on the accelerator and squeezed into the shrinking space between the truck and the curb, then whipped around a corner. Behind him he heard a crash and screams. Two cars remained on his tail.

He took several sharp turns, pulled over on a deserted street, and proceeded on foot, creeping through alleys and hopping fences until he was home.

The next morning he phoned Locke.

"I am carrying a .45," he said, "and I've run from your gang for the last time. When I shoot, I shoot to kill."

He carried the pistol in a shoulder holster for months. A year or so later, he had a confidential conversation with a Klansman who claimed to have been one of his pack of pursuers that night. The man said that the group had planned to kidnap him and castrate him, but the presence of the Catholic firemen had made them hesitate. They figured they would have better luck catching up with him on the streets. Then the water truck got in the way, he said, "and your damned Ford was too fast."

9

—

Tonight We See the Mob

The Visible Government ticket took out newspaper ads to announce its big event at the City Auditorium, scheduled for September 4, five days before the primary. Van Cise would be the featured speaker, holding forth on "Morley and the Courts: The Klan Boycott." "Do YOU want YOUR business at the mercy of a boycott?" one ad blared. "Do you want ANY secret order to dictate whom you may employ?"

The notices were aimed at the business community and its concerns about getting caught in the crossfire of the Klan's economic warfare. But the speech Van Cise was preparing touched on much more, from jury-rigging to the Klan takeover of the public roads outside Golden to the duplicity of Morley and Locke. Two days before the auditorium event, he gave a truncated version of his remarks to a thousand people at a packed West Colfax theater.

"If the Klan wins this election, its membership will be doubled," he warned. "Everyone will say, 'Well, we can't beat it. We'll just join.'"

He was met with thunderous applause. But this was only a test run before a favorably disposed audience, one that included many people from the surrounding Jewish neighborhood. At the auditorium he would be facing a much tougher crowd. He fully expected the Klan to try to disrupt the event. A spy report from Castle Mountain on September 1 noted that Locke had mentioned Van Cise's upcoming talk and "wanted as many of the Klan to be there as could. All he asked them to do was not to clap the speaker."

Van Cise couldn't picture a horde of Kluxers sitting passively through his talk. Things could get ugly. He was told that forty police officers would be handling crowd control, but he had more confidence in the handful of men from his office—including Otto Moore, Ken Robinson, and Bob Maiden—who would be helping out. As an additional precaution, he made photographic "lantern slides" of internal Klan documents and other paperwork backing up his claims, so he could project them on a screen during his talk, as if he was presenting a closing argument to a jury. The facts would be right before their eyes, impossible to deny, no matter what stunts the Kluxers pulled.

It was not a bad plan. If it had worked, a great deal of unpleasantness might have been avoided. But Van Cise underestimated the viselike grip the Klan already had on the functions of city government. Because his group had rented the auditorium for the evening, he assumed that they controlled access to the place. The doors were supposed to open at 7:15 p.m., forty-five minutes before the speeches started. Men and women began showing up at the auditorium much earlier than that, flashing yellow tickets. The Visible Government organization had issued no such tickets, but police and staff were under orders to admit the bearers. By the time the doors opened to the general public, the four-thousand-seat theater was almost full. The remaining seats were quickly occupied, and thousands of others were turned away.

An organist played interludes while the clock ticked away toward eight. Then the curtain rose, revealing the Visible Government candidates, Van Cise, and other speakers, seated in a half-circle on the stage. A trickle of applause was quickly swallowed in the cavernous silence. The organist played "The Star-Spangled Banner." The crowd stood, listened stonily, then sat down again.

Benjamin Griffith, a former Colorado attorney general, was the first speaker. He outlined the goals of the Visible Government ticket and noted that all three major presidential candidates—Coolidge, Davis, and the Progressive Party's Robert "Fighting Bob" LaFollette—had denounced the Klan. As if on cue, the word "Klan" triggered a chorus of shouts and shrieks from the audience. Startled, Griffith appealed for a chance to be heard. The shouts subsided. Griffith tried again. The shouting resumed. Griffith stumbled through his ten-minute pitch and sat down.

The second speaker, attorney Henry McAllister, didn't fare much better. His presentation on the judicial races was met with boos. "Yah-yah-yah-yah!" a woman screamed. Then a man in the middle of the main level stood and raised his arms. The crowd fell silent. McAllister concluded his talk.

Griffith introduced the night's featured speaker. Van Cise stood up—and was greeted by an impenetrable wall of boos, jeers, hoots, and catcalls. He waited for the din to subside.

"The issue is this," he said. "Shall the Republican party be turned over to the Ku Klux Klan?"

The audience exploded. A chant—"It will! It will!"—rippled through the hall.

"Three cheers for Morley, you traitor!" someone screamed.

"Get out of here!"

"We want Morley!"

Van Cise waited for his next opening, but the noise kept building. Some people had brought whistles and horns. Others chanted Morley's name. Sitting on the stage, looking out on the pandemonium, Forbes Parkhill was transfixed by the shrieking of one large woman in the front row. "You ain't Ah-murrikins!" she howled repeatedly. "You ain't Ah-murrikins!"

Sidney Whipple of the *Express* had never seen anything like it. The scene was like something out of an insane asylum, or maybe the French Revolution. People were standing up and hollering their lungs out, their eyes glittering. A woman in brown in the front row was screaming something about Americans and shaking her fists—not once, not twice, but *constantly*, as if possessed. Far in the back, a youth with greasy blond hair kept up a monotonous, rhythmic hand-clapping. A few Klan officials strolled the aisles—trying to keep a lid on things, it seemed to Whipple, rather than excite more frenzy. But the uniformed and plainclothes police officers just stood around, arms folded.

"Police—hell! There were no police," Whipple wrote in his account of the event. "For the police themselves were Klansmen, sneering, grinning Klansmen, winking at the disorder and leering at their friends in the mob."

The sole police action Whipple witnessed that night came shortly after Van Cise responded to the chants demanding Morley. The Klan's candidate for governor only spoke at Klan meetings, Van Cise noted. "Your candidates do not dare come on this platform," he said.

"You're a liar!"

The shout came from Carl DeLochte, a state labor official.

A Canadian by birth, DeLochte was not "native-born" and thus was ineligible for Klan membership, but he had been a close friend of Morley's for years. He also headed the Colorado chapter of the Royal Riders of the Red Robe, a Klan affiliate for Protestant immigrants. Either because of his sensitive state job or his prominence among the Kluxers, the enraged DeLochte was quickly escorted out of the theater by police. But the uproar resumed.

"Dirty traitor!"

"Morley! Morley! We want Morley!"

"You ain't Ah-murrikins!"

Van Cise put on the screen a list of Catholic businesses that had been distributed at Klan meetings—a list supposedly drawn up by the Catholic hierarchy to insure the faithful did business only with fellow Catholics. The list was a hoax, he explained. He pointed out names on the list of Masons and Protestants. Much of the explanation was drowned out by boos and abuse. It was like trying to lecture a room full of unruly toddlers who clamp hands over their ears and sing to themselves to avoid hearing what they don't want to hear.

"Morley! Morley!"

"You ain't Ah-murrikins!"

"Liar!"

Van Cise denounced the Klan boycotts as a form of mutually assured destruction. An excerpt from the Klan doctrine on klannishness appeared on the screen to cries of outrage. "I'll read you this section of the oath," Van Cise began.

"Read it all! Read it all!"

"That's not it! Where did you get it?"

"What about Ludlow?"

Now they actually were singing. Someone had started a sing-along that swept the entire place. "The Old Gray Mare."

Then "California, Here I Come." (Locke had boasted that Van Cise would be moving to California after the election.) Van Cise kept talking, even though his words couldn't be heard beyond the first row, where the woman in brown was still shrieking and shaking her fists.

"This meeting shows that the Klan does not believe what it professes," he said, "and is afraid of free speech and the truth."

California, here I come

"What you are doing tonight is a better argument against the Klan than any I could make!"

Right back where I started from

Slowly, methodically, he pressed forward. The skills he'd acquired on his high school debate team were useless here, but he had other tricks. He folded his arms and beamed at the crowd, as if he'd just thought of a witty remark. When they quieted down, he made it through another sentence or two before a fresh tide of noise buried him. He turned his back to them, as if giving up the fight, then whirled back around and resumed. The lantern slides helped too. A new image appeared on the screen, and the tumult ebbed until the crowd figured out what they were looking at: a Klan program that listed city attorney Rice Means and "Klailiff-elect" Clarence Morley as speakers. Cheers and whistles, followed by blasts of disapproval as Van Cise detailed Morley's numerous public denials of Klan membership.

Whipple could feel the energy of the place shifting, spiraling into confusion. For the first hour or two, the disruptions had consisted mostly of well-orchestrated chants and sing-alongs. Now it was all breaking down into incoherent shouts and paroxysms of rage. Those who had come to hear Van Cise and couldn't hear anything had left. Young men were taking off their coats and huddling together, like street toughs getting ready for action. In the lobby, Whipple found the police chief, strutting around in his gold braid and pretending to be in charge. "I could stop it in five minutes if I wanted to," Chief Candlish said.

Locke was nowhere to be found.* From what he could see, Whipple surmised that phone calls were being made from the lobby to the lair of the Grand Dragon on Glenarm Place, apprising him of the situation and seeking guidance. At half-past ten Clarence Kirkling, a close associate of Locke's and the Grand Dragon of the North, overseeing Klan operations in northern Colorado and Wyoming, walked to the front of the auditorium and raised his hand. The place fell silent immediately.

"I have been reliably informed," Kirkling announced, "that a number of rowdies have been planted here by some organization, not the Klan. I call upon all good Klansmen to be silent and let Philip Van Cise vent his spleen."

Kirkling walked away.

Van Cise resumed.

Whipple checked his watch. For two minutes the district attorney managed to pick up the frayed thread of his speech, with only occasional hoots and hisses. Then the noise level shot up again. Kirkling couldn't control them, Whipple realized.

---

* Some histories of the KKK in Colorado assert that Locke was at the City Auditorium that night, directing the crowd's actions from the mayor's box. Their source appears to be a statement made by Forbes Parkhill in an interview conducted forty years after the event. None of the contemporary accounts make this claim, and Whipple's account in the *Express* remarks on the Grand Dragon's absence. The available evidence suggests Parkhill was mistaken, possibly confusing the Visible Government debacle with the raucous GOP county assembly at the same venue a few weeks earlier, during which Locke directed his forces from the mayor's box.

Nobody could. And whatever happened, true to form, the Klan would blame the chaos on "planted" rowdies.

"I shall continue to the end of my speech," Van Cise said, "if we stay here until morning."

For a solid fifteen minutes, he couldn't get a word in. The crowd bellowed out "Onward Christian Soldiers." Then "America (My Country, 'Tis of Thee)." Halfway through the latter, the woman in brown left her seat and approached the stage, shaking her fist at the Visible Government candidates and berating them for failing to stand during the patriotic song. "You ain't Ah-murrikins!" she shrieked.

Van Cise responded that the woman in brown had arrived in Locke's car—a very distinctive car. "Your Grand Dragon poses as '100 percent American,' but Dr. Locke uses a coat of arms on his automobile," he said. "What real American uses a coat of arms?"

More howling at the mention of Locke's name. The woman in brown wandered back to her seat. On her way there she lashed out at attorney Clarence Wortham, sitting in the row behind her, striking him twice in the face. Shrewdly, perhaps, Wortham didn't respond in kind, but he was quickly surrounded by policemen descending from the stage.

"He tried to trip her!" someone yelled.

Wortham denied it. Juvenile Court Judge Ben Lindsey, who had witnessed the assault, demanded that the officers arrest the woman in brown. One of them started to grab Wortham. "Don't touch that man!" Lindsey barked.

"Something is wrong," Van Cise shouted, "when the police department of Denver is afraid to keep order at a public meeting! When policemen in uniform are standing in the aisles, afraid to arrest disturbers!"

The police withdrew. Soon Lindsey and his wife were

surrounded by Kluxers. The couple sat meekly, heads bowed, while taunts and insults were hurled at them.

"The Klan advocates mob action," Van Cise continued. "Tonight we see the mob, and we see what mob rule means!"

He was speaking now mainly to the reporters in the front row. Nobody else could make out any of it as he plowed ahead with his speech, describing how Locke had been rejected for membership by Denver's medical association. Every time he mentioned Locke's name, the noise intensified.

"We'll stick till you quit!"

Hail, hail, the gang's all here . . .

Shortly after midnight, Robinson called him to the wings, where Chief Candlish and Louis Ormsby, the Stapleton appointee in charge of the auditorium, were waiting. The Visible Government ticket's lease of the facility had expired at the stroke of twelve.

"I think it's about time to stop," Candlish said.

"I will not stop," Van Cise replied.

He returned to the rostrum and started in on the story of Morley's illegal grand jury. An account that would have taken ten minutes, under normal circumstances, consumed the next hour. It had come down to a contest of wills—one man onstage, voice ragged, defying the tyranny of the mob. Four hours and forty minutes after he began, Van Cise closed with a hoarse plea to vote the straight Visible Government ticket at Tuesday's primary.

He had just wrapped up and the crowd was pouring out when a disheveled and furious Mayor Stapleton arrived on the scene, summoned from his slumbers by Candlish. "What's this building doing open at this hour?" he demanded.

Van Cise slipped out the stage door in the company of Bob

Maiden, who was assigned to get him home safely. Years later, Deputy District Attorney Otto Moore would maintain that Maiden and Van Cise had to flee for their lives that night in a speeding car, exchanging gunfire with pursuing Klansmen. But neither Maiden nor Van Cise left any account of such a denouement.

In the next day's *Express*, Sidney Whipple described the showdown at the auditorium as "a scene never duplicated in Denver in all its history . . . a meeting hall packed with enraged, shouting, shrieking men and women gone mad with fanatic klan-frenzy . . . It will do more to win votes for Van Cise's ticket than all the speech-making in the world."

Three days later, on the eve of the primary, an estimated five thousand Kluxers gathered on Castle Mountain. According to a spy report, Locke was in a celebratory mood. He declared that the "rowdies" who did all the yelling at the City Auditorium the other night "were brought in by Van Cise himself. He said that personally he wanted the meeting to go on."

———

IT SHOULD NOT HAVE COME DOWN to one man on a stage, shouted down by a mob. The most startling revelation of the City Auditorium showdown wasn't the Klan's ability to disrupt the proceedings. It was the inability of the anti-Klan forces to present any kind of coordinated resistance, to put aside differences and unite to defeat a common enemy.

Klan membership in Colorado was approaching its peak at the time of the 1924 elections, yet the raw numbers were not so overwhelming as to make a Klan victory inevitable. The remarkably intact Klan membership books for the Denver area contain close to thirty thousand individual entries, leading some researchers to claim that nearly a third of the eligible adult white males in the city were Klansmen. Others have noted that some Klan membership cards bore numbers exceeding sixty thousand. But many of the names in the membership ledgers are repeated, while others may be those of men who joined early, expecting to remain anonymous, and dropped out as the group fell under greater scrutiny. Historian Robert Goldberg's analysis of the membership books concludes that the number of active Klan participants in Denver in 1924 was around 17,500, with roughly another 17,000 elsewhere in the state. Even the most generous estimates of the group's size, including affiliated organizations such as the Women of the Ku Klux Klan and the Royal Riders of the Red Robe, suggest that it represented less than 8 percent of Colorado's one million residents. Compare that with the state's 125,000 Catholics, 11,000 Blacks, and 20,000 Jews. Or its 117,000 white immigrants. On paper, it's the Klan that was outnumbered—which makes the lopsided outcome of the 1924 elections all the more remarkable.

Many people did actively oppose the Klan, but they were not always on the same page or seeking the same outcome. Black activists in Denver had recognized the Klan threat from the outset, protesting the screening of *Birth of a Nation* and opposing the KKK's application to incorporate in the state. The threat of Klan retaliation did not dissuade them. George Gross's successor as head of the local NAACP, dentist Clarence Holmes, was so outspoken in challenging segregation in housing and schools that the Klan burned a cross on the lawn outside his Five Points home. Like Van Cise, Holmes carried a gun for months after the incident but refused to back down. Instead, he threw himself into plans to host the NAACP's national convention in Denver in 1925. Yet the Black community's most daring response to the Klan was one that couldn't be discussed with outsiders. NAACP stalwart Joseph Henry Peter Westbrook was a blue-eyed, light-skinned African American physician. At great personal risk, he attended Klan meetings for years, passing for white and sharing what he learned with Holmes and others. Dr. Westbrook's undercover operation was entirely independent of what Van Cise and other whites were attempting to do, and it remained largely unknown and unheralded for decades.

Even though one Black newspaper, the *Colorado Statesman*, urged readers to stick with the Republicans, the party of Lincoln, many Black residents regarded Locke's organization and its takeover of the GOP as an existential threat. Surprisingly, many Jewish and Catholic leaders didn't share that view. Attorney Charles Ginsberg, one of the Klan's more militant opponents, complained that most prominent Jews were reluctant to condemn the group. To Ginsberg, it seemed like the Jewish business community wanted to tiptoe around the Klan's anti-Semitism, not wanting to stir up more trouble. He sharply ridiculed a proposal by the B'nai B'rith service organization to sit down with Grand Dragon Locke and explain Jewish rituals. Ginsberg regarded the offer as a gesture of appeasement.

Many influential Catholics, too, appeared hesitant to get in a brawl with the Klan. Father Smith occasionally took a poke at the Kluxers in the *Denver Catholic Register*, usually in response to some outrageous claim, such as a Klan newspaper's assertion that Catholic arsonists were torching public schools to force students into parochial schools. But most members of the church hierarchy steered clear of commenting on the Klan's escapades, perhaps concerned about appearing to be exactly what the Klan accused them of being: a grandiose religious bureaucracy, meddling in politics.

Personal as well as ideological disputes kept the anti-Klan factions from forging an effective alliance. Ginsberg and Van

Cise, for example, both wanted to eradicate the Klan, but there was bad blood between them dating back to the district attorney race in 1920, when Ginsberg, a Democrat, connived to put an independent candidate on the ballot, as part of an elaborate plan to draw votes from the Republican challenger, Van Cise, and reelect William Foley. Van Cise had gone to court to defeat the move and had exposed Ginsberg's efforts to bankroll a sham candidate to run against him. (One of the prospective candidates Ginsberg had approached was Rice Means, now running as the Klan's choice for U.S. Senator.) That legal squabble, along with other feuds between Van Cise and Democratic leaders, may have played a part in keeping the Visible Government effort from becoming a more aggressive and far-reaching coalition.

Partisan politics within the GOP also undermined the battle against the Klan. Many mainstream Republicans thought it was bad form to openly attack other Republicans. Lieutenant Governor Robert Rockwell, who was vying against Morley to become the GOP's candidate for governor, was one of them. A wealthy West Slope rancher who had spurned Klan attempts to recruit him, Rockwell privately admired Van Cise's battle against Morley and what he stood for. But he refused to denounce the Klan publicly, insisting that to do so would simply create dissension in the ranks and aid the Democrats. "I do not regard the Ku Klux Klan or any other secret organization an issue in this campaign," he wrote to one rival, "and I will not be drawn into any controversy over the merits or demerits of any such organization."

The Klan had no such scruples about delineating the merits and demerits of the candidates. On the day of the primary, voters found pink sheets in their mailboxes that identified every candidate as Protestant, Catholic, or Jew. Unacceptable

Protestants had stars next to their names, either because of "Roman Catholic Affiliations" or because they were "Known Enemies of American Institutions."

The disarray among the anti-Klan forces was reflected in the primary returns. Morley lost to Rockwell in several Western Slope counties but comfortably carried Denver and its suburbs, as well as Pueblo and Canon City, to win the Republican nomination for governor. Rice Means defeated two challengers to become the GOP candidate for the short-term Senate seat. Van Cise's Visible Government slate of proposed state senators and representatives, comprising neophytes like Parkhill and old-time GOP loyalists dragged out of retirement, was crushed by the Klan ticket.

In several statewide races, the margin of victory consisted of a few thousand votes. The deciding factor may have been the Klan's ability to get its members to vote in lockstep, regardless of party affiliation. The state's open primary system allowed Democrats to vote in Republican primaries and vice versa, and the unusually high turnout in the '24 GOP primary suggests that the Stapleton machine rallied many registered Democrats to the Klan cause.

After the primary, momentum was on the Klan's side. The group could ride on the coattails of Coolidge's popularity, urging Coloradans to "vote the straight Republican ticket"— while avoiding mention of the KKK altogether. Morley was up against an unpopular liberal Democratic governor, William Sweet, a former securities dealer whom Van Cise had attacked for being too generous with pardons; by contrast, Morley portrayed himself as a humble servant of the people, committed to law and order. To his credit, Sweet denounced the Klan's racism and bigotry repeatedly, insisting that the Klan issue could not be ignored. He described his party as "a cross section of the common people of America," one that included Blacks and whites, immigrants and natives, Catholics and Jews as well as Protestants. The Klan's notion of Americanism would disenfranchise half the country. "If we follow the advice of the Ku Klux Klan," he declared, "we would soon emulate the example of the Kansas merchant who hung out his placard: 'I AM 200% AMERICAN. I HATE EVERYBODY.'" More pungent critiques could be found in broadsides circulated by Democratic activists, including an alleged collection of KKK "hymns" that played off stereotypes of Kluxers as illiterate, white-trash degenerates:

> *Benedikt Arnold, Morley, Massie,*
> *Luk us over, ain't we classy*

> *We're the Bunch of kommon Asses*
> *Taken from the lown-down Klasses . . .*

> *A little Huch, a little Wisky*
> *Makes us Kluxers rather frisky*

> *We rase Hell and then the Flag*
> *Ain't it grand, a Kluxers Jag.*

In the final weeks leading up to the election, Van Cise focused his efforts on trying to reelect as many non-Klan judges as he could. It didn't matter if they were Democrats or Republicans, as long as they weren't in Locke's pocket. He spoke at several public events, usually with better security than he'd had at the City Auditorium. The Kluxers still tried to interfere, shutting off the lights at one church gathering in support of Judge Ben Lindsey. Lindsey, who'd established one of the first juvenile courts in the country in Denver and was nationally celebrated as a judicial reformer, was a prime target of the Klan; his advocacy of women's rights, sex education, and "companionate marriage"—a kind of test-run relationship that could be undone without the stigma of divorce—were an affront to the Invisible Empire's notions of morality. Short, abrasive, and imperious, Lindsey sometimes alienated his own most loyal supporters. But at the GOP county assembly, Van Cise had attempted to nominate Lindsey (the Democratic incumbent for the past twenty-three years) as the Republican choice for juvenile court judge, insisting that he was a far better choice than the Klan's pick to challenge him, a shady attorney from a mountain town who hadn't even established proper residency in Denver. Lindsey had repaid the favor by showing up at the City Auditorium for Van Cise's talk and getting harassed by Kluxers himself. Politically, the two men were at opposite ends of the spectrum, but they were logical allies in the battle to keep the justice system out of the hands of the Klan.

Election day arrived. So did more pink-sheet smears, accusing various Democratic candidates of having Catholic wives or other impediments. Morley and Means won by substantial margins; Morley carried 54 percent of the votes cast in the gubernatorial election, more than twenty-five thousand votes ahead of Sweet. Senator Phipps and the Klan's Secretary of State, Carl Milliken, breezed to reelection. The Klan slaughtered the opposition in statehouse races, giving the Republicans control of both houses of the General Assembly.

Stunning as it was, the victory wasn't absolute. Congressman William Vaile, an old-school Republican and Van Cise ally, managed to hold on to his seat against a challenge from a Democrat Klansman. Van Cise's efforts helped save three out of seven district judges; the four newcomers were all Klan. And Judge Lindsey defeated his Klan challenger, Royal Graham, by a mere 137 votes—touching off a legal battle, with each side accusing the other of election fraud, that would go on for years.

The Klan enjoyed many successes in local elections that fall, but nowhere else in the country had it prevailed so thoroughly, taking control of the executive and legislative functions of state government—and backing the winners of both U.S. Senate seats as well. A week after the election, on a crisp November morning, Imperial Wizard Evans stepped off a private train car in Denver's Union Station, accompanied by several other Klan leaders, including the grand dragons of Kansas and Georgia. They were met by Grand Dragon Locke, Governor-elect Clarence Morley, and other VIPs. A squad of city detectives escorted the group to breakfast at the Brown Palace, where Locke announced a special event, to celebrate the Colorado Realm's remarkable achievement and the visit of its honored guests. That night Klansmen would gather in a newly acquired indoor venue along the Platte River, a former cotton mill transformed into a stadium, and hold an initiation ceremony for five thousand new members.

Post reporter Frances "Pinky" Wayne, Locke's favorite journalist, wrote an awestruck account of the meeting. At one point she asked the Imperial Wizard if he could compare the Ku Klux Klan to the *fascisti* movement in Italy. Evans demurred. Foreign politics had nothing to do with what was going on in America, he said, and any movement "founded on force," like the *fascisti*, was bound to fail.

"The Klan is not interested in politics," the Imperial Wizard said. "Its specialty is patriotism."

10

The New Regime

At a quarter past noon on January 13, 1925, the Ku Klux Klan took control of the executive branch of government for the State of Colorado. Accepting the reins of power on behalf of the Invisible Empire was Clarence Joseph Morley, who was sworn in as Colorado's twenty-fourth governor by James H. Teller, the chief justice of the Colorado Supreme Court, before a crowd of thousands at Denver's City Auditorium. It was the first time in more than thirty years that the ceremony was held somewhere other than the Capitol building. Morley's inaugural committee had deemed the gold-domed statehouse too puny to accommodate the multitudes seeking to attend the historic event.

Festooned with stars-and-stripes bunting from the stage to the rafters, the auditorium opened to the public two hours before the ceremony. There was no need for special yellow tickets this time to insure a Klan-friendly audience. The election returns showed strong support for Morley among working people as well as business interests, among farmers and suburbanites—and in counties that usually voted Democrat as well as Republican strongholds. Add to that the thousands who, as Van Cise had predicted, were just now hopping on the bandwagon. By noon the place was packed to the upper balconies with people eager to cheer on the new regime.

Some of them may have had little conception of what the new order stood for and had come to learn more. But those who'd been on Castle Mountain every Monday night and listened to the speeches had come with certain expectations. The Klan leadership had outlined a broad agenda, and now it had the opportunity to turn its words into action. Measures that Morley's team and Klan lawmakers were eager to see enacted included tougher restrictions on immigration; compulsory sterilization programs for epileptics and the feebleminded; abolition of the civil service system, so that state agencies could be purged of Blacks, Catholics, and Jews, to be replaced by Klansmen; and a series of bills, clearly targeting Catholics, that would outlaw the use of wine in religious services, require orphans to attend public schools, and add a mandatory course of religious instruction to the public-school curriculum.

Except for closing the Prohibition loophole that allowed for the use of sacramental wine, none of these proposals received any mention in Morley's inaugural remarks. With members of both houses of the legislature seated behind him, he delivered an exceptionally dull, colorless speech. He praised the state's "commercial stability" and its "high standard of citizenry." He listed several boards and commissions, boiler inspectors and library supervisors and such, that he wanted to eliminate in the name of efficiency. He spoke vaguely of reviving the mining industry and called for a minimum wage law "for the benefit of women employed in industry." He looked forward to a legislative session that would be notable for its "fairness to all the people" as well as its brevity.

There was little that was provocative or inspiring in what he had to say, but the crowd cheered mightily anyway. The line that got the loudest response was his declaration that the state's most critical need wasn't more houses or railroads, not more laws or education, but "more spirituality." He made no mention of the Klan, but the passing reference to spirituality touched on something that was central to the Klan's promises, something Morley himself fervently believed—that with the right kind of leadership, America could purify itself of sinful influences and become the country it was meant to be, a country ruled by proud, manly white men clad in white robes, serving the white Protestant God.

The new governor stayed onstage after the ceremony ended, holding an impromptu reception for a crush of well-wishers. The gesture had a nice man-of-the-people touch, and it marked the zenith of Morley's popularity, the abrupt ascendancy of a nondescript nobody.

Yet even at that moment of triumph, a shadow hung over the proceedings. The Morley administration had scarcely begun, and trouble was already smoldering backstage, a whiff of scandal wafting from the wings, like the first acrid fumes from a short in the wiring that could turn the whole place into a raging inferno. John Galen Locke, the governor's spiritual mentor, his most trusted adviser—in short, the brains of the operation—was under attack by dark forces. Dr. Locke was facing charges of kidnapping and conspiracy. Just four days before his inauguration, the governor-elect had paid a thousand dollars out of his own pocket to bail his Grand Dragon out of jail.

———

THE DAY OF MORLEY'S INAUGURATION also marked the changing of the guard at the Denver district attorney's office. Van Cise devoted considerable time during his last two weeks in office to preparing reports and recommendations for his successor. His office had filed 3056 criminal cases in 1924. In the 637 most serious cases, the ones filed in district court, more than half had resulted in convictions at trial or plea deals; 84 defendants had been acquitted or freed on directed verdicts; 108 cases had been dismissed; and the rest were still pending. More startling, perhaps, were the number of search warrants his office had obtained for private residences—1023, nearly double the number sought in the previous record year.

The surge in search warrants was a direct result of the escalating war on bootleggers, and Van Cise was unapologetic about it. In a final report to the legislature, he proposed that officers of the law should be allowed to search automobiles without a warrant, if the state wanted to get serious about enforcing Prohibition. He made a case for easing the prosecution's burden in other ways, too, including allowing juries in misdemeanor and minor felony cases to render a verdict on a majority vote, rather than requiring a unanimous decision; establishing a statewide fingerprint identification bureau; simplifying the process involved in prosecuting abortionists for killing their patients; doing away with the "barbaric" practice of jailing indigent material witnesses until trial; eliminating loopholes in banking laws that allowed embezzlers to escape serious punishment; taking steps to prevent judges from tampering with grand juries; and yes, tightening up the sacramental wine exemption, which sometimes resulted in wine being diverted to the black market. Like the Klan's wish list for legislative action, some of his bolder recommendations would require significant changes in state law, if not in the Constitution itself. But the report made waves, especially a passage that drew attention to an issue Van Cise was keen to highlight, the need for drastic reform of Chief Candlish's Klan-infested police force: "I would be remiss in my duty to the public, did I fail to call attention to the police department in Denver. It is in a badly disorganized condition, torn into two factions, lacking in leadership and teamwork, with many of its own members more faithful to other organizations than their own where the enforcement of law is concerned."

The barbed comments reflected the exasperation of a crusader who was about to lose his bully pulpit, a man in search of a legacy. It wasn't so long ago that he was the celebrated gangbuster, the man who beat Blonger. But what was he now? An object of fun, a target for harassment who had to carry a gun everywhere he went. An annoyance that would soon be removed, like a pebble from a shoe. He had thwarted Morley's secret grand jury and salvaged a few honest judges, but he had failed miserably in his efforts to keep the Klan from taking over his party, his city, and his state. Years later, he would describe his brief political career as "an excellent illustration of mob favor" and its fickleness—hero one day, goat the next.

Yet in the final days of his term, the wheel turned again. A lanky teen walked into his office, accompanied by his mother, and told a bizarre story of an abduction and a forced midnight wedding, orchestrated by none other than John Galen Locke. It was one last gift, the opportunity Van Cise had been seeking for the past three years—a chance to bring criminal charges against the Grand Dragon himself.

Keith Boehm, a nineteen-year-old East High School student, lived at the Southard Hotel, a rooming house for bachelors that his parents operated. On Tuesday evening, January 6, six men entered the Southard, flashed badges, and identified themselves as police officers. They told the boy's mother, Evelyn Boehm, that they were responding to complaints about liquor and prostitution. Three of the men went upstairs with Mrs. Boehm to search the guests' rooms. The others stayed behind, guarding the exits and questioning her son. When he admitted that his name was Keith Boehm, they hustled him into an automobile and took off.

Boehm was taken to Locke's office, only two blocks from the rooming house, where the Grand Dragon and several other men were waiting. Mae Nash, the seventeen-year-old daughter of a Klansman, known to be in a "delicate condition," was also present, along with her parents. Questioned about his relationship with Mae, Boehm denied impregnating her. Asked if he would marry the girl, he said he would rather be killed. According to Boehm, he was then taken into Locke's surgery, stripped of his clothes, and strapped to an operating table. A large man brandished a knife and asked, "Will you marry the girl, or shall I operate?"

Boehm explained to the district attorney that he didn't believe he had much choice. "Why, Mr. Van Cise," he said, "I'd have married *you* to get off that table in one piece."

The county clerk was summoned to issue a marriage license. The ceremony was performed in Locke's office by an unshaven Methodist clergyman Boehm didn't recognize. Boehm arrived back at the Southard after midnight and told his mother what had happened. Evelyn Boehm called Chief Candlish, who denied sending any officers to her rooming house. Candlish assigned two detectives to look into the boy's claims, but didn't report the incident to the district attorney. The next day, the Boehms decided to go directly to Van Cise.

Van Cise could hardly believe it—not the kid's story, which he found quite plausible, but Locke's incredible blunder. The

Grand Dragon's contempt for those who succumbed to the sins of the flesh, his tendency to get personally involved in meting out punishment and humiliation to those who strayed from his teachings, had finally caught up with him. By trying to assert his supreme authority over his followers—despite his age, young Boehm was apparently a Klansman—Locke had left himself open to prosecution for kidnapping and assault. Even better, he'd committed these felonious acts in front of multiple witnesses. After talking to the Boehms, Van Cise took additional statements from the county clerk and the minister who'd performed the ceremony. He soon had the names of others who were in Locke's office that night, including Clarence Kirkling, the high-ranking Klan official who had addressed the crowd at the Visible Government debacle at the auditorium last September; William Pritts, one of Locke's enforcers; and H. A. Calvert, a newly elected district judge (Klan membership #601), who claimed to have popped in for "a private business talk with Dr. Locke" and hastily exited. Several of the witnesses told conflicting stories. The county clerk insisted he had no knowledge of any forced wedding and had merely prepared a duplicate license to replace one Boehm had been issued a year before but never used. Boehm claimed the previous license was just a joke, while Mae Nash claimed Boehm had shown her that license in a previous wooing session to convince her that they were already married.

Locke wasted no time giving his version of events to the press. He said Boehm came to his office willingly, in the company of several men whom he described as "friends of the girl." Boehm admitted to him that he'd obtained a marriage license a year earlier for the sole purpose of deceiving and seducing Mae Nash. "I told Boehm plainly what I thought of him as a man and what I thought of him as a Klansman," Locke said, "and I told him that the only manly thing for him to do would be for him to marry the girl." No force, threats, or coercion had been used, he insisted.

The murkier aspects of the narrative didn't worry Van Cise. Boehm may have been a seducer; he also had committed perjury by claiming to be twenty-one years old in his original application for a marriage license. But the district attorney doubted that even a Klan jury could swallow Locke's account of all these people just happening to converge on his office to amicably settle their differences. Based on the evidence he'd assembled in a few hours of investigation, Van Cise was prepared to charge Locke, Kirkling, and Pritts with kidnapping and conspiracy, along with several "John Doe" defendants to be identified later.

Filing such a case was a risky move, even under the best of circumstances. Doing so as he was heading out the door might be considered irresponsible. He would have no say in how it was prosecuted, or whether it was prosecuted at all. That would be up to his successor, a man whose loyalties were difficult to discern. Since Van Cise had declined to seek a second term, the race for district attorney had pitted Republican Lewis Mowry against Democrat Foster Cline. Both men had been approached by the Klan to join, and claimed to have repudiated the group. Locke had initially backed Mowry, a deputy DA in Van Cise's office, hopeful that the Klan could blackmail the candidate over an extramarital affair. But Mowry publicly acknowledged the affair rather than give in to Locke's demands. Locke had then urged his followers to vote for Cline, who was described at one Klan meeting as "a white man and a Mason . . . who after the election would probably be a Klansman." Cline won by less than four thousand votes.

Van Cise didn't know if Cline would drop the kidnapping

case like a hot poker. He didn't know if a Klan judge would deep-six it, or if a Klan jury would hang it up in mistrials. To give the case the best possible chance for survival, he filed it in the juvenile court, making use of a statute that granted concurrent jurisdiction to juvenile and district court in cases involving a minor. That move put the case in the hands of Judge Ben Lindsey, who had barely held on to his seat on the bench in the recent election, fending off a ferocious Klan effort to oust him. Lindsey promptly signed arrest warrants for Locke, Kirkling, and Pritts.

Kirkling donned a disguise and fled the city; he and Pritts would not turn themselves in for several days. Locke was arrested at his office by Lindsey's probation officer. He appeared in court on a Friday afternoon with his attorney, Ben Laska— the same resourceful criminal lawyer who, almost exactly a year before, had claimed to have been abducted, beaten, and threatened by Klansmen himself. A glum Clarence Morley paid the one-thousand-dollar cash bail.

It was Van Cise's second-to-last day on the job.

———

CLARENCE MORLEY'S FIRST OFFICIAL ACTIONS as governor did not go well. He issued executive orders firing the head of the state militia, Adjutant General Paul Newlon, along with two of his top aides. But Newlon and his men refused to be fired.

Governor Sweet, Morley's predecessor, had tried to get rid of Newlon, too, viewing him as a partisan holdover from a previous administration. Sweet, too, had failed. A 1921 law, intended to protect the Colorado National Guard leadership from political interference, shielded Newlon from dismissal without a court-martial conviction. When Morley sent his hand-picked replacement to give Newlon the heave-ho,

Newlon declined to vacate his office. Captain Alphonse Ardourel, a disbursement officer whom Morley also tried to dismiss, slept in Newlon's office that night to prevent the insurgents from moving in. The "siege" of Newlon's office became the kind of low comedy that provides grist for editorial cartoonists. Newlon ultimately prevailed in court. It would take six years, a change in the law, and a much wilier governor to dislodge him.

Morley's inability to seize control of the militia was a portent of greater failures to come. The administration had expected little resistance to its legislative initiatives, given the hefty Republican majority in both houses of the Colorado General Assembly. In the House, the GOP advantage was an overwhelming 52–13; in the Senate, the tally was a more modest but still comfortable twenty-one Republicans to fourteen Democrats. The deck was so heavily stacked in the new regime's favor, it seemed, that it should have been able to enact its slew of social reforms and fill state government offices with Klansmen without breaking a sweat.

But party affiliation didn't translate into blind obedience to party leadership—especially when the leadership's agenda was as extreme as what Morley and his team were proposing. Nine of the Senate Republicans, including six who'd been elected in 1922, had no Klan ties. They had made no deals with Locke, never submitted to the Grand Dragon any undated letters of resignation, like the ones Locke reportedly demanded from candidates the Klan backed, as a way of insuring their loyalty. The nine senators were an independent bloc, which gave them the strongest hand in the game.

Morley's team found out they were in trouble in the opening days of the session. The rogue Republicans balked at undesirable committee assignments and refused to participate in the caucus process, which would have bound them to the majority vote. They allied themselves with the savvy Senate minority leader, Billy Adams, who'd been a key player at the statehouse for an astonishing thirty-eight years. The Klan could count on perhaps a dozen Republicans in the Senate, as well as two or three defectors among the Democrats, but that still left the anti-Klan coalition with a firm 20–15 advantage. Efforts by the Klan leadership to mollify the dissenters by offering them plum committee assignments only strengthened the anti-Kluxers' position.

Morley saw many of his favorite bills sail through the House, only to be scuttled in the Senate. Some were killed outright; others were dispatched to obscure committees to perish of neglect or linger in a vegetative state, awaiting a hearing date that was never scheduled or eternally postponed. Minority leader Adams was a master at sabotaging legislation he didn't like, and in the Klan bills there was a lot not to like. The group's crusade against immigrants alarmed agricultural and industrial interests that depended on cheap labor. The effort to ban sacramental wine offended Episcopalians as well as Catholics, and even some temperance groups spoke out against it. (It never got out of a House committee.) Other bills, pushing sterilization of epileptics or compulsory religious instruction, raised awkward humanitarian and church-state issues.

As for Morley's proposals to reorganize state government, it soon became apparent that the targets were not merely redundant or archaic commissions, but vital oversight of food safety, health care professionals, and the government itself. The larger plan seemed to be to abolish many posts that Morley couldn't control, then reconstitute them with Klan members in charge—returning state agencies to the spoils system long enough to populate them with Kluxers, who would remain on the job long after the Morley administration was over.

Billy Adams and his allies throttled many of these efforts. Over the next twelve weeks, the impotence of the new regime became apparent. Far from the brief, robust collaboration Morley had predicted, the 1925 legislative session was the most contentious and least productive in state history. More than eight hundred of the thousand-plus bills introduced went down in flames. Of those that passed, many were so inconsequential that they could scarcely be described as Klan victories. The Board of Horseshoe Examiners was abolished. Colorado schools were now required to fly the American flag. The individual bag limit for ducks was increased from ten to twenty-five per day. The blue columbine was designated as the state flower and protected from reckless pickers.

Morley sulked and plotted revenge on the anti-Klan faction in the Senate. He paid back a few of his opponents by punishing their constituents, holding back appropriations for the University of Colorado, the Pueblo state fair, and the teachers' college Billy Adams had launched in Alamosa, the Adams State Normal School. The tantrums only alienated more lawmakers and highlighted how ineffective Morley had been. He purged various boards of perceived enemies and named as many Klan appointees as he could to replace them. Many of these actions were later challenged and undone in court.

His critics began to refer to him as Clarence the Little. If that government is best that governs least, they quipped, then the Morley administration was the best bunch the state had ever seen. But mockery from outsiders wasn't nearly as worrisome as the reaction within the Klan itself. Locke's arrest for kidnapping, followed by defeat after defeat in the statehouse, had sown doubts about the Colorado Realm among the rank and file as well as the national leadership. If the Klan couldn't provide jobs for real Americans, save orphaned babies from the clutches of the Catholics, or keep its own Grand Dragon out of the pokey, what good was it?

Despite the carping, many people were still fiercely loyal to Locke, including the governor. A couple of weeks after posting his hero's bail, Morley appointed Locke to the position of colonel in the Colorado National Guard's medical corps, assigned to the governor's staff as a recruiting and publicity officer. The commission was problematic; for one thing, the available ranks in the medical corps didn't extend as high as colonel. But it provided an opportunity for Locke, so fond of dress-up, to be photographed for the newspapers in full dress uniform, staring calmly into the distance, chest beribboned and jodhpurs neatly tucked into gleaming black riding boots. It was the image of a man in complete command of his troops, his faculties, and his cunningly minimized waistline. In the presence of such crispness, discipline, and authority, it was hard to detect the turmoil behind the scenes, the factions forming, the internal bickerings and betrayals gnawing away at the organization he had built—an empire that he'd once compared to the U.S. Army, "where the command of a superior officer is never questioned when given, and where the honor of one is the honor and responsibility of all."

THE WAY IT WAS EXPLAINED to Adolf Hecker, if you wanted a job with the City of Denver, particularly a job that dealt in any way with Prohibition enforcement, you had to go along with the graft. If you wanted to keep the job, you had to join the Klan. And if you wanted to stay healthy, you didn't double-cross the bootleggers or the Klan.

At least, those were the rules when he signed up. But it all changed in the spring of 1925, and people you never thought had it in them started going against the Klan, jumping ship like rats.

The son of a former state senator, Hecker used his father's political connections to obtain a job with the city shortly after Stapleton's election. The first position he landed, working at the city hospital, didn't appeal to him, so he asked the mayor to find him something better. Stapleton arranged for Hecker to work as a health inspector out of the Manager of Safety's office, a job that paid $180 a month. One of his duties was inspecting soft-drink parlors. Many of the parlors were serving something stronger than Coca-Cola. At first, when Hecker came across whiskey, he would seize the parlor's license—only to find it back on the wall on his next visit. He soon realized that the parlors were paying off someone above his pay grade and that he was depriving himself of extra income by bucking the system. "I went to taking their money and leaving their licenses on the wall," he explained in a memoir published nearly sixty years later.

At the prompting of police officers he knew, he also joined the Klan. It was the only way to hold on to his job, he was told. Locke befriended him, presented him with a special purple robe with silver lining and gold trim, and asked him to join the elite squad of Klansmen who patrolled the Castle Mountain meetings on horseback, making sure no interlopers made their way onto the mesa. Hecker, who'd learned horsemanship at a local riding academy, was happy to oblige.

His rising status in the Klan helped Hecker expand his shakedown schemes, and his growing connections and influence as a city employee made him an increasing asset to the Kluxers. He took payoffs from taxi drivers who delivered hooch all over town and from madams seeking protection for their girls. He claimed to have persuaded Stapleton to give him temporary authority over some police assignments, in hopes of turning up the heat on the bootleggers; instead, Hecker used his position to rake in payments from Klan cops seeking easy beats or a posting to the bootleg squad, where there was real money to be made. As a token of their esteem, bootleggers arranged for a two-carat diamond to be set in Hecker's Manager of Safety badge.

Stapleton quickly grew tired of Hecker's empty promises, just as he'd soured on Chief Candlish's assurances that his men were winning the rum wars. At heart the mayor was a puritanical man, uncomfortable around any displays of vulgarity or vice. He didn't appreciate his administration being turned into a laughingstock by the bootleggers while his Klan-riddled police force grew fat on the graft. He had needed Locke and his lot for the election, and again for the recall. But now, with the instincts of a veteran politician, he sensed the group's vulnerability and resolved to distance himself from them. It was time to try something else—something that would clarify, once and for all, who ran City Hall.

On the Friday before Easter, Stapleton shocked the city by overseeing a massive sweep of bootlegging operations and related criminal enterprises, dispatching dozens of officers to conduct hundreds of arrests. A *Post* reporter described the Good Friday raids as "a gargantuan mop-up of bootleggers, moonshiners, gamblers, lewd women and human dregs of the underworld." The action had been months in the making. The mayor had borrowed heavily from the playbook Van Cise had developed for the bunco investigation three years earlier. Like the Fighting DA, Stapleton kept the police chief and his top detectives out of the loop; relied heavily on police from other jurisdictions, volunteers, and other outsiders to make the arrests; and even used a church as a command center to keep word of the raids from leaking out too soon. The suspects piled up in the county jail, where they were held without bail through the Easter weekend.

Not much actual booze was seized in the raids, but that wasn't the objective. The mayor's team had identified numerous bootleggers who'd been paying cops for protection—and might be persuaded to testify about the arrangements, now that they were guests of the state. A few days after the raids, Stapleton ordered Chief Candlish to suspend three sergeants and eleven patrolmen, for offenses ranging from bribery to selling confiscated whiskey and helping themselves to cash seized in gambling raids. Most of the suspended officers were soon fired, and several faced criminal charges.

More raids followed. Hecker's thin memoir doesn't explain how he escaped the dragnet, but he was hardly the only one. The corruption and money-making opportunities associated with Prohibition enforcement were simply too pervasive to be eradicated by gangbusting tactics. Still, Stapleton's raids boosted his popularity; they were also a repudiation of the Klan. Several of the disgraced members of the bootleg squad were Klansmen. Candlish, the Klan police chief, had been exposed as unreliable and would soon be out the door. The criminal side of the Klan, jarringly at odds with Locke's sermons on the evils of rum-running and the Klan vows to clean up the town, was now too obvious to ignore.

Just how much Locke knew about the corruption on the force is debatable, but he clearly tried to shield Klan members from jail. Otto Moore, who'd stayed on at the district attorney's office after Van Cise's departure, handled many of the prosecutions stemming from the Good Friday raids, including one larceny case against several officers of the bootleg squad, who were accused of seizing seventeen cases of whiskey from one bootlegger and selling them to another at forty dollars a case. Shortly before the case came to trial, a *Rocky Mountain News* reporter visited Moore and told him he'd just come from Locke's office. He had hoped to interview the Grand Dragon, but Locke was in conference with the police defendants, their lawyer, and Henry Bray, the Klan judge who would be trying the case. The transom was open, the reporter said, and he listened as Locke instructed the defense attorney to make a motion for acquittal in his opening statement—and ordered the judge to grant it.

At trial the defense attorney argued that because whiskey was illegal, no property right could be asserted in connection with it, and thus there was no larceny. Over Moore's strident objections, Judge Bray granted the motion for acquittal. Moore took the case to the Colorado Supreme Court, which shredded Bray's ruling into confetti: "Defendants' position was that by reason of this statute intoxicating liquor is so completely outlawed that if a home be broken into to get it, there is no burglary; if a citizen be held up at the point of a pistol and deprived of it, there is no robbery . . . the construction given the act in question by the trial court is fraught with such momentous and disastrous results that we would need go no further than invoke against it the fundamental rule that absurd interpretations will not be given statutes when reasonable ones may be resorted to."

———

Van Cise followed his enemies' legal troubles from a frustrating distance. The gangbuster was a private citizen now. Whether Stapleton cleaned house, whether Locke went down for kidnapping—it was all out of his hands. But he still had a part to play, and he took comfort in a strange private ceremony held a few months after he left office.

One spring evening he was taken in hand—"in custody," he later called it—by a trusted friend, who insisted on accompanying him home. The man made him wait outside the house, which had all the shades drawn, until seconds before six o'clock. Then he hurried him inside, where a group of men in black robes and black masks sat around the dining room table. The room was lit only by candles, casting a warm glow on an expensive radio at the center of the table. Van Cise sat down in front of it, just in time to hear a speech being broadcast from a local studio. It was a tribute to him for his years of public service, prepared by the donors who had funded his bunco investigation. Several of them had come in person, albeit in disguise, to honor him.

The costumes may have been an allusion to the judiciary, or perhaps a show of support for Van Cise's battle against the white-robed Kluxers. Either way, he was quite moved by the whole business. He wrote to one of the instigators to thank the group for "your wonderful and unexpected gift." The letter made it clear that the gift he cherished the most wasn't the radio but the compliment they had paid him by their presence and the surprise on-the-air homage. "All I can say is that I was glad to have an opportunity to do my duty as a public official," he wrote. "I appreciated your support at that time, but value far more highly your present interest as friends. I hope that I may never disappoint your confidence in me."

———————

MAYOR STAPLETON'S BREAK WITH LOCKE was one of several public ruptures that left the Grand Dragon marveling at the treachery and ingratitude of his subjects. Another turncoat was state senator Harry Saunders, a criminal attorney and former close friend whom Locke had cast out of the Klan in 1924 for disloyalty. With Stapleton's encouragement, Saunders became involved in trying to incorporate a rival group called the Knights of the Ku Klux Klan of Colorado. The dispute over who had the rights to the KKK name in the state led to a federal lawsuit, ultimately decided in Locke's favor.

Locke had a knack for smoothing over disagreements with people he deemed useful, and he and the well-connected Saunders eventually reconciled. But the doctor's biggest worry was also his finest creation: Rice Means. A perpetual political also-ran before he joined the Klan, Means had, with Locke's help, moved quickly from manager of safety to city attorney to a seat in the U.S. Senate. Means was a dynamic speaker and an accomplished gladhander; he was also just about the only one of the Colorado Klan's Spanish-American War heroes who could plausibly claim to have seen combat.* He and Locke had been in an uneasy rivalry for years, and Locke believed he was owed more consideration from Means than he was getting, now that the latter was in Washington. He confided to his most trusted aides that he suspected Means of plotting against him, meeting with the Imperial Wizard behind his back, and seeking to have him removed as Grand Dragon.

The intrigues led to a visit to Denver that spring by William Zumbrunn, the national counsel for the Klan. Locke and Means both threw receptions for Zumbrunn and his wife, but Locke was excluded from a dinner party that Means hosted. In a conversation with Locke's chauffeur, Zumbrunn expressed his admiration of Locke and hinted that the good doctor might

---

* The fact that people referred to both Means and Van Cise as "Colonel" may have influenced Morley's appointment of Locke to the rank of colonel in the Colorado National Guard. Locke didn't like being outranked.

be invited to join the Imperial Kloncilium, an advisory board that also functioned as the Klan's judicial arm. It was one of those promotions that were actually demotions, reminiscent of the way Imperial Wizard Evans had disposed of his predecessor, Joe Simmons, by making him Emperor.

Locke wasn't planning on going anywhere. But the national Klan's concerns about his leadership extended beyond the poor showing at the statehouse or even the kidnapping charge—which was still hanging over Locke's head, despite his lawyers' efforts to get the case moved out of Judge Lindsey's courtroom. In May, court filings revealed that Locke was under federal investigation for tax evasion. The law required any unmarried individual with annual income of one thousand dollars or more to file a tax return. Locke had not filed a return in the past eleven years—not since the Sixteenth Amendment, granting Congress the power to tax personal income, was first passed.

Locke loyalists suspected that Rice Means had sicced the tax men on their beloved leader—or had, at the very least, failed to use his influence to block the investigation. Others believed that the investigation was triggered by gossip about the money Senator Phipps paid Locke to buy the Klan vote in the 1924 election, or possibly by reports that Locke had profited handsomely from the sale of tens of thousands of Klan robes at $6.50 each. Tax problems would bedevil numerous Klan officials over the next few years; such troubles weren't surprising among leaders of a cash-heavy organization with loose accounting and many opportunities for skimming, both at the local and national level. In his 1925 exposé *The Maelstrom: The Visible of the Invisible Empire*, Klan insider Edgar Fuller, the former aide of Imperial Kleagle Edward Clarke, estimated that tens of millions of dollars flowed through the

national KKK—from initiation fees, robes, dues, and more—
with little chance of ever being traced:

> A statement showing receipts and disbursements
> has never been made. Any number of audits by expert
> accountants have been made, but these audits have
> shown, simply, assets and liabilities of the organiza-
> tion. A record has never, or, for that matter, will never
> be given to the Klan or to members of the Klan, or to
> the public, as to the amount of money received from
> any state in the Union, and how it has been disbursed.

In Locke's case, the elegant car and diamonds, the stories
about bags of cash and buried treasure chests, the aura of luxury enveloping a man who claimed to subsist on the humble
fees of a homeopath, were bound to attract attention sooner
or later. How much Locke was making off Klan operations
in Colorado and whether he was declaring the income were
matters of endless speculation among friends and foes alike. "I
certainly would like to see his income tax return," one of Van
Cise's undercover agents remarked in a surveillance report.

Locke's lawyers responded to the tax investigation with
stall tactics. A court pleading claimed that his personal
financial records from 1913 through 1918 were destroyed
by "the Japanese housecleaning force" that tidied his office.
Locke missed one examination appointment because he was
in Colorado Springs, attending a hearing on the Boehm kidnapping case; Judge Lindsey had refused to transfer the case
to one of the Klan judges in Denver, moving it to El Paso
County instead. Locke fended off other inquiries from tax
examiners by claiming his account books contained confidential information, such as his patients' names. His lawyers
argued that the tax probe was a vendetta against the Klan,

and that allowing federal inspection of certain bank records would violate the Klan's rights.

U.S. District Judge Foster Symes was not impressed by this barrage. He ordered Locke to produce his records and meet with tax agents. But when Locke next appeared in court, he had no records to offer. One of his lawyers provided a confusing account of how Locke's ledger books had been accidentally left in an automobile parked outside the courthouse, then mysteriously disappeared before they could be retrieved. Judge Symes listened to the dog-ate-my-homework tale with mounting irritation and disbelief. Not even the eloquent pleadings of attorney Ben Laska, who insisted his client was a victim of circumstance, could placate the judge. Symes declared Locke to be in contempt of court and sentenced him to confinement in the Denver county jail "until he has purged himself of such contempt, or until further order of the court."

A federal marshal escorted Locke to his cell. Locke continued to protest his innocence as he was being booked. "I am a martyr to the Klan," he said. (Nearly two years later, former Klan enforcer Joseph Bushnell would provide an affidavit to private investigators that touched on the mystery of the missing ledgers. Bushnell described how Locke vacillated over surrendering what financial records he did have, fearing that the government could prove that they were backdated and false. At the last minute, he turned the ledgers over to Bushnell and another Klansman, who returned them to Locke's office. Another witness recalled Locke boasting, "I guess we gave them a good screwing on the books, didn't we?")

At the county jail, Locke was treated with a deference usually reserved for movie stars. He had dozens of visitors every day, male and female, bearing boxes of cigars, bouquets of flowers, and bags of candy. Governor Morley was one of the first and most frequent callers. Right after his inauguration, the governor had set up a special telephone and messenger at his office so that he could keep in constant communication with his mentor. Now that Locke was behind bars, the governor had to visit him in person, giving onlookers the all-too-accurate impression that the most powerful man in the state took his marching orders from a jailbird. It was an unsuitable arrangement all around, putting pressure on Locke's defense team to find a way to spring the Grand Dragon as soon as possible.

Attorney Laska asked Judge Symes to impose a definite sentence for the contempt charge. Symes agreed, sentencing Locke to ten days in jail and fining him fifteen hundred dollars. Since Locke claimed to have no funds of his own to pay the fine, Morley ordered the state auditor to issue a check to Locke in the amount of $1599, a sum that was supposedly his salary over the past six months as a colonel in the Colorado National Guard. The notion that taxpayers should pay Locke's fine for failing to cooperate in a tax investigation drew outraged editorials, thinly disguised as news stories. Locke had done nothing to earn his salary, and nobody in the Guard seemed to think his colonelship was anything but an honorific. The Colorado attorney general blocked the payment, ruling that Locke's appointment wasn't properly authorized. Soon Locke's commission was revoked, too; he could not continue to be an officer in the Guard after being sentenced to a term of imprisonment by a civil court.

Halfway through the ten-day sentence, the fine was paid with funds raised by unspecified friends of the Grand Dragon. On the morning of June 22, Locke emerged from the jail a free man, purged of contempt. He was met by top aides Joe Bushnell and Jack Martin and whisked away by automobile. The tax problem still lingered, but within a few weeks he would agree to pay $14,700, the arbitrary amount the Bureau of Internal Revenue had assessed against him for delinquent income tax. Presented in cash to the tax collector by Governor Morley, the $14,700 came from a few generous donors, eager to see Locke's tax problems resolved. (Morley would later testify that most of the money came from an oilman, whom Morley subsequently appointed to a state board, and Locke's sister; according to the governor, he was "nothing but an errand boy" in the transaction.)

The newspapers reported that the cash payment settled the matter, but that wasn't accurate. The payment only covered the Grand Dragon's tax liability through 1922. The government would eventually seek another $30,000 in taxes on purported income in 1923 and 1924, based on the discovery of a bank account containing close to $150,000. Locke maintained that he was merely the agent overseeing the account, that the funds on deposit belonged to the Klan, and that he never received a penny in recompense for his services to the Invisible Empire. The dispute would drag on for years, raising questions about how a fraternal organization, chartered for benevolent and patriotic purposes, managed to have that kind of cash sitting around; how much actually went to charitable activities; and which local or national Klan officials ended up pocketing the rest.

Locke had more success extricating himself from the kidnapping charge. Laska got the case moved back to Denver from Colorado Springs and placed in the hands of a Klan judge, who threw it out on the grounds that it had endured too many changes of venue. District Attorney Cline chose not to refile the charges. No longer of much interest to the press, the marriage of Keith Boehm and Mae Nash was not a happy one—Mae's baby girl died before her second birthday—and was eventually annulled.

It was a season of troubled unions and messy divorces. The Grand Dragon may have thought that he was finally in a position to put all these misunderstandings about money and kidnapping behind him, but he had badly shaken the confidence of people who had once been quite smitten with him. Imperial Wizard Evans, for one, had had enough. A week after he was released from jail, Locke had another visit from William Zumbrunn, the national Klan's chief attorney, bearing a message from Evans. This time the Imperial Klonsel was accompanied by two other Klan officials, a sizable delegation sent for the sole purpose of hand-delivering a letter from a Dallas dentist to a Denver physician.

Imperial Wizard Evans thanked Dr. Locke for his loyalty and his service. Then he demanded that Locke resign immediately as Grand Dragon of the Colorado Realm of the Ku Klux Klan.

11

Collapse

Zumbrunn delivered the Imperial Wizard's letter on a Sunday. Locke called for an emergency meeting of the Colorado Realm on Tuesday night at the Cotton Mills stadium. It was the largest gathering the venue had ever seen, filling the surrounding vacant lots with cars and drawing an overflow crowd that listened to the unfolding drama on loudspeakers outside the building. As usual, the newspapers couldn't agree on the actual numbers. The *Denver Post* estimated the crowd at upwards of thirty thousand. The skeptical *Express* pointed out that the building's capacity was about one-fifth of that figure.

Locke was in fine form. He deplored the disloyalty of Means, Stapleton, and several other feckless Klansmen and announced that their memberships had been suspended. The horde heartily approved. He read Evans's letter demanding his resignation and drew howls of protest. He insisted that he would resign, like a good soldier, and was greeted with even more strenuous objections. This evolved into an energetic, possibly spontaneous outbreak of applause for the Grand Dragon, a deafening show of support that drowned out any discussion. During lulls in the demonstration, puffed-up titans and kligrapps declared that if Locke's resignation was accepted, they too, would leave—and take their klaverns with them. One admirer squeezed onto the crowded platform long enough to present Locke with a costly imported gold wristwatch, a bauble that was clearly not 100 percent American.

Zumbrunn and the two national Klan officials he'd brought with him stayed until the wee hours, watching the crowd rally around Locke. The national organization had rarely meddled in Colorado's affairs, and many of the assembled seemed to regard Zumbrunn and his men as interlopers, conspirators with Means and Stapleton in a plot against their beloved leader. To appease them, Zumbrunn announced that Locke's resignation would not proceed until he'd had a chance to consult further with the Imperial Wizard. On that conciliatory note, the meeting finally broke up at one in the morning.

The next day the Grand Dragon received a stream of visitors at his office on Glenarm Place, imploring him not to resign. To most of them, he gave a standard response about being a humble servant of the Invisible Empire, a soldier whose duty is to obey. "I know there are a dozen men in this city more capable than I to direct the affairs of the Klan," he told his favorite reporter, Frances Wayne.

Alone with his closest lieutenants, he was more candid. He told Joseph Bushnell that, regardless of what Zumbrunn said, the Imperial Wizard would not back down. Evans wanted him gone. This business about further consultation was just a ruse to buy time, he explained, while the boys in Atlanta tried to figure out how to avoid a schism that would cost them most of their Colorado membership and property. They wanted to ease him out while keeping what he had built. But they had not expected the emphatic show of support at the stadium, and Locke had a few other surprises in store for them. He gave Bushnell instructions and dispatched him on a secret mission to the Secretary of State's office.

For two weeks, a delicate truce prevailed. Rumors circulated that most of the klaverns in Colorado were poised to secede, or that Locke, with the backing of other disgruntled Grand Dragons, would lead a coup and supplant Evans as Imperial Wizard. But Evans didn't press for Locke's resignation, and Locke continued to profess his undying allegiance to the Invisible Empire. Then on Friday, July 17, in the span of a few minutes, the Ku Klux Klan of Colorado split into two unreconcilable camps.

That evening Coca-Cola Candlish, recently fired as police chief by Mayor Stapleton, addressed a crowd of thousands at the Cotton Mills. He read a telegram from Imperial Wizard Evans, instructing the local leadership to hand over all Klan funds and property to his representatives, who would be arriving shortly in Colorado. This news was met with boos and another demonstration on behalf of Locke. The Denver klavern, Klavern No. 1, voted to secede on the spot. Men removed their hoods. A few of them tore down an electric fiery cross and carried it away. The aggrieved were directed to line up in front of booths at one end of the arena, where Klan cards could be exchanged for membership in something called the Minute Men of America.

Supposedly ill at home, Locke didn't attend the meeting. Contacted by reporters, he expressed dismay at the revolt and claimed to have no involvement in the Minute Men. He insisted he was still loyal to the Klan and its principles. As with many of Locke's public utterances, these were brazen lies, designed to sow confusion among his enemies. Acting on Locke's orders,

Bushnell had filed incorporation papers for the Minute Men of America on July 3, listing himself as president. A filing for the Minute Women of America soon followed.

The Minute Men was Locke's conception, a patriotic organization that would be much broader in scope than the Klan—and much flashier, its members decked out in Revolutionary War uniforms, including a tricorn hat, waistcoat, and knee breeches. No masks, no Southern hoodoo, just good old Yankee Doodle stuff. The group would be open to all white, native-born adult males, not just Protestants. Although clearly based on the Klan template and its creed of white supremacy, the Minute Men mission statement emphasized tolerance rather than hate: "To cultivate the worship of God, according to the dictates of individual conscience, to maintain law and order, protect our pure womanhood, promote charity, support the sovereignty of states' rights, freedom of speech and press, separation of church and state, closer relation between American capital and American labor, limitation of foreign immigration."

Once again Zumbrunn and a contingent of national Klan officers flew to Denver to deal with the evolving crisis. Over the past four years, Klan executives had acquired considerable experience dealing with insurrectionists and splinter groups. Zumbrunn moved quickly to file court papers, seeking to establish a receivership for the Denver klavern and to impose a restraining order on Minute Men officers, prohibiting them from disposing of Klan property, divulging Klan secrets, or recruiting current Klan members. Locke rejected a proposed sit-down with national Klan officials at the Brown Palace, hinting that some further treachery was in the works. A meeting was then arranged on "neutral ground"—Governor Morley's office. Zumbrunn huddled with Locke, the Denver city attorney, and a Klansman state senator for three hours. Morley popped in and out of the room during the discussion.

Locke once again tendered his resignation as Grand Dragon. This time it was accepted. Imperial Wizard Evans reinstated Means, Stapleton, and the others Locke had summarily purged. Then he issued a decree banishing Locke from the Invisible Empire, claiming that he "did knowingly and willfully violate the laws of this order," but declining to make public what his offenses had been. His banishment led to another angry pro-Locke demonstration at the Cotton Mills, amid renewed calls for secession. At the last minute, Evans reportedly had second thoughts and offered Locke reinstatement, only to be rebuffed.

Locke turned over to Zumbrunn a cache of records and $23,535.43 in cash, represented as the entire amount of the Klan treasury for the Colorado Realm. In return, Zumbrunn provided Locke with a release from any claims against him by the national office and an effusive letter, praising him for "building one of the most effective and powerful state organizations; this you have accomplished only through giving your every thought and energy to the work; you served the Klan without personal reward or compensation and because you loved the things you were doing."

The matter of the Klan's real estate in Colorado would not be so easily settled. The most significant asset by far was the Cotton Mills stadium, but its ownership was in dispute. It had been acquired for Klan use through the sale of $57,000 in bonds to hundreds of individual backers—many of whom were now Minute Men. Thanks to some paperwork filed shortly before Zumbrunn's team arrived, the title to the property was held in the name of Locke aide Jack Martin, and the mortgage holder on behalf of the bond investors was the former police chief,

William Candlish. It was the Minute Men's position that Zumbrunn couldn't take control of the venue until the Klan had reimbursed the bondholders. The Klan officials soon discovered that the records of the bond sales were fragmentary and poorly maintained. What they could piece together from receipts and sales books indicated significant shortages of cash that had been received and never deposited in the building account.

The bond sales weren't the only records problem. While Locke was negotiating his exit, his lieutenants were hard at work covering his tracks. Joe Bushnell would later recall removing records and robes stored at the Cotton Mills and hiding them at another member's ranch. On another night, he participated in a midnight bonfire at the home of Clarence Kirkling. The two men burned armfuls of Klan records—membership applications, kleagle reports, receipts for initiation fees, orders for robes, and more—in an effort to make the national Klan's takeover of the Colorado Realm as difficult as possible.

Many Klan members in southern and western Colorado elected to stay with the national organization. But the mass exodus in Denver and other northern cities hollowed out the state's largest klaverns and deprived the Klan of much of its political clout. It's estimated that a third of the Klan members in Colorado defected to the Minute Men. But thousands of others responded to the schism by shunning both organizations.

Secretary of State Carl Milliken was in the latter camp. A Kluxer since 1921, he severed ties with the group shortly after Locke's departure, claiming that Klan officials had tried to pressure him to discharge his chief deputy, the son-in-law of a Klan enemy. "I am all through with this kind of an organization," Milliken told reporters. He then fired his deputy labor commissioner, Carl DeLochte, for being "influenced by outside interests."

DeLochte, the head of the Royal Riders of the Red Robe, the Klan subsidiary for foreign-born Protestants, had many outside interests to consider. On one hand, the Klan under Doc Locke had treated him well. On the other, his close friend Governor Morley and the Doc himself were siding with the Minute Men, a group DeLochte would not be allowed to join because he was born in Canada. Asked where he might land, DeLochte conceded that his group would probably ally itself with the Minute Men anyway, for the betterment of Colorado. Other prominent figures in the Colorado Realm, including former Great Titan Gano Senter, former Exalted Cyclops Rex Yeager, and several Klan judges, decided to cross over to the Minute Men, too. They were all loyal to Locke—who, after several weeks of feigned reluctance, was finally "persuaded" to head the organization.

His grand inauguration as supreme commander of this new national movement took place at the Cotton Mills, amid much pomp and ceremony. Locke appeared in a magnificently ornate costume, inspired by George Washington's livery: a voluminous waistcoat with red trim, cuffs and collar of fine lace, doeskin vest and breeches (made from the hide of a deer the doctor had potted himself), plumed tricorn hat. More than anything he said that night, his outfit declared his intention to create a fraternal order that would utterly eclipse the Klan, not only in size and influence but sartorial splendor.

The ovation that greeted him raged for half an hour.

———

THE INTERNAL WARFARE THAT DECIMATED the Colorado Klan that summer was not an isolated phenomenon. Across the country, the organization was convulsed by scandals, schisms, lawsuits, and criminal prosecutions that signaled the beginning of the end of the Klan's viability as a mainstream political entity. The group was shedding members even more rapidly than it had acquired them. After reaching its peak strength of between two and four million people in 1925, the Invisible Empire lost more than 80 percent of its following in a matter of months. By the end of the decade less than one hundred thousand active Klansmen remained.

Law enforcement efforts to crack down on masked demonstrations and vigilantism may have played a role in the decline, but most of the wounds were self-inflicted. In Oregon, squabbling between Grand Dragon Fred Gifford and rival factions led to accusations of fraud and rounds of expulsions. In Georgia, the protracted feud at headquarters between backers of Joe Simmons and those who supported Hiram Evans spilled into local klaverns and drove away prospects; it also led to the fatal shooting of Simmons attorney William Coburn by a mentally unstable Evans supporter, *Imperial Night-Hawk* editor Philip Fox. In Pennsylvania, the Klan took several banished members to federal court, alleging fraud and theft, only to be denounced as a criminal enterprise by an unsympathetic federal judge, W. H. Seward Thomson. The KKK was brutal, despotic, and "a continuing menace to the public peace," Thomson found, and Evans was "directly responsible" for a riot at a 1923 Klan rally in the town of Carnegie, which left one person dead.

In Arkansas, Little Rock Klan No. 1 seceded from the Invisible Empire, spearheading a general revolt against Grand Dragon James Comer. Comer, who had worked closely with Evans on the palace coup that removed Simmons from power, stood accused of feathering his own nest at his followers' expense and having the audacity to propose, as a money-making scheme, the establishment of "a Negro Ku Klux Klan." There were also ugly rumors that Comer's wife, Robbie Gill, used her position as Imperial Commander of the Women of the Ku Klux Klan to embezzle seventy thousand dollars of that group's funds for personal use; a photo of Robbie Gill wearing a thirty-thousand-dollar diamond-studded crown, allegedly a gift from Imperial Wizard Evans, didn't help matters. The Arkansas Realm and the national WKKK never recovered from the infighting that followed.

The most grotesque fall from grace was in Indiana, where Grand Dragon David Stephenson lorded over the largest, loudest state organization in the country. At the height of its power, roughly a third of Indiana's adult white males were loyal to the Klan, and few Hoosier politicians would dare to make a move without first consulting Stephenson, a charismatic salesman in his early thirties. Stephenson balked at taking orders from Atlanta, and in 1924 the Indiana Klan severed ties with the national office and went on to victory after victory in the November elections. But Stephenson's plans to build his own empire were soon derailed by his violent treatment of women, which escalated from drunken rages to bizarre forms of sexual assault. On March 15, 1925, he insisted that a young woman named Madge Oberholtzer, a recent acquaintance, accompany him on a trip to Chicago. On the train, he attacked her repeatedly, raping and mutilating her, biting her face and neck, tongue and breasts, back and legs. Denied medical help by Stephenson, who kept insisting that she marry him, Oberholtzer slipped away from her captor long enough to consume a deadly amount of mercuric chloride, used for treating syphilis. She died in agony at her parents' house weeks later, after dictating a detailed account of her ordeal. The horrific case drew national attention and sent Stephenson to prison for twenty years for second-degree murder. Subsequent investigations into campaign finance violations led to prison sentences for the mayor of Indianapolis and the chair of the state Republican Party, as well as the indictment of the Klan governor. By 1929 Klan membership in the state had dropped from a quarter-million to four thousand.

Other Klan leaders lacked Stephenson's cannibalistic tendencies, but their arrogance, greed, hypocrisy, and blundering were enough to drive many out of the organization. The leadership had promised so much, with its dreaded boycotts and ambitious legislative agendas, and delivered so little. The Klan's most significant contribution to national policy was its fervent support of the Johnson-Reed Act of 1924, which greatly restricted immigration and imposed quotas designed to preserve the country's existing racial makeup. Asian immigrants were barred entirely, while the quotas for Europeans were skewed in favor of British and German applicants and against southern and eastern Europeans. The bill's passage was a triumph for the guardians of what Simmons called "Anglo-Saxon American civilization." But it didn't make up for all the other ways the Klan had disappointed and misled its followers—while relentlessly dunning them for dues, donations, and klecktokens. Sooner or later, even the most credulous mark begins to rumble to the true nature of the game. Compared to other Big Con operations, the Klan was remarkably short-lived.

Marks get wise, and times change. Most Americans scarcely noticed the Klan's implosion in the summer of 1925. They were too busy savoring the culture war being waged in Dayton, Tennessee, where high school science teacher John Scopes was on trial for defying a state law that prohibited teaching the theory of evolution. The Scopes Monkey Trial was conceived as a media event—local officials wanted to promote the town of Dayton, and Scopes volunteered for the role of defendant to challenge the state law. The trial soon developed into an entertaining inquisition into the fuzzier aspects of fundamentalist Christian cosmology, vigorously prosecuted by attorney Clarence Darrow and feebly defended by ailing demagogue William Jennings Bryan. (Bryan died of a stroke days after the trial ended.) As expected, the verdict went against Scopes, but the press coverage was a catastrophe for the fundamentalist cause. H. L. Mencken and a pack of lesser pundits mercilessly ridiculed Biblical creationism and the backwoods "half-wits" who embraced it. Many Klan leaders tried to stay clear of the controversy, but the incessant mockery of their close allies in the Evangelical community was another blow, more evidence that the Klan was out of step with the frantic pace of the twentieth century.

The most compelling reason for leaving the Klan, though, had nothing to do with the group's stand on evolution or immigration or other policy issues. It was the beatings, bombings, arson, kidnappings, tar-and-feather parties, and other mayhem perpetrated by the self-appointed crusaders for law and order. The prospect of "taking action" had been part of the appeal of the group in its furtive early days, but its continuing reliance on brute force undermined its claims to legitimacy as a political movement. Business-minded Kluxers were embarrassed and alarmed by the threats, bloodshed, arrests, and lurid headlines. Although Evans had attempted to rein in the rough stuff, the essential thuggishness of the Klan couldn't be denied. Violence was in its genes, in its lineage of white supremacy. It was implicit in its pledges to defend and avenge a social order that no longer existed.

Even in Colorado, where the Klan devoted most of its energy to boycotts and rigging juries and elections, violence was never far away. Walter Walker, editor and publisher of the Grand Junction *Daily Sentinel*, contributed cash and publicity to help establish the Klan on Colorado's Western Slope. After being passed over for the position of Exalted Cyclops in favor of another candidate, he broke with the Klan and began writing editorials critical of the group's takeover of city and state government. On September 3, 1925, a Klansman deputy sheriff confronted Walker on Main Street, cursed him, and proceeded to beat him, punching him every time he tried to get up from the sidewalk. Far from striking fear in the populace, the assault generated sympathy for Walker, a jail sentence for the deputy, and assertions that the Klan was on its last legs.

"The Klan is scotched," commented the Colorado Springs *Gazette* in an account of the Walker beating. "It blazed up as quickly as its kerosene-soaked fiery crosses, and for a time it found Colorado a golden harvest. But it could not hide its greed, nor could it control its viciousness."

"The Klan is on the down grade—busted into several different parts," Judge Ben Lindsey observed in a letter to an Indiana journalist a few months later, "with the old timers fighting each other like cats and dogs and each ready to squeal on the other."

———

SHORTLY AFTER LEAVING the district attorney's office, Van Cise opened a law firm with his former chief deputy, Kenneth Robinson. They turned down many criminal defense cases; both men wanted to avoid becoming mouthpieces for the people they once put away, the fate of so many ex-prosecutors. With their background in fighting white-collar crime, they soon attracted a core clientele of fraud victims enmeshed in civil cases, including shareholders who'd been burned in stock swindles or bank failures that Van Cise had investigated as DA. It was steady, reliable work, and it paid much better than being a gangbuster.

Yet there was a certain bitterness in his outlook now. His skirmishes with the Klan and its corrosive influence had convinced him that the justice system was rotting from within and needed drastic reform. His cynicism was on display when, in September of 1925, he appeared as a featured speaker at the Colorado State Bar Association annual meeting in Colorado Springs—and delivered a diagnosis of the nation's crime ills that seemed designed to offend just about everyone.

"America, though saved for democracy, is chained fast to judicial precedent, terrified by criminals of all kinds, and mentally unbalanced by swarms of social theorists, who have delegated to themselves the task of making martyrs out of lawbreakers," he declared. "We are said to have more criminals than any other country in the world. We catch a few and then mollycoddle most of them, probably to make the penitentiary so attractive that the balance will flock in.

"We sentence a man to life and pardon him in a few years. The stench of our cesspool of crime nauseates all nations, while we wallow in our filth and seem to like it . . . Modern civilization is but a veneer over savagery. Men still fear power, and the law is respected only where real force is ready to strike."

The solution he proposed was to take the serious crime fighting out of the hands of petty local officials—sheriffs and magistrates, constables and coroners—who were too easily corrupted. Instead, create a far-reaching state police force under the authority of the attorney general. Give the state supreme court the power to reverse an acquittal or enhance a sentence. Pass a three-strikes law that would send chronic offenders to prison for life, and make prison sentences for other crimes indefinite, so that miscreants would have to demonstrate good behavior to obtain a release date. In the absence of such changes, he added, the "strongest deterrent to gang crime" that law enforcement officials had was the ability to cut deals with one criminal to testify against another, just as he had done in the bunco case: "So I say all praise to the squealer, the only law enforcement agency that the criminal really fears."

The caustic diatribe made headlines. Doubtless some members of his audience wondered if Van Cise had lost his mind. But, as events would soon demonstrate, he was not wrong about the cesspool of crime and widespread abuses involving sentencing and parole. The corruption went all the way to the top, to the highest elected official in the state, who was doing his best to undo much of what Van Cise had accomplished.

———

LEADING THE PEOPLE OF COLORADO to the promised land was proving to be more difficult than Clarence Morley had expected. The governor was surrounded by naysayers, bent on frustrating his every move. His greatest consolation was his conviction that he was on the right side of things. On the burning issue of the decade, the question of alcohol, he had no doubts whatsoever. He believed in bone-dry Prohibition and was encouraged by what he saw as a great awakening among his constituents, a growing respect for the ban on booze as a first step on the journey to a better world.

"This change has its roots in a great spiritual impulse that is gradually and surely taking hold of the public conscience," he declared in a 1925 speech. "The day of the hip-pocket flask is passing into the oblivion that must eventually claim it wholly . . . the voice of the people raised in a concerted demand for strict enforcement is everywhere heard, its tone unmistakable. I believe the Prohibition law will never be repealed, and that the Twentieth Amendment will remain a part of our great Constitution as long as that instrument itself exists."

Morley's reach often exceeded his grasp of details. It was the Eighteenth Amendment, not the Twentieth, that sanctioned the national crusade against demon rum. Whatever you called it, the machinery of Prohibition provided the governor with fresh opportunities to reward his friends and punish his enemies. Colorado had created a modest state agency, the Law Enforcement Department, and staffed it with paid agents to help enforce its Prohibition statute. But it was also possible to appoint volunteers, answerable only to the governor, to aid the cause. Morley's predecessor had shied away from doing so, leery of overseeing an amateur police force, but Morley had no such qualms. He appointed dozens of volunteer Prohibition agents. Many were Klansmen—or Minute Men, after the schism—who'd been promised a job in the new regime. Some were ex-convicts whose only experience with police work was being on the wrong side of it. The volunteer agents didn't receive a salary, but they could put in for expenses and enjoy the perks a state badge could bring, which were considerable.

The complaints poured in from sheriffs, district attorneys, and private citizens. Morley's men were drunk on duty. They invaded people's homes, threatened local cops, made arrests on the flimsiest of pretenses, and extorted bogus fines. It was as if Coca-Cola Candlish's corrupt bootleg squad had been reincarnated statewide. After a series of midnight raids in rural Weld County, Greeley attorney Robert Winbourn wrote to Morley threatening civil action against the agents who shook down his clients:

> Without the semblance of warrants (either criminal or
> search) their homes were entered in the night time,
> women and men were compelled to arise from beds,

where they had retired for the night, and be subjected
to search, accompanied by the flourish of firearms
and the application of profane and insulting epithets
and demands; bureaus, closets, attics and rooms were
unceremoniously searched and in a few instances liquor,
in small quantities, was found. Whereupon twelve
of these people were arrested . . . taken to the City
Jail at Lafayette in Boulder County, where they were
incarcerated and ill-treated until the following day at
1 p.m., when they were brought to the town of Dacono.
A Justice of the Peace was there obtained and a farcical
and clandestine purported judicial hearing was held
on Sunday, where fines were illegally imposed on these
defendants to the extent of and in excess of $1200.00 . . .

At the end of his first year in office, Morley declined to renew the appointments of his rogue Prohibition enforcers. Instead, he issued an executive order abolishing the entire Law Enforcement Department. The debacle was one more layer of stink in the heap of failures that was the Morley administration. Five months before the end of his two-year term, the governor announced, to no one's surprise, that he would not run again. "The people determined quite a while ago that when his present term ends, he will be retired," a *Post* wag observed. "His announcement indicates that even he senses the futility of trying to fool them again."

Most statehouse reporters had dismissed Morley as a mere figurehead long before he threw in the towel. Anyone who observed him on the phone with Locke, a frequent occurrence, knew where the real power resided. Morley was a rubber stamp, an echo. Early in his governorship, he had taken a mysterious business trip to California—and no reporters, much less his own lieutenant governor, noticed his absence for several days.

As his time as chief executive ticked down to its final weeks, few journalists bothered to drop by his office on their rounds. But a couple of them began to pick up clues that something funny was going on, the first inklings of a scandal that would dwarf all the rest.

Back when he was the Klan's law-and-order candidate, Morley had sharply criticized Governor Sweet for his liberal use of his office's powers to pardon or parole prisoners and commute sentences. But after taking office, Morley proved to be an even more forgiving fellow. He commuted the death sentence of Arthur Mitchell, slayer of two, to life in prison. He paroled Maurice Mandell, the twenty-six-year-old "boy broker" who'd engineered a scheme to loot $465,000 from the Hibernia Bank. Van Cise had prosecuted the case and obtained a twenty-year sentence for Mandell; scarcely two years later, he was free.

Van Cise conveyed his outrage to reporters and predicted that Mandell's release was only the start of a "pardon and parole orgy which will shortly be indulged in by the present incumbent of the gubernatorial chair."

He was right. Morley paroled other swindlers, as well as bootleggers, still operators, armed robbers, and worse. According to three witnesses, the governor showed up at the state penitentiary one night with an ex-convict named Bert Donaldson and demanded that the warden arrange a private interview between Donaldson and Jackie French, the notorious bookmaker for the Blonger bunco ring. French was paroled a few months later, after serving little more than two years of a seven-year sentence. Orders for release were issued for other prisoners who had never even applied for parole. Many of these actions were kept secret for months, but in the final days of the Morley administration the *Denver Post* ran a series of stories on the "pardon orgy." By the newspaper's count, Morley had issued pardons or paroles for 149 prisoners in two years, including twenty-three lifers, nineteen murderers, and several rapists. The series strongly insinuated that money had changed hands for these mercies. Many of those who obtained the governor's pardon were represented by Ben Laska or Harry Saunders, Locke's personal attorneys and bribe brokers.

Morley sued the *Post* for libel, seeking $117,000 in damages and insisting that he'd never personally profited from the prisoner releases and reprieves. That may have been true, but the lawsuit was ill-advised. It exposed the governor's activities and related Klan follies to a degree of scrutiny they had never received before. The case went to trial three times. The first time around, Judge Henry Bray blocked testimony on many subjects, including his own Klan membership, and a deadlocked jury resulted in a mistrial. The second trial produced a $15,600 judgment in Morley's favor, but that verdict was thrown out after Judge James Starkweather ruled that Morley had failed to establish a foundation for damages. (The *Post* also argued that the verdict was tainted by the presence of Klansmen or Minute Men on the jury.) By the third trial, the *Post* had fine-tuned its devastating defense, as well as the shrill press coverage that went with it.

Testimony from former Locke associates suggested that Morley did whatever Locke asked. George Minor, the former Klan lecturer, said that Locke had shown him the undated letter of resignation he'd extracted from Morley before he became governor, just in case the chief executive ever was tempted to defy him. Minor also recalled a discussion with Locke about starting a klavern at the state penitentiary, since so many Kluxers were serving time there. A *Post* managing editor detailed how the paper's parole series had scuttled a scheme that would have released Alfred Max, an abortionist serving time for murder, in exchange for $30,000 doled out to various interests, including $12,500 to Locke. Attorney Charles Ginsberg recounted how he'd tried to save the life of Ray Shank, a mental case facing execution for killing his wife and son; he was told by Locke attorney Laska that it would cost $5000 for a commutation from the governor, money the condemned man didn't have. Shank's hanging proceeded as scheduled.

When it was his turn to take the stand, Morley displayed little knowledge or concern about the men he had released. He denied the late-night visit to the pen on behalf of Jackie French and contradicted himself about when, if ever, he'd publicly disclosed his membership in the Klan. He admitted to being an "errand boy" in the Locke tax case and seeking Locke's advice on pardons and paroles. He did nothing to correct the impression that he was precisely the man the *Post* had made him out to be—a stooge, a dupe, a bag man, a tool.

The jury found in the newspaper's favor. By that point Morley had left office and moved to California. His friendship with Locke had unraveled over the parole mess and other difficulties, but he was still willing to serve as a front for others, to loan out his name and connections to get some business done. Minor details, such as whether the business was legal or not, continued to elude him. That failing would eventually land him in a federal penitentiary, where he would write plaintive letters to powerful men, seeking a pardon of his own.

―――――

VAN CISE COULDN'T LEAVE IT ALONE. Another man in his position, newly retired from public life, would have been content to take a seat in the bleachers and watch the Ku Klux Klan devour itself. But his obsession with the hooded order was as robust as ever. He was still determined to fight them, to expose them. If they were truly on the run, then he would give them whatever push he could to send them on their way.

Six months after the Klan's triumph in the 1924 elections, a group calling itself the Constitutionalists began organizing a broad-based campaign to defeat them. The organization wasn't aligned with any single party or ideology, other than a commitment to the Constitution; the aim was to avoid the divisiveness among anti-Klan forces that had led to the Klan victory, to form new alliances rather than stoke old rivalries. Van Cise joined the group, whose officers included his long-time ally, former Republican governor Oliver Shoup, and his nemesis from the bunco trial, defense attorney Horace Hawkins. Other prominent political leaders and activist attorneys, including Phil Hornbein and Charles Ginsberg, also enlisted. The *Rocky Mountain American*, a Klan newspaper, immediately began mocking the group and Van Cise in particular, reporting that he'd been named the Constitutionalists' "Official Bugler," thanks to "years of arduous practice 'blowing his own horn' . . . Mr. Van Cise, after the limelights had been suitably adjusted to suit his particular temperament, assured the gathering that he was as he always had been, ready to die (theoretically speaking) in 'any old cause,' so long as he could do so in the full view of all the people, all the time."

The new coalition was a more serious threat than the Klan cared to acknowledge. The Constitutionalists held a public meeting at a Denver theater, warning an overflow crowd about a Klan plot to take over the commission overseeing the construction of the Moffat Tunnel, a $15-million project that would create a key rail link west of the city, under the Continental Divide. The Kluxers aimed to replace the current commissioners with their own crew in an upcoming election. One component of the campaign was a bogus report, issued by a

Klan grand jury, accusing the commission of malfeasance. Van Cise went to court on behalf of the incumbent commissioners to get the report expunged. His clients were reelected, the Klan plot foiled.

Now that he was in private practice, Van Cise could be selective about the people he chose to represent. The fraud cases paid the bills, but he was also on the lookout for cases that would feed his obsession, give him a shot in a courtroom at Locke and company. The Moffat Tunnel flap was one instance. The case of attorney Edward Sabin, who claimed that Locke owed him money for services rendered, was another.

The services at issue stemmed from the litigation surrounding Royal Graham, the Klan-backed candidate for Denver's juvenile court judge in the 1924 election. Graham had a history of misconduct and financial mismanagement as a probate court judge, and Van Cise had bitterly opposed his effort to unseat Judge Ben Lindsey. Officially, Lindsey had narrowly won the contest, but recounts reduced his margin to a few dozen votes and led to a court challenge, alleging election fraud. The convoluted case persisted for years; after Graham committed suicide in 1925, his widow Cora continued to press it, arguing that Graham's estate was owed the salary he would have earned on the bench if the election hadn't been stolen.

Sabin had represented Graham and his widow in the fight, but he claimed that it was Locke who had hired him. Locke had paid him some money but still owed him $445. Locke insisted that it was the Klan that had hired Sabin; any money he was still owed was the Klan's debt, not his. The good doctor no longer belonged to the Klan.

It wasn't a lot of money—hardly enough to justify a lawsuit—but Van Cise pursued the case like a hound from hell. He demanded the right to depose Locke. The doctor's attorneys opposed the move. Van Cise pointed out that Locke's answer to the suit had made vague references to an "invisible empire," but failed to state its location; a deposition would help clear up this and other matters. Locke sat reluctantly for his deposition while Ben Laska popped up and down, swatting away questions about his client's finances like flies. Van Cise deposed Brown Harwood, former Imperial Klazik of the national KKK, as well as Imperial Wizard Evans. Both men stated that Locke had no authority to hire attorneys on behalf of the Klan.

The first jury to hear the case deadlocked on a key piece of evidence, two checks paid to Sabin that bore Locke's signature. The panel couldn't decide if they were Klan checks or personal payments by Locke, since the doctor apparently used the same account for personal expenditures and Klan business. A second jury found that Locke had hired Sabin and owed him the remaining $445. Locke paid it. The case took two years from complaint to judgment and was a Pyrrhic victory at best, but Van Cise didn't regret it. Obtaining a jury verdict against Locke was like finding a white rhino in your basement. It just didn't happen.

By the time the case was resolved, Locke was under siege on several fronts. Federal tax agents were back on his case, digging around and asking questions about the whereabouts of hundreds of thousands of dollars in dues and robe fees collected back in his days as Grand Dragon. According to the *Post*, some of the digging took place in the backyard of a Denver home, where "important records" were unearthed. Someone attempted to break into Charles Locke's crypt in Fairmount Cemetery, apparently in the belief that his son had stashed plunder there. A few days later, a burglary was reported at the Cotton Mills, which the Minute Men were leasing from the Klan for their meetings while the bond mess got straightened out.

The Minute Men had failed to become the coast-to-coast patriotic movement Locke had envisioned. One hurdle seemed to be the elaborate costume, which lacked the simple anonymity of a robe and hood. People didn't want to be caught dead in knee breeches and a funny hat. Uniform sales were disappointing, and after the first few raucous gatherings, the crowds began to dwindle. The group also lost face after a raid on its downtown headquarters, led by District Attorney Foster Cline. The DA had complained for months about the frequency with which criminal defendants affiliated with the organization achieved hung juries or acquittals. He had been spurred into action by a tip from a former jury commissioner, who said he'd been pressured to pack the jury pool with Minute Men; when he resisted, he was replaced by a more compliant bureaucrat. Seized in the raid were two typewriters—which, tests soon confirmed, had been used to compose the official list of two thousand names of prospective jurors. Cline couldn't prove that the list had been prepared on Locke's orders, and his investigation failed to produce charges against anyone, but the uproar confirmed suspicions that Locke's new venture was proceeding along the same crooked lines as his old one.

More allegations about Locke's schemes and backroom deals came from disillusioned Kluxers and Minute Men. The most damaging account was provided by Joe Bushnell, formerly one of the doctor's closest friends and an adjutant general of the Minute Men. On October 1, 1926, Bushnell admitted in open court that, while acting as conservator for a mentally ill soldier, he'd stolen $2680 from the man's estate. Prior to making his confession, Bushnell had gone to Locke, seeking help. Locke had refused any assistance and told him to take his medicine. He was sentenced to a term of eighteen months to three years in the state pen.

Bushnell stewed over his situation for three months. As he saw it, he would not have been in the desperate circumstances that led to the embezzlement if Locke had paid him what he was owed for all the dirty jobs he'd undertaken. He decided to unburden himself in an eight-thousand-word affidavit, provided to private investigators looking into allegations of fraud in the 1926 elections.

The former henchman had plenty to say. He described the shenanigans involved in hiding Locke's tax records from federal examiners and the destruction of Klan records as Locke orchestrated the mass defection to the Minute Men. He touched on the shady bond sales, his encounter with one of Keith Boehm's kidnappers a few hours before the teen's forced wedding, and a conversation with a prominent Denver banker, who confided that Dr. Locke had saved his family from disgrace by performing an abortion on his daughter. He admitted to compiling lists of names of Klansmen and Minute Men with another Locke aide, the same man who was accused of rigging the lists used in Denver jury selection. He recalled Locke flashing large wads of money while stiffing his lieutenants on promised salaries. He accused the doctor of scheming to insert himself in Klan feuds elsewhere, including the Arkansas schism, as well as trying to take over the local chapter of the Shriners. As for the Minute Men, Bushnell believed the organization was little more than a personality cult.

"It is my honest opinion that very few men who are now closely connected with Dr. Locke know of his falsities," Bushnell stated. "The secret service staff of the Minute Men actually amounts to the numerous hangers-on who believe Dr. Locke has the power to do anything he wishes. They get nothing for their services but abuse in the end."

Like little Len Reamey, the star witness in the bunco trial, Bushnell was a prosecutor's dream—a high-ranking member of a criminal conspiracy who was prepared to tell all. An aggressive district attorney could have used his revelations as a launching point for a far-ranging case against Locke, one that would encompass kidnapping, bribery, jury tampering, election fraud, and much more. Such a case wouldn't have to hinge on Bushnell's word; he had named several other disaffected insiders who could verify his claims. All it would take was a prosecutor willing to do the legwork. But Cline wasn't that prosecutor. One possible explanation for his reluctance can be found in Bushnell's affidavit, which hinted that Locke had something salacious on Cline and was blackmailing him. But it's also possible that Cline didn't see much percentage in chasing a foe that was doing a good job of destroying itself.

The decline of the Minute Men and the Klan was glaringly evident in the 1926 elections. Both organizations tried to operate as power brokers, dangling the support of their legions before those candidates who promised to provide the best quid pro quo. But since their legions had been drastically reduced by desertions, they had little of the leverage the Invisible Empire had enjoyed two years earlier. Even in his reduced circumstances, Locke was determined to thwart the reelection bid of his arch-rival Rice Means, the only member of the U.S. Senate to have been publicly outed as a Klansman. Locke initially backed George Luxford, a county judge and fellow Minute Man, in the Senate race, but soon shifted his support to Charles Waterman, a well-heeled corporate lawyer who'd lost to Means in the Republican primary in 1924. According to Bushnell, Locke collected thousands of dollars

from Luxford for his support, then abandoned him and collected even more from Waterman. Waterman went on to beat
Means in the primary and former governor William Sweet in
the general election. Whether Locke's maneuvers had much
impact on the outcome is difficult to say, since Waterman had
strong backing from corporate interests, too. It was, in any
event, the doctor's last bit of kingmaking. He frittered away
his waning influence in intrigues over city council races and
failed utterly in his efforts to stop Ben Stapleton's reelection
as Denver's mayor a few months later.

The Klan fared even worse than the Minute Men in the
1926 elections. The group lost the Senate, the governorship,
and any semblance of control of the state legislature. Outnumbered and outmaneuvered at county assemblies, the
group no longer had the delegates to head off the Constitutionalists and other anti-Klan forces within the GOP. Con-
stitutionalist Oliver Shoup emerged from the primary as the
Republican choice for governor; he was defeated by Democrat Billy Adams, who'd led the anti-Klan coalition in the
statehouse. Now commanded by a Baptist preacher based in
Canon City, the rag-tag remnants of the Colorado Klan were
in retreat and headed back to the shadows.

Van Cise's last skirmish with the night riders came
five months before the election. The Denver klavern had
announced a "klorero" (large gathering) and parade through
downtown for Memorial Day weekend. Despite predictions
that up to sixty thousand Klansmen would show up for the
festivities, the turnout was shockingly low. The previous
summer, a Klan picnic at Lakeside Park had attracted an
estimated fifty thousand people. Earlier parades through
downtown had lasted for up to four hours, the Klan legions
marching four abreast and bringing commerce to a standstill.

But less than five hundred men and women showed up for the 1926 parade.

Van Cise had been invited to speak at Memorial Day services in honor of military veterans at Crown Hill Cemetery. He began by observing that Denver was in the peculiar position of having two parades that weekend. One was for veterans of the Grand Army of the Republic and the Spanish-American War, "men who do no not need to boast of their achievements because their deeds speak for themselves." The second was the puny pageant the Ku Klux Klan had staged in an attempt to "usurp" the holiday.

"Another parade came in white, shrouded and masked, yet proclaimed itself American," Van Cise said. "A day dedicated to the heroic dead should not be outraged by a group of cheap politicians, organized as a secret society, trying to obtain advertising for themselves."

Some Klansmen in the audience began to mutter. But they'd had no chance to pack the house, and Van Cise was just getting started.

"Those of us who have been in the service, who encountered shot and shell or the horrors of the trenches as part of our job, as a duty of citizenship, were glad to do it," he said. "Unfortunately, not all the great battles are fought in war, and some of the major struggles come in peace. In Colorado, for the last two years—and now—we are facing a battle as serious, as terrific, as any we fought in the Civil War or in the World War. We are face to face with a gigantic battle of peace—the battle for Americanism . . . Secret political organizations are un-American in every possible particular. They strike at the foundation of our liberty. They strike at the integrity of our manhood. I call on you who are here today to denounce this highhanded proceeding on the part of these ghostlike intruders, to rise up and fight the battles of your country against those who are too cowardly to come out in the open and declare what principles they possess and what candidates they have."

The mutterings were drowned out by cheers and applause. But the Kluxers couldn't let such an affront pass. Van Cise had impugned their patriotism. Worse, he'd questioned their manhood. The insult had to be avenged. Six nights later, the Klan struck back, erecting and burning a large cross in the former district attorney's front yard.

There are two versions of how this story ends. In the first version, the Van Cise family was out of town on the Sunday night that the Klan attacked. Neighbors called the fire department, which extinguished the fiery cross. Van Cise told a reporter that he was sorry he missed the show and vowed, "If the Klan has nerve enough to let me know when it intends to call, I assure it a warm welcome from a reception committee of one."

The second version was told by Edwin Van Cise, Philip's son, many years later, a vivid memory from his childhood that he shared with his own children. In this account, the children and Sara were at home that night. Standing at the living room window, completely oblivious to the sinister significance of the event, seven-year-old Edwin and his eight-year-old sister, Eleanor, greeted the blazing, night-defying cross with shrieks of delight, as if the Fourth of July had arrived early.

Both versions can't be true. Edwin would have been nine in June 1926, so perhaps he was recalling some other event. Or perhaps there was more than one episode of cross burning at the Van Cise home. In the end, it doesn't matter. Both accounts take us to the same place. What was once a deadly threat, a symbol to strike terror in the hearts of the Klan's enemies, had become a mere act of vandalism, an impotent gesture, a spectacle for the kiddies. Van Cise and others like him, the ones who would not abide infamy in silence, had challenged and ridiculed the men in hoods at every turn, until they could no longer hide their own absurdity. The group would linger, increasingly fractured and directionless, but there was no longer anything to fear from the Colorado Realm of the Knights of the Ku Klux Klan.

The Klan was finished.

12

—

Legacies

A milkman discovered the body at half-past two on a Monday morning. Drawn by the clatter of an idling automobile engine, he wrestled open the stubborn sliding doors of a Capitol Hill garage and found the place thick with fumes, the driver door of a coupe wide open, the occupant sprawled across the seat, dead from carbon monoxide poisoning. The deputy coroner ruled out foul play but declined to choose between accident and suicide as the manner of death.

Despite the official waffling, there was no mystery surrounding the demise of Adolph Duff. It was hard to picture the former manager of Denver's Big Store taking the trouble to close those garage doors, then crawling back into his car on a chilly November night to take a nap—and "accidentally" leaving the motor running. But this was scarcely a month after Black Tuesday, the great stock market crash of '29, and no one was inclined to look too closely at the death of a washed-up confidence man amid so many more notable sad cases.

Back in the old days, Kid Duffy had bragged of having

such ironclad protection that no one could touch him. Five years in prison had taken the starch out of him, but the real problems began after his release. He gambled heavily, burning through the cash and investments he'd left in his wife's care during his incarceration. She filed for divorce. He mortgaged his remaining property, blew the proceeds at cards and craps, and ended up in the garage without a dollar in his pocket. He was fifty-five years old.

Other confidence artists who had once thrived in Duff's operation also struggled to make ends meet. Following his early parole, Jackie French teamed up with a new badger-game partner, the daughter of Billy Arnett, Blonger's former connection in the Justice Department. But Dapper Jackie soon landed in federal prison on an old mail-fraud beef; after serving five years, he died of pneumonia shortly after his release. His former lover and partner in crime, Buda Godman, was nabbed in New York while trying to fence $300,000 in jewels stolen in an armed robbery and was sentenced to four years. Elmer Mead, the Christ Kid, emerged from the Colorado pen and went right back to working scams across the country and in England, keeping one step ahead of federal agents, but life on the run took its toll. The feds slapped liens on his properties. British authorities deported him. When he was arrested for a minor traffic violation in Boston, it was discovered that he had mutilated his fingerprints with acid.

The confidence racket wasn't what it used to be. Van Cise's investigation had exposed cherished trade secrets to suckers everywhere, and no major American city would ever again be as well-fixed as Denver had been before the gangbuster showed up. The Big Con would endure, but the touches were smaller, the risks greater—and the Payoff, the most elegant and lucrative con game of them all, was now hopelessly dated. You couldn't sell marks on a red-hot stock exchange that churned out stacks of cash, not when the real market was in shambles and the deepening Depression had robbed people of their confidence. The brokers on Wall Street had spoiled things for hard-working grifters everywhere; they had, as the saying goes, *ranked the joint.*

Len Reamey picked the right moment to walk away from the game. Van Cise saw to it that his star witness in the bunco case was quietly released, his trail obscured. Reamey returned to his home state of Arkansas with his wife, Nina Hansen. The couple opened a hotel and prospered. He died in 1959, two months shy of his seventieth birthday.

Another key witness would outlive Reamey and just about everyone else involved in the case. A few months after the bunco trial, rancher turned avenger Frank Norfleet crossed the last name off the list of confidence men who had swindled him; Charles Harris, the elusive roper he knew as Spencer, had finally been captured in Salt Lake City. His mission accomplished, Norfleet could have stepped away from the limelight at that point, but he'd grown fond of it, and he had bills to pay. In 1924 he published a larger-than-life account of his adventures, *Norfleet: The Actual Experiences of a Texas Rancher's 30,000-Mile Transcontinental Chase After Five Confidence Men.* He went on the lecture circuit, starred in a never-completed movie adaptation of his book, and offered his services as a manhunter to other swindle victims. He claimed to have apprehended ninety-three criminals by 1940, the year he turned seventy-five. "Memory is a luxury only those who go straight can afford," he declared. He died in 1967 at the age of 102.

Van Cise and Norfleet became lifelong friends, but their memories differed regarding certain aspects of the bunco case. Possibly to correct the record, as well as dispel some popular myths about confidence men, Van Cise eventually got around to writing his own book on the Blonger investigation, *Fighting the Underworld*, published in 1936. Scrupulous in many details and not without a mordant sense of humor, it's also an oddly circumspect work. Van Cise changed or omitted the names of many important players, including several police officers, corrupt officials, and unindicted coconspirators. Even the mayor at the time, Dewey Bailey, is never named. It's likely this was done to avoid libel claims. (After the arrests, several of the con men filed civil suits against Van Cise for allegedly violating their rights; all their claims were soon dismissed, but the prosecutor had a keen appreciation of how litigation could be used as a tool for harassment.) The author also refers to himself in the third person, as "the Colonel" or "the District Attorney," draining color and emotion from what should have been a vivid first-person account.

Its aloof tone didn't discourage reviewers, several of whom hailed *Fighting the Underworld* as an important work in a much-neglected area of criminology. ("Despite a somewhat dry style the book is steadily interesting," Robert Van Gelder wrote in the *New York Times*.) Its influence extended well beyond its press run. Not long after its publication, Van Cise was contacted by David Maurer, a linguistics professor at the University of Louisville who was obsessed with underworld slang and subcultures. Maurer consulted with Van Cise and interviewed numerous crooks while researching his classic survey of grifter lingo and scams, *The Big Con: The Story of the Confidence Men*, published in 1940. A generation later, Maurer's book provided source material for one of the most popular movies ever made: *The Sting*.

How much the movie owes to Maurer is disputed. In 1974,

shortly after the movie's release, Maurer filed a $10 million copyright infringement suit against Universal Pictures, claiming that *The Sting* contained too many similarities to his book. David S. Ward, who received an Oscar for best original screenplay, acknowledged turning to several nonfiction sources in his research but denied any plagiarism. The case was settled out of court for a reported $600,000. The movie went on to become one of the highest-grossing blockbusters of the 1970s. Its success owes a great deal to a feat of Hollywood trickery that would have astounded even the most jaded grifter—transforming the hard-eyed predators who ran the Big Con into lovable scamps, played by Paul Newman and Robert Redford.

———

FIRING COCA-COLA CANDLISH and distancing himself from the Klan did wonders for Benjamin Stapleton's political career. In 1927 he handily won reelection as Denver's mayor against a pack of challengers, including a city councilman backed by the Klan and the Minute Men. Voted out in 1931, Stapleton bounced back four years later and went on to serve three more terms as mayor, dominating city politics well into the 1940s. He died three years after leaving office.

Under Stapleton, Denver acquired a municipal airport and completed the Civic Center complex of public buildings started by Boss Speer. But Stapleton's shrewdest move may have been hiring Van Cise's former classmate and patron, George Cranmer, as manager of Parks and Improvements. Like Stapleton, Cranmer had impeccable timing; he cashed out of the stock market months before the crash and retired from the brokerage business at forty-four. He became Stapleton's campaign manager and then his point man on several projects that would help define the city, including expansion of its mountain parks system and the construction of the Red Rocks amphitheater and concert venue. In 1940, he launched a city-operated "winter sports park" on a mountainside seventy miles from town, consisting of a rope tow and T-bar for skiers, a few warming sheds, and not much else. Winter Park became a lynchpin of Colorado's nascent ski industry, which now employs thousands of people and generates close to $5 billion a year in economic activity.

A park in Denver's Hilltop neighborhood with expansive views of the Front Range is named after Cranmer. The airport that was built on Stapleton's watch carried his name from 1944 until it was closed in 1995. The residential community that replaced it continued to be called Stapleton for another twenty-five years, even as controversies surfaced elsewhere about naming monuments, streets, and public buildings after leaders with ties to white supremacy. Stapleton's Klan affiliation was no secret to historians, but it didn't prompt much public discussion until 2018, when Walker Stapleton, the Colorado state treasurer and the mayor's great-grandson, made an unsuccessful run for the governor's office. In 2020, the Stapleton Master Community Association voted to change the neighborhood's name to Central Park.

No similar act of erasure has been directed at the Klan governor of Colorado, Clarence Morley, because there is no memorial that needs to be erased. No airport, neighborhood, park, plaza, alcove, alley, or outhouse was ever named after Morley—which is ironic, perhaps, since he was so amenable to loaning his name to dubious ventures when it still meant something. While serving as governor, Morley had been persuaded to become president of the Fall River Mining Company, a business that was more focused on stock manipulation and inflated dividends than producing ore. He made a short-term profit on his involvement before the stock price cratered, driven down to a fraction of a cent by regulatory probes, bad press, and lawsuits. A few years later, reeling from losses in the market and struggling to keep his law practice afloat, he fell in with other stock hustlers who opened a reputed brokerage agency, Clarence J. Morley & Company, in Indianapolis, listing the former governor as president.

The company was a complete fraud, bilking its clients out of cash for stock purchases that were never made. Customers in Indiana, Ohio, and Kentucky lost substantial sums, but the scam continued for a full year, until federal agents raided the place. In 1935 Morley was arrested and charged with mail fraud; two of his six codefendants took it on the lam. Morley didn't dispute the fraud but insisted he had no knowledge of it or intent to participate in it. He'd never set foot in Indiana, he pointed out, and his attorney claimed that a series of strokes had impaired his ability to understand what was going on. A jury didn't buy his defense, and neither did the Seventh Circuit Court of Appeals. Given Morley's background as an attorney, judge, and governor, "it is impossible to believe that the defendant was not aware of the character and practices of his associates," the circuit judges concluded.

Tried on twenty-one counts of mail fraud, Morley was convicted of only one, but that was enough to draw a five-year prison sentence. He was paroled in 1940 after serving twenty-one months at the Leavenworth penitentiary and continued to insist that he was guilty of nothing—except being a dupe. He died in Oklahoma City in 1948.

His death came shortly after that of another Leavenworth graduate, former Locke attorney Ben Laska. In 1935, Laska was accused of accepting ten thousand dollars in ransom money from a kidnapping as his fee for defending Albert Bates, a career criminal. Laska denied that he'd knowingly taken the tainted money—which, under the Lindbergh Act, would make him an accessory to the crime. He was found guilty and sentenced to ten years. He served close to half that amount before obtaining parole. With his typical nimbleness, the ex-magician returned to Denver and began to work on reviving his law career. A pardon signed by President Truman arrived in 1947, but by that point Laska was contending with health problems and losing hope that he would ever get his law license reinstated. One night he retired to his bedroom, wrote six suicide notes, downed a box of sleeping pills, and pulled his last vanishing act.

The man who had once commanded Laska and Morley preceded them into the darkness. On April Fool's Day, 1935, John Galen Locke wandered into a suite of rooms at the Brown Palace that comprised the campaign headquarters of Denver mayoral candidate Charles Armstrong. In the reception area he encountered ex-undercover agent Robert Maiden, a good friend of Armstrong's, who was just leaving. The former Klan infiltrator was one of the last people to see the former Grand Dragon alive.

Other men passed through the anteroom and greeted Locke. One attempted to strike up a conversation with him, but Locke abruptly slumped to the floor. A doctor was summoned, artificial respiration attempted, but it was no use. He was dead from a heart attack at the age of sixty-three.

Competing stories soon emerged about what Locke was doing in Armstrong's suite. It's possible that he had other business at the hotel that evening and had dropped in on the candidate on a whim. But many suspected that he had an appointment with Armstrong and was trying to get back in the game, building his political base in Denver before trying to exert his influence statewide.

Former Exalted Cyclops Rex Yeager, who'd visited Locke at

his home earlier that day, favored the latter explanation. Locke had never stopped plotting his comeback. He had smoothed over past misunderstandings and acquired influential friends wherever he could. Governor Morley had appointed him to the state board of medical examiners, drawing protests from the medical establishment; two governors later, Locke was still on the board, making nice. And his tax problems were finally behind him. Just two months before he dropped dead, a tax appeals board ruled that the government had failed to prove that Locke had skimmed from the Klan and owed thirty thousand dollars in taxes on that income. Instead, he was issued a three-thousand-dollar refund for overpayment.

He had also revised his history, representing himself as a champion of religious tolerance. The Minute Men had been a disappointment; a much-heralded branch in California had quickly withered, and Catholics and Jews failed to take advantage of its generous membership provisions. (Locke had appointed Laska as the first Jewish Minute Man, but the backlash from former Kluxers had been so vocal that he hadn't been eager to add more.) Refusing to concede defeat, Locke had recently started yet another fraternal society, the Order of Equals, open to white men of all faiths, that he predicted would one day be bigger than the Klan. He boasted to Yeager that Hiram Evans had contacted him a few months back, inviting him to return to the Klan fold and lead the Colorado Realm, and he'd rejected the offer.* Whatever Locke had in mind for the Order of Equals, it was not klannishness.

---

* Evans continued to lead the depleted Klan until he resigned as Imperial Wizard in 1939, shortly after attending the opening of a Catholic cathedral on the site of the former Imperial Palace in Atlanta. In 1944, what was left of the national organization succumbed to longstanding tax troubles and was disbanded. It was soon replaced by other, more marginal incarnations.

The doctor would have relished the front-page press coverage of his death. The stories were full of whoppers and exaggerations he'd propagated over the years about his military record, his education, and other accomplishments. One claimed that he'd served in the Philippines during the Spanish-American War (he spent the entire conflict stateside). Another explained that his break with the Klan had been the result of his refusal "to enter upon a program of persecuting Catholics, Jews, and Negroes." Hundreds turned out for his memorial service. The roster of honorary pallbearers included eight judges and a Catholic priest.

He remained an enigma, a changeling whose true shape was always hidden. He had taken on a fanatic's job, but there was nothing fanatical about him—just a schemer's love of scheming, a liar's habit of lying. Whatever his true beliefs, they mattered far less than what he could persuade others to believe. Men like him embraced any infernal bargain that could bring them the power they sought and never bothered to read the fine print.

═════

SEVERAL OF VAN CISE'S ALLIES in his battle against the Klan went on to enjoy long and distinguished careers. After filing his last KKK meeting spy report, Robert Maiden left the district attorney's office and served as a federal law enforcement agent for the next thirty years. He worked narcotics and tax investigations and as a probation officer. He came out of retirement to take the job of marshal of Empire, a small mountain town, for six years. He died in 1976.

Otto Moore left his job as assistant district attorney to open his own law practice. His concerns about the economic struggles of his clients, especially the older ones, prompted him to work with members of Congress on drafting legislation that would eventually become the Social Security Act of 1935. In 1948, he was elected to the Colorado Supreme Court. When he retired from the bench twenty years (and five thousand court decisions) later, he went back to work as a prosecutor at the request of Denver District Attorney Dale Tooley, and stayed at it until he was eighty-nine. He died in 1990, at the age of ninety-four.

Sidney Whipple, the Klan-taunting editor of the *Denver Express*, moved on to bigger outfits. He reported on the Lindbergh kidnapping trial for United Press and authored two books about the case; worked as a drama critic for the *New York World Telegram*; covered the war in the Pacific for Scripps-Howard; and wrote a column for *Stars and Stripes* until shortly before his death in West Germany in 1975 at the age of eighty-seven. *Denver Post* star reporter Forbes Parkhill left the newspaper business for magazine and film work. He wrote short stories for the slicks and the pulps, a couple of screenplays, at least one novel, and several books of nonfiction about the Old West. Several of his cowboy stories were adapted into movies in the 1930s. He died in San Diego in 1974, at the age of eighty-one.

Van Cise, too, had an eventful journey after the collapse of the Klan. His legal career was rich in drama and occasional, inchoate bursts of violence. Yet it was an oddly muted second act, his accomplishments largely unsung. No judgeship awaited him, no invitations to run for public office, no political intrigues beyond the petty power struggles within the state bar association. His name vanished from the newspapers for years at a time. He was not simply passed over but shunned, as if the powers that be had decided that he should be consigned to oblivion early and for all time.

What could turn a local hero into an exile in his own

town? Part of it, surely, had to do with Van Cise's voice-in-the-wilderness role in an episode that many Denver citizens were not keen to revisit. After Locke's death, the Klan's two-year reign in the state was hardly ever mentioned in polite society—not for decades. People didn't want to be reminded how many prominent members of the community, including Mayor Stapleton and several distinguished judges, had gotten their start under a sheet. Although he rarely spoke about his battle with the Klan, Van Cise's very presence was a reproach to those who had gone along to get along.

Van Cise's inflexible notions of right and wrong didn't help matters. His uncompromising sense of rectitude, so central to his defiance of the Klan, frequently exasperated colleagues and allies. He prepared for litigation like a general prepared for war, and his scorched-earth campaigns against two of the city's most influential leaders may help to explain how he came to be treated as a pariah himself.

In 1927, after a series of court battles, Judge Ben Lindsey was toppled from his perch in Denver's juvenile court, a fiefdom he'd held since the turn of the century. The Colorado Supreme Court ruled that Lindsey's reelection in 1924 had been tainted by vote fraud in one closely contested precinct; although the Klan-backed challenger in the race, Royal Graham, had since committed suicide, a new judge had to be appointed immediately. To add insult to injury, Lindsey was also ordered to turn over a portion of the salary he'd received since the election to Graham's widow. Lindsey vowed to contest the bizarre decision and regain his seat on the bench.

Van Cise had business in the juvenile court shortly after Lindsey's ouster. He found records missing, staff absent, and the new judge overwhelmed. He filed a complaint with the bar association, accusing Lindsey of leaving the place in a state of "anarchy" and orchestrating a walkout of his loyal employees. Lindsey hotly denied any misconduct and insisted that it was his duty to remove confidential records on hundreds of juveniles so that they didn't fall into the wrong hands. He invited the press to attend while he burned piles of files in a bonfire in a vacant lot. At a bar committee hearing held to investigate the complaint, he told Van Cise to go to hell.

"Just calm down there, mister," Van Cise said. "I'm not through with you yet."

He wasn't. The bar committee cleared Lindsey of wrongdoing in his tumultuous exit, but Van Cise soon leveled more serious charges. He'd learned that while serving as a judge, Lindsey had received $47,500 from a longtime friend for representing her children in a multi-million-dollar battle over her ex-husband's estate. Lindsey insisted that he had not asked for any compensation for his "arbitration services" and that the money was a gift, not a fee for legal work; furthermore, he had sought another judge's advice on whether to accept the payment and was told there was nothing improper about it. But Van Cise maintained that Lindsey had acted as a private attorney in the matter, violating his oath of office. In 1929, the Colorado Supreme Court ruled that Lindsey had been less than truthful in his account of the transaction and disbarred him.

Lindsey soon obtained a law license in California and spent his last decade as a judge in Los Angeles Superior Court. His Colorado license was reinstated in 1935, but he never returned to the state. He and his supporters blamed Van Cise for his expulsion, accusing the former gangbuster of working with the Klan and archconservatives to discredit the judge and destroy the compassionate, innovative juvenile justice system he'd developed over decades. "I deeply resent any suggestion that this proceeding was brought to uphold

the honor of the bar," Lindsey said, shortly after his disbar-
ment. "Its sole purpose was revenge."

His feud with Lindsey didn't win Van Cise any friends
among Democrats and Denver's reform-minded elite. But
it was his assault on another sacred cow, one of the state's
most powerful and feared men, that probably had the greatest impact on his future career. In 1932, the owners of the
Rocky Mountain News retained Van Cise to defend the newspaper against a libel suit brought by Frederick Bonfils, the
cantankerous publisher of the *Denver Post*. The cause of the
action was an article in the *News* that had quoted liberally
from a speech delivered by Walter Walker, the state Democratic chairman.* Walker had called Bonfils a vulture, a rat-
tlesnake, and "a public enemy that has left the trail of a slimy
serpent across Colorado for thirty years." Bonfils wanted
$200,000 for the blackening of his good name.

Van Cise had no love for the *Post*, Bonfils, or his late partner, Harry Tammen, a longtime pal of Lou Blonger's. During
the Klan's rise to power, the region's dominant newspaper had
been wildly erratic in its response, tweaking Morley for his
pardons scandal but also spewing obsequious articles about
Locke that sounded like they were dictated by a press agent.
The libel suit was a chance for some payback. Van Cise told
the *News* executives that he would offer truth as a defense—
in fact, it was his intention to amass overwhelming evidence
that Bonfils was every bit as slimy as Walker had made him
out to be and worse, that he had no good name to protect. It
would be expensive, he cautioned, and he wanted a free hand

---

* Walker was also the publisher of the Grand Junction *Daily Sentinel*—
and, as noted in chapter 11, was attacked on the street following his break
with the Klan in 1925.

to investigate the plaintiff's entire sordid history. "If I'm going into this case, I'm going in it to win," he told them.

Roy Howard, the chairman of Scripps-Howard newspapers, agreed to Van Cise's terms. The attorney set up a command center in a building next door to the *News* and hired a research staff to rake through the muck of decades of local scandal-sheet journalism. ("We're yellow, but we're read, and we're true blue," Tammen boasted.) The team quickly established that Bonfils had been referred to in print in far worse terms than the ones Walker had used; a list of 188 colorful names the publisher had acquired over the years included *assassin, traducer, felon, cuttlefish, cootie-covered rat, ghoul, vermin,* and *devil's paramour.* To establish that the name-calling had ample justification, two *News* reporters working under Van Cise's direction hit the road and traced the serpent's trail, from Bonfils's boyhood in Missouri to fraudulent land deals in the Texas panhandle and running phony lotteries in Kansas City. But those were mere youthful indiscretions compared to what the publisher had accomplished since he and Tammen took over the *Post.* He had blackmailed advertisers, threatened and assaulted competitors, and purportedly extorted money from Harry Sinclair, one of the principals in the Teapot Dome oil-leasing scandal, in exchange for dropping his paper's aggressive coverage of him. In a court filing, Van Cise detailed forty-three allegations of bad behavior by Bonfils, from the criminal (bribery, jury tampering, stock fraud) to the boorish (hogging his favorite fishing hole on the North Platte River). It was capped off by the jaw-dropping claim that Bonfils "is subject to violent nightmares and fears that in one of them he may reveal some of the shady transactions of his past, and requires a constant companion when asleep, so that he may be instantly awakened when seized by such a spasm."

When Van Cise attempted to take his deposition, Bonfils refused to answer even the most innocuous questions about his personal history. Van Cise sought a court order compelling him to answer. Bonfils's attorneys requested delays. Like Morley before him, the publisher was finding out how a libel suit can blow up in the face of a complainant who has something to hide. Before the case could get to court, Bonfils abruptly died at his home, at age seventy-two. According to his front-page obituary, an ear infection "worked its way into his brain," leading to toxic encephalitis.

Bonfils had seemed despondent in his last weeks, and some of his friends and relatives believed that Van Cise's relentless investigation of the man contributed to his death. Helen Bonfils, who inherited the bulk of her father's estate and control of his newspaper empire, was not above seeking some payback of her own. The *Post* blacklisted Van Cise—his name was banished from the newspaper, and members of his family found a chilly reception in social circles friendly to the Bonfils family. No formal decree was issued, but the shunning persisted for years.

Even in his banishment, trouble kept calling for him. In 1943, he chased the would-be kidnappers from his front porch. Two years later, he was in his office, advising a socialite client on her divorce case, when her husband, stockbroker Charles Mangan, burst in. Van Cise whipped around his desk just as Mangan pulled a .32 automatic and pointed it at his wife. Van Cise grabbed his arm, and the two men wrestled for the pistol. A janitor entered the fray and jumped on Mangan's back. Mangan fired two shots before they could disarm him. One bullet grazed Van Cise's knee.

In 1946 he ended his long partnership with Kenneth Robinson and went into practice with his son Edwin, a graduate

of Harvard Law, just back from service as a lieutenant colonel
in the army in Europe during World War II. A new editor,
Palmer Hoyt, had been brought aboard the *Post* with the aim
of boosting the paper's quality and credibility; one of his first
moves was to end the blacklist. Van Cise was no longer per-
sona non grata. After he and Edwin successfully defended the
Better Business Bureau in an $11-million libel case brought
by a chiropractor who claimed to have cured patients of cancer and polio, they found themselves in regular demand as
the *Post*'s libel attorneys. In 1953, the father-son team served
as special prosecutors in a bunco case against brothers Clyde
and Eugene "Checkers" Smaldone, members of a notorious
Denver crime family. The gangbuster failed to secure a conviction this time, but the brothers went to prison for jury
tampering in another case soon afterward.

"My only hobby is work," Van Cise told a reporter. That
wasn't strictly true. He still fished and hiked in the mountains
on occasion and was said to have one of the most impressive
stamp collections in the state. But he was seen less and less
outside his home, where Sara had been bedridden since the
early 1940s, battling the debilitating effects of multiple scle-
rosis. She passed away in 1955. A few months later, Van Cise
announced his engagement to Mildred Kyffin, a Denver voice
teacher. On the way to a Christmas Eve wedding in Salt Lake
City, the couple's car skidded off an icy road in Wyoming and
tumbled down a ten-foot embankment. The car was a wreck.
Van Cise's ribs were bruised. Mildred was knocked out. The
wedding took place as scheduled.

Edwin was the best man. He was a skillful attorney, adept
at salvaging cases whenever his father's famous stubbornness
threatened to torpedo a reasonable compromise. He would
one day have the judgeship that eluded his dad, a seat on the

Colorado Court of Appeals, but the Colonel wouldn't live to see it. In 1958 the elder Van Cise became "of counsel" in his son's firm, slipping into the twilight of semi-retirement. He still went to the office, but work wasn't nearly as exciting as it once had been. The past loomed large, yet even its bright edges were fading. He was beset with health problems related to diabetes, the same disease that had claimed his father.

On December 8, 1969, he died of a urinary obstruction at St. Luke's Hospital in Denver. He was eighty-five.

His death did not attract the crowds of mourners or the weepy tributes that had attended Blonger and Locke. Virtue—"cold and odorless and tasteless virtue," as Faulkner called it—is inherently less interesting than vice, and Van Cise had managed to outlive most of his admirers as well as his enemies. But a tribute to his virtue would eventually be offered. It would only take another forty years.

In 2008 Mayor John Hickenlooper invited the public to help in naming Denver's new justice center complex. Nominations of several neglected trailblazers were submitted to a task force charged with making a final recommendation. One group pushed for honoring the much-maligned Ben Lindsey. Other contenders included James Flanigan, the city's first African American district judge; 1970s District Attorney Dale Tooley; former manager of safety John Simonet; retired judge and civil rights activist Roger Cisneros; and Philip Van Cise, whose inclusion was supported not only by members of the Van Cise family and local historians, but by descendants of the Blonger clan. The task force snubbed Cisneros and Van Cise, prompting debate in city council over the selection process. Ultimately, the council decided to dole out pieces of the complex to all six finalists, naming the courthouse after Lindsey and Flanigan and the fifteen-hundred-bed detention center after Van Cise and Simonet. Councilwoman Jeanne Faatz abstained from the vote, saying she was troubled by the juxtaposition of the Van Cise and Lindsey names across a plaza: "They're going to be facing off from each other, just as they did in life."

Naming the jail after Van Cise was presented as a form of poetic justice. After all, he had been an innovator in the field of detention, transforming a church basement into an effective holding cell. But locking up offenders had been the least of his achievements. His name on a building could not explain who the man was or the stand he took in the dark days, when his entire city seemed to teeter on the edge of an abyss.

Twenty-first-century Denver is a very different place than the town Van Cise knew—the population more diverse, the economy more robust, the political climate less provincial and paranoid. The speakeasies and clip joints have been replaced with government-approved brewpubs and marijuana dispensaries. Graft is no longer a given in civic affairs, and people are genuinely shocked when allegations of payoffs surface. Van Cise wouldn't recognize the place, but he had something to do with altering its course.

He didn't conquer the underworld, but he exposed the systemic corruption that allowed organized crime to thrive. He didn't eradicate the Klan, but he stripped off its hood and displayed its criminal nature for all to see, until it scurried back into white America's dark corners. He met lies and hysteria with cold facts and the law. Even when it led him to wild and lonely places, he kept to his path, convinced that he was on the road to redemption.

Author's Note

This book is nonfiction. There are no composite characters, no embellished scenes or invented dialogue. The
actions, statements, conversations, and attitudes attributed to
Van Cise and others derive from eyewitness accounts, court
documents, newspaper reports, surveillance notes, memoirs,
correspondence, oral histories, private papers, and other
archival records. When credible firsthand sources are in dispute regarding key facts, I have sought to alert the reader to
the conflict rather than print the legend.

At the same time, I have chosen to forgo the scholarly
apparatus of citation, as well as the nuanced debates in aca-
demic circles about whether the 1920s Klan was, say, a per-
version of populism or a precursor of fascism (or both), in
favor of focusing on the *story* I wanted to tell. Those looking
for a comprehensive history of the Ku Klux Klan or the evolution of the confidence game in America are encouraged to
look elsewhere. This is a work of narrative nonfiction, a journalist's book. It's a story that happens to be true.

To tell that story, I was fortunate to be able to draw on the
work of many dedicated researchers and authors who came
before me. My greatest debt is to Van Cise's own account of
the bunco investigation, *Fighting the Underworld* (1936). I

have tried to compensate for that book's omissions and evasions by turning to press coverage, the substantial investigative files found in the Robert R. Maiden Papers at the Denver Public Library, the even more substantial bunco trial transcripts (long thought to be lost, but recently located by an intrepid state archivist in a matter of minutes), and other sources. David W. Maurer's *The Big Con* (1940) is required reading for anyone seeking to decipher the language and rituals of the grifter's trade. The adventures of Frank Norfleet, freelance undercover agent, are trumpeted in Norfleet's 1924 autobiography and parsed entertainingly in Amy Reading's *The Mark Inside: A Perfect Swindle, a Cunning Revenge, and a Small History of the Big Con* (2012). The Blonger Brothers website (blongerbros.com) launched by brothers Craig and Scott Johnson is an excellent resource as well.

Van Cise never wrote a book about his battle with the Klan, but he did retain some souvenirs of his investigation, including several pieces of Klan literature and internal documents that help to illuminate a past that many Denver citizens were eager to forget. The spy reports submitted by his undercover operatives are a priceless record of the pomp, lunacy, and circus atmosphere that prevailed at the Castle Mountain gatherings, and I am surprised that historians haven't made more use of them. Two other pioneering preservationists, *Rocky Mountain News* Associate Editor Lee Casey and Denver Public Library researcher James Davis, deserve special recognition. Working on his master's thesis in the early 1960s, Davis recorded interviews with several witnesses to the Klan's rise and fall, including Charles Ginsberg, Robert Maiden, Forbes Parkhill, and Otto Moore. The oral histories that Davis compiled are available to listeners on the Denver Public Library website. In 1946 Casey donated the official membership ledger of the Denver

Klan, obtained from a former Klan official, to the Colorado Historical Society. The book was kept under wraps for three decades, until a persistent grad student named Robert Goldberg obtained access to it. In 2021 a digitalized database of the ledger, searchable by name, was finally made available online at the History Colorado website.

Goldberg went on to write *Hooded Empire: The Ku Klux Klan in Colorado* (1981), the first book-length study of the Klan's spread across the Centennial State. Forty years later, it remains an essential text on the subject, along with Phil Goodstein's highly detailed *In the Shadow of the Klan: When the KKK Ruled Denver 1920–1926* (2006). There are many books on the Klan as a national phenomenon in the 1920s. For my purposes, particularly helpful were *Hooded Americanism: The History of the Ku Klux Klan* (1965), by David M. Chalmers; *The Ku Klux Klan in the City, 1915–1930* (1967), by Kenneth T. Jackson; *The Fiery Cross: The Ku Klux Klan in America* (1987), by Wyn Craig Wade; and Linda Gordon's *The Second Coming of the KKK: The Ku Klux Klan of the 1920s and the American Political Tradition* (2017).

The materials I relied on the most in researching *Gangbuster* won't be found in any bookstore. They are artifacts, such as the Joe Bushnell affidavit, the spy reports, and the typescript of the speech Van Cise tried to deliver to an audience of four thousand howling Kluxers—the kind of live-wire, high-voltage connections to the past that can only be found in public and private archives. My thanks go out to the employees of several institutions who managed to make their special collections available to researchers despite the many challenges posed by the pandemic, including librarian Brian Trembath and other staffers in the Western History & Genealogy Department of the Denver Public Library; collections access coordinators Jori Johnson and Bethany Williams and the rest of the team at the

Steven H. Hart Research Center at History Colorado; archivist Richard Elsom of the National Archives at Denver; and Jennifer Simmons, Jordan Gortmaker, and other super-helpful folks at the Colorado State Archives.

I am profoundly grateful for the assistance provided by Cindy Van Cise, granddaughter of Phil and daughter of Edwin. Cindy, along with her late husband Simon Peter O'Hanlon and Denver County Court Judge Larry Bohning, first introduced me to aspects of the Van Cise story in 2007, and this book would not exist without the family scrapbooks, letters, photos, reminiscences, diaries, and other materials she has shared with me. Van Cise may have been shortchanged by the Denver establishment, but his descendants have done him proud in their efforts to preserve and celebrate his legacy.

Dennis Gallagher and Robert Goldberg were kind enough to share their time and insights and guide me to additional resources. *Westword* editor Patricia Calhoun provided a congenial home in print and online for my early forays into archival reporting, including a dive into the Van Cise story that left me wanting to know more. Many family members and friends offered aid, comfort, and moral support along the way. Deserving of special mention: the generous spirit of Frank Azar, the editorial comments of Keith Andrew, William Gibson and Michael Grano, and the encouragement and hospitality of John and Elizabeth Carver. Most of all, I want to acknowledge the assistance of my first and most devoted reader, researcher extraordinaire, and heart's companion, Lisa Flavin, whose help over the years this project took shape went far beyond the call of spousal duty.

Finally, I want to thank my agent, Frank Weimann, and my editor at Kensington, Denise Silvestro, for their faith in me and this book. In these cynical, con-crazy times, a genuine vote of confidence is a rare thing. I am doubly blessed.

Index